THE
AUTHOR'S
APPRENTICE

THE
AUTHOR'S
APPRENTICE

*Developing Writing Fluency,
Stamina, and Motivation
Through Authentic Publication*

Vicki Meigs-Kahlenberg

Foreword by Jeff Anderson

Stenhouse Publishers
Portland, Maine

Stenhouse Publishers
www.stenhouse.com

Library of Congress Cataloging-in-Publication Data

    Names: Meigs-Kahlenberg, Vicki, author.
    Title: The author's apprentice : developing writing fluency, stamina, and
       motivation through authentic publication / Vicki Meigs-Kahlenberg.
    Description: Portland, Maine : Stenhouse Publishers, 2016. | Includes
       bibliographical references and index.
    Identifiers: LCCN 2016000430 (print) | LCCN 2016016591 (ebook) | ISBN
       9781571109415 (pbk. : alk. paper) | ISBN 9781625311016 (ebook)
    Subjects: LCSH: Authorship. | Mentoring of authors.
    Classification: LCC PN151 .M39 2016 (print) | LCC PN151 (ebook) | DDC
       808.02--dc23
    LC record available at https://lccn.loc.gov/2016000430

Cover and interior design by Lucian Burg, Lu Design Studios, Portland, ME
www.ludesignstudios.com

Manufactured in the United States of America

 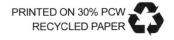

For all of my young writers . . .

*May your voices continue to soar and
your words continue to inspire.*

Contents

Foreword

I'm jaded.

When I read a new professional book about writing I ask myself, What's new? Is there anything I want to know more about? Is this book about quick fixes or is it about the true, long path of the writing process, messy and imperfect and glorious? Does it have some practicality and a breath of fresh air to keep me trudging down the road to writing success?

I flipped open *The Author's Apprentice* and saw what was tried and true and bold and new. I'd heard about NaNoWriMo—National Novel Writing Month—being applied in classrooms, and I was curious, both as a novelist and as a teacher of writing. But it was these words that made me continue reading:

> This is the one opportunity in their school career for your students to write un-
> apologetically, to write fiercely about whatever they want without the fear of their
> words being imperfect. They suddenly look forward to our language arts period
> and beg me for writing time. Really. How awesome is that?

I felt a friend in the voice of Vicki Meigs. I felt the strength of someone who knows what she's talking about—a real writing teacher, probably with a messy desk (I picture everyone I like with a messy desk). I felt the strength and depth of an educator who acknowledges those whose shoulders she stands upon.

As a writing teacher, I follow the research base that points us to the writing process, to let students do what professional writers do: Face a blank page at the beginning of a project with a mixture of excitement, fear, and wonder. Play with words and ideas and organization. Look closely at favorite novels and discover craft and style, and try successfully and unsuccessfully to apply this craft to their work. And when they want to give up, they don't. Instead they write through to the end. Writing through is the way to transform.

As a middle grades novelist, I also have an idea of what writers do, and I know that what Meigs suggests works on both fronts. We get better by diving in and doing the work. I wrote six novels before *Zack Delacruz: Me and My Big Mouth* (Sterling, 2015) was published. Writing those six novels was not wasted time. I learned through writing and feedback and struggling and attempting and, finally, succeeding. That is the work of a writer. What a gift Meigs gives her students (and now perhaps yours) to experiment and grow. To find the joy of honest, long-term work.

Not convinced your students can write novels? Not convinced the work outlined in this book is true to curriculum standards, Common Core or otherwise? Then you've got to read this book, try it out in your classroom, and see what happens. Meigs gives you the tools that the novelist and the writing teacher in me adores—it's dripping with hard-won truths and the grit it takes to be a writer and reviser.

I started writing novels, off and on, when I was twenty-six. I was first published as a teacher who wrote about teaching. Now, by doing much of the work described in *The Author's Apprentice*, I'm also a published fiction writer. Give your students the gift of the real writing process—that ever-evolving, upward-spiraling path of discovery.

Jeff Anderson: Author of
Zack Delacruz: Me and My Big Mouth (Sterling, 2015)
Zack Delacruz: Just My Luck (Sterling, 2016)
And a few books about teaching writing and grammar for **Stenhouse Publishers**

Acknowledgments

*I*t takes a village to raise a writer. It takes mentors—authors who inspire us as readers with their stories and awaken us as writers to possibilities with their advice. It takes words—in books and poems, in newspapers and songs—to stimulate us to refine our writing style. It takes teachers, colleagues, students, friends, and an entire community of writers to motivate, encourage, and support us through every step in the writing process. Without any one of these, this publication would not have been possible. I have so many people to thank for helping me to bring this work to the world.

Although I know that many of you will never see this, I must acknowledge all of those who have come before me—all of those extraordinary writing teachers who have paved the way for quality teaching and learning and have influenced writing instruction across the country and in my own classroom. Nancie Atwell, Kelly Gallagher, Ralph Fletcher, Katie Ray, Georgia Heard, Jeff Anderson, Lynne Dorfman, Rose Cappelli, and so many others: I proudly stand on your shoulders. With your passion, you continue to inspire, challenge, and deepen my understanding of writing and what it takes to rise above the tide. To all of those YA and middle-level writers who have touched my world with your words: Your fingerprints remain on all of the writing work that I do.

Sincerest gratitude to my first real writing teachers, all of the remarkable educators, mentors, and colleagues at the Pennsylvania Writing and Literature Project (PAWLP) in West Chester, PA, especially former director Dr. Andrea Fishman for taking me under your wing and helping me to get this project off the ground, and to current director Dr. Mary Buckelew for being my cheerleader from day one. The work that all of you do to keep reading and writing alive in our schools and communities through PAWLP institutes, courses, staff development, and youth programs is immeasurable.

I need to thank all of my teacher friends and colleagues, most notably Denise Dugan, for always nodding and smiling at all of my crazy classroom ideas (and for being my eternal voice of reason), and Ryan Hohman for so often coming along for the ride without question or hesitation. I feel blessed to have lived across the hall from you both for so many years. Your knowledge and camaraderie have been an inspiration. I am eternally grateful for Sally Poletick, my partner in crime, who has taught me, among other things, that sometimes there is no better word choice than the f-word. You have helped shape my classroom and my heart in so many ways.

My classroom would not have been the same without all of the folks of National Novel Writing Month. Grant Faulkner, Executive Director, and Chris Angotti, COO, it has been a pleasure collaborating with you over the years. My sincerest gratitude for all of your support, both with this book and for all of the work that you do to make novel writing and the possibility of publication attainable for students and adults alike. You have transformed my teaching and my writing forever.

To all of my students through the years who have come in curious and eager, excited to grow and learn together, thank you for helping me to become a better writer. And to those of you who entered my classroom filled with dread, apathy, or attitude, thank you for making me a better teacher.

I am so thankful for my breakfast buddy, Rasul. Now, it's your turn. Enough said.

Thank you to my family. To my mom, Lynn, thank you for being a part of our *I Survived NaNoWriMo* parties and documenting our classroom and celebrations in pictures. To my own young writers, Riley, Halle, and Connor, thank you for being my guinea pigs and test-drivers when I needed them, for understanding when I needed to spend hours in front of my computer instead of doing things that would have been way more fun, and for being so proud of your mom for finally sending her own words out into the world. You are truly amazing. To my husband, Dave, you always knew that this book was one that needed to be written. Somehow, you understood the power of publication long before I realized the true impact it has on students and on teaching. Thank you for putting up with my office explosions and all of those days when my entire bookshelf ended up splayed across the floor as I searched to find just the right lesson, sample, or mentor text. These past few years have been a roller coaster, and I am so glad to have had you right there in the front seat next to me.

Bill Varner, when you found me in a crowded hall of poster sessions at NCTE in Philadelphia, my teaching and writing life changed forever. While I have spent years teaching my students to write fearlessly and share their words with the world, you were the one who believed that my ideas needed a stage for my voice to be heard. Thank you, Bill, Holly, Chandra, Louisa, Chris, Jay, and all of the amazing people at Stenhouse for all of your work and dedication to this project every step of the way.

Introduction: Why Write?

*I*t was mid-February when Bill walked into my classroom. I was buried under a pile of papers, trying to squeak out a little grading before I headed home for the day, so I hardly noticed his quiet entrance.

"Hey, Mrs. Meigs," a barely audible, yet recognizable voice spoke from beyond the desks and chairs. I looked up to see Bill, standing nearly six feet tall, with broad shoulders, no longer a child but a young man, lingering in the doorway.

"Bill Harvey?!"

Bill was the last student I ever thought I'd see back in my classroom. He was tough, a kid who never really cared much for the academic side of school. Back in eighth grade, when I taught him, Bill was there for only one reason: sports. And that was just to pass the time until he could drop out. As with many of the students we teach, Bill had no idea how intelligent he was. But I knew. Thinking back, I can remember having extreme power struggles with this child about his lack of effort. Every day, I pushed. And every day, he pushed back. I was sure I had made his eighth-grade year miserable; at least, I was sure that's how it must have seemed to a fourteen-year-old who did not want to accept responsibility for his learning. And yet, four years later, here he was.

"Wow. It is so great to see you!" I said, rising from my desk and smiling. "So what on earth brings you back *here*?"

"I know, right? And the custodians almost didn't let me in," he said, smiling back. "I spend three years tryin' to get outta this place, and now they wouldn't let me *in*. That is, until I told them I just *had* to see you."

"You had to see *me*? Gosh, it's been so long. You must be a senior now, right?"

He nodded yes.

"You graduating?" I asked, raising my eyebrows in hope.

He nodded and smiled.

"Good for you! I'm really proud of you!" I said. "And *you* should be proud of you. You did it!"

"Yeah, I did," he acknowledged.

"So what are your plans?" I asked hesitantly.

"I enlisted in the Marines. I just got my papers. I start basic training the first week of July, then in six months, I'm shipping out."

"Oh, my God, how are you feeling about that?" I asked.

"About the deployment? I kind of wish I had longer than six months to train. I hope it's enough, but I'm ready to do something with my life. I didn't really have any other options."

He paused a long time before he began again, shifting his weight from one foot to the other, digging his hands deeper into his pockets, and gathering courage. "You know . . ." He broke off, took a deep breath, and collected his thoughts once more. "Since it's my senior year and all, my mom and I have been going through all of my old stuff. And we found the book in the box. You know, *the book*. The one that I got my poem published in?"

I knew then exactly the book that he meant. I had a copy of it on my bookshelf. It was a beautiful bound edition with black and gold scrolling letters: *Celebrate! Young Poets Speak Out!* As a matter of fact, I have many of these books—one from every year that I have been teaching. The publication receives tens of thousands of entries every season, but it only sends the best to the presses. I am proud to say that nearly 90 percent of my students who submit entries make the cut each year—that's hundreds of students throughout my teaching career.

I remember Bill working on this poem, *crafting* this poem, in the hallway near my classroom. He would pretend to act up, just enough that I'd have to kick him out of the room because he didn't want anyone to see him writing a *poem*. His poem was about baseball and the passion he had for the sport. It was one of the only things that mattered to him then, and, more importantly, for once he'd found a place to express his passion in school.

It took Bill a long time to share his writing with me. When he finally did, I praised him over and over and then encouraged him to send it in to the editors of the poetry anthology. He fought me, but then, begrudgingly, he gave in, in his own way. He left the poem on my desk. I sent it out in the afternoon mail.

"That poem, Mrs. Meigs," he said, bringing me back to the present moment. "I think that poem was the only thing I did in your class all year—except maybe drive you crazy." He smiled and then dropped his eyes to the floor, outlining a floor tile with his sneaker. "Yeah, my mom and I found the book and we read the poem." He glanced up for a moment, then his eyes looked back to the floor. Bill shrugged his shoulders. "It was pretty good."

"You're right. You really are an amazing writer when you put your mind to it."

"See, the thing is, Mrs. Meigs, I had to come and see you," he said. "My mom and I were looking through the box, and, *that* book, *that poem* . . . it's the only thing that I have to show for all twelve years of school. It's the only thing I ever did in school that really mattered. It was the only thing that I was ever proud of. I never got good grades, never really did any projects or anything, but this is kinda cool, now. And I just needed to come and see you and *thank you*. I know I didn't even want to write it at all, but you made me do it, and now . . . I never cared about grades, so college wasn't an option, and I wasn't interested in any trades. I didn't want to start my life in a go-nowhere job; I know I'm smarter than that. Enlisting was my only choice, and I wanted to come and see you and say thanks, and all, before I go. Just in case."

My heart was in my throat. In that moment, I knew that Bill would make an excellent soldier, because his introspection had taken more courage than the heroics of a thousand men.

Writing That Matters

Moments like these are *real.* They matter. Publishing does that for students. It helps adolescent writers realize that they have amazing potential. It helps them feel confident, even years later, when a difficult high school or college English class or some other situation later in life challenges them. They realize they have what it takes to succeed. After all, they are published authors. Each year, dozens of kids like Bill come back to visit after they've been in my classes. Not one of them remembers his or her scores on the standardized

tests they took during our year together. But they all remember the experience of becoming authors. And for those who were accepted for publication, their work provides tangible evidence of success that will last forever.

At the middle school level, in-class writing instruction typically shifts from the narrative focus of the elementary grades to sophisticated informational writing,

> *Learning to write a single word or sentence or paragraph really, really well (meaning, like Wow!) is the key to learning to write well—then you can apply these skills to a larger assignment.*
>
> —Carole Marsh, children's author and the founder of Gallopade International, a children's book publishing company

literary analysis, and argument-writing techniques. This is an appropriate evolution that reflects the influence of the Common Core State Standards and other initiatives that aim to mirror writing beyond the classroom. However, we cannot expect our students to *apply* these new strategies in addition to the more complex grammar, punctuation, and stylistic techniques that are also expected in the middle grade unless we also help them to develop the habits of real writers.

That is, they must write: frequently, to develop stamina and fluency; attentively, to notice and practice the techniques of skillful writers; and authentically, to analyze and engage diverse audiences. As teacher and author Kelly Gallagher shares in *Teaching Adolescent Writers*, "If we want students to become lifelong writers, students must see writing as intrinsically important—not just another school assignment. Students must find writing assignments to be relevant and meaningful" (2006, 11).

So how do we accomplish these lofty goals?

First, we research and establish "writerly" routines, which include contributing to a writer's notebook three times per week for twenty-minute sessions and reading like a writer to explore language and voice and inspiration. My *flexible* "any three days of the week for writing" assignment allows for busy schedules, outside activities, and "I just couldn't focus today" kinds of days. The *inflexible* amount of time that must be spent on writing (twenty minutes each session) levels the playing field for all of my students and gives those who need the most practice the opportunity to improve at a rate that is commensurate with their peers. This approach helps to build writing stamina and fluency for all. It also helps students learn how to produce the on-demand writing that is required by high-stakes tests.

"Students who write regularly learn about their own writing process," Ralph Fletcher and JoAnn Portalupi share in *Writing Workshop*. "They know whether it takes them longer to generate ideas or to refine those thoughts on the paper . . . Students who write regularly develop the habit of rereading their own work" (2001, 109).

Second, we learn writing conventions, explicitly and in context through a balanced grammar instructional approach that Judith Langer recommends in *Effective Literacy Instruction* (2002). For example, after mini-lessons about conventions, we apply and reinforce new grammar and mechanics skills within the pages of our writer's notebooks and our novel excerpts. Instead of speculating about a student's understanding through inauthentic worksheets or forced practice sentences, I encourage students to "play" with new usage. Free from judgment, they can more naturally experiment in their own writing, regardless of the genre. As Regie Routman affirms in *Writing Essentials* (2005), "Your students learn about sentences and paragraphs not by studying about them in isolation, but through reading widely, hearing good literature read aloud, and writing for audiences and purposes that matter" (154). When students have the opportunity to practice and refine their newly acquired skills within their own writing, it matters to them. The grammar and mechanics lessons are no longer viewed simply as proficiencies to be tested and forgotten. Instead, students begin to see these concepts as tools for enhancing their own writing style and effectiveness.

Third, we work toward publication in a variety of forms. Each of my seventh graders writes a novel in November. That's right! They write a first draft of between seven thousand and fifteen thousand or more words in conjunction with National Novel Writing Month (NaNoWriMo), which involves more than eighty-one thousand other teachers and students from two thousand classrooms in fifty different countries and every state in the United States. NaNoWriMo "winners" (those who reach their word-count goals) are eligible to receive free paperback copies of their finished book when they independently publish their novel through CreateSpace, FastPencil, or other publishing opportunities provided by the generous sponsors of National Novel Writing Month. Seeing their self-published novel in print is tremendously cool, but my students also work toward authentic, editor-selected publication in the spring through a variety of literary anthologies, including *Poetic Power*, *Anthology of Short Stories by Young Americans*, and well-known magazines such as *Highlights*, *Creative Kids*, *American Girl*, and *Boys' Life*. Students research publishers' submission guidelines in the student writer's market that I've compiled (see Chapter 8); decide on the form (poetry, memoir, mystery, historical fiction, fantasy, or perhaps an editorial or essay); and then submit their writing to selected publications they have researched.

As a result of their relentless practice, both independently and collaboratively, my students are better able to manage their time on structured writing assignments, and they rarely experience a debilitating bout of writer's block, because they know that inspiration can come from anywhere. It's up to them to seek it and get the job done.

> *Persistence. This is the hardest point to master. Writing consistently is the best way to improve. Write, write, write until the words no longer seem jarring, until you have confidence in dealing with various parts of the craft—dialogue, description, action, grammar—and until you can achieve whatever effect or emotion you want.*
>
> —Christopher Paolini, author of *Eragon* and the rest of the Inheritance Cycle series

Becoming a Better Writing Teacher

Much has changed in education and in my own teaching style since Bill was my student a lifetime ago. What hasn't changed is my dedication to offering students authentic writing experiences and my students' desire to work harder when their writing matters. I don't *have* to teach my students the fundamentals of manuscript formatting, nor do I *have* to teach them to feel proud of producing a piece of writing for the purpose of publication. But I do. It is important to make writing real to our students—to give them real purposes and audiences and opportunities. Keeping it real has nothing to do with writing for a grade or for a teacher. It's doing the work of real authors—the people whose writing we read by choice. It's about the validation that comes with giving students a stage and making their voices heard.

Why write? To be read, to be heard, to be someone. After all, that's what *authors* do. So let's make it matter.

PART 1

The Writing Apprenticeship Model

In this section, you will gain an understanding of the writing apprenticeship model and how the author-to-author approach can yield huge gains that extend far beyond the walls of the classroom. This workshop model integrates the advice and theories of literacy gurus and published middle level and young adult authors as well as ideas from business leaders and contemporary thinkers who can help us prepare students for success in college and careers. Be forewarned: this is the "heavy lifting" chapter. All of the background and theory is frontloaded here. We will explore the organizational structure and management of the apprenticeship model as well as the role of writer's notebooks, which provide a passport to authentic writing experiences.

Chapter 1

The Power of "What If?"

I get my ideas from everywhere. But what all of my ideas boil down to is seeing maybe one thing, but in a lot of cases it's seeing two things and having them come together in some new and interesting way, and then adding the question "What if?" "What if" is always the key question.

—Stephen King,
author of *The Stand*, the Dark Tower series, and many other titles

What if you are a master teacher fluent in the best practices of teaching reading and writing, but you feel bound by well-intentioned state and district testing?

What if you are a new teacher who came into the profession to share your love of the art of writing and the craft of reading, but you can't seem to find the window to do so in your already overstretched curriculum?

What if in spite of these factors, you are still passionate about cultivating choice and voice for your students? *What if* you are searching for a solution that enables you to meet your curriculum requirements while allowing you to breathe in the fresh air that workshop time offers?

What if you believe that real writing matters?

You may have found your answer.

In recent years, much emphasis has been placed on testing and assessment, seemingly for the purpose of ranking our schools, rating our teachers, and comparing our students.

In this atmosphere, it's difficult not to feel as if we—teachers and students alike—are competing against each other rather than collaborating with one another and celebrating the accomplishments and contributions of individuals.

I have been in education for twenty years. Back in the day, I can remember the excitement of learning something new and then sharing that new lesson with my students and peers. There was a real sense of collegiality and an importance and purpose to everything that we did. It feels different today, and I don't think it is simply because I am older and wiser, as they say. When I talk to teachers of English and language arts in school, at workshops, and at conferences, I hear from many that they are just *tired*. They are exhausted by ever-changing expectations and demands of their curriculums and stressed by the potential impact of the tests. Even younger teachers are feeling burnt out way too soon. Many are leaving the profession without ever having that feeling that they positively impacted a child's life. Those moments when we know that we have connected to kids are what teaching is all about.

Clearly, we need some balance.

I recognize the importance of contemporary texts that contain helpful lessons and strategies for addressing Common Core writing and other newer initiatives. I have many of these resources on my bookshelves, and they have proven invaluable in helping me to navigate today's classroom demands. Yet I want this book to remind teachers of important historical works that can still be transformative today. I think it is time that we stand tall on the shoulders of those who have paved the way for us as teachers of writing. I think it is time to reclaim our classrooms and to show our students why real writing matters, and how their voices can be heard.

Back in the Day

During a holiday break one year, my friend and colleague found a book in a used bookstore and bought it for me. Sarah placed the gift on my desk with a note saying she knew I'd love the book, and I found it when I returned to school. This was a great way to start my first day back on a frigid morning. I peeled back the worn book cover and immediately smiled. Sarah was right. I did love the book, which was filled with quotes about writing from authors. I thought these words of wisdom would be just the change my been-up-since-the-first-day-of-school bulletin board needed. I was sure the quotations would inspire my young writers and give them a second wind for the new semester.

That afternoon, I frantically photocopied dozens of my favorite quotes from the book and stapled the sheets to that worn-out bulletin board underneath a banner that I had created and laminated during my lunch break. I just knew these additions would be great talking points for my writing workshop.

I was wrong.

Class after class came into my room, but my students were not impressed. A few made comments such as "Oh, nice board" or "Hey, you put up something new"—if they noticed at all. Yes, it was *nice*, and yes, it was *new*, but that wasn't the *point*. The problem was that not one student knew who the authors were, so no one cared. As cool as *I* thought the quotes were, they held no real meaning for my seventh graders. Here's the thing about seventh graders: If you can't make learning relevant to their world and give them a greater purpose as a reason to take notice, it just won't stick. How could I have overlooked that fundamental principle of middle school teaching?

I started the next school year with an attitude that mirrored my students' thinking: *Fine, then. You don't like my quotes? Find your own.*

The bulletin board in the center of the cinderblock wall of my classroom remained empty. When the new group of seventh-grade language arts students walked into my classroom on the first day of school, I handed each of them a vibrantly colored index card and their very first homework assignment of the year: The Backstage Pass (more on that in Chapter 3). By the following Friday, they had to check out the official website of their favorite middle level or YA author (or any appropriate author that they had heard might be good—a consideration for those who hadn't read all summer and weren't planning on doing so anytime in the near future) and find a quote that had something—anything—to do with writing.

When Friday arrived, I asked each student to go to the bulletin board (which still had the previous year's banner, "Writers' Words of Wisdom," across the top), read aloud their quote, and name the author before stapling their entry to an empty space. To my surprise, this process was the catalyst for wonderful whole-class conversations that I never could have planned. Here's a snippet of their comments:

"Who's E. L. Konigsburg?"

"What did she write?"

"The whole book is *poetry*?"

"Do you think I'd like it?"

"What was it about?"

"Yeah, his books are banned in some places."

"Oh, I think I saw the movie."

"Did you know that *my* author got his first book published when he was in ninth grade?"

"Really?! That's just two years older than us."

"No way! That's so awesome."

The last line was mine. I was completely in awe of the conversations that the students in my classroom were having. They were buzzing with excitement. All of the "Words of Wisdom" provided sincere insights, strategies, and advice from real authors, just as before. But this time, the quotes mattered. They were suddenly interesting and relevant, because the students selected them and they came from authors whose books my students had read or now planned to read.

Keep in mind that I don't exclusively teach students classified as gifted and talented. I would argue, however, that all of my students are both gifted and talented in ways that traditional IQ tests may not reveal. Having been a former gifted coordinator, I recognize the need for all students to be expected to complete rigorous work, to have opportunities to feel successful, and to feel that the work they are doing matters. Although I do teach one honors class, the remainder of my classes now consists of a fairly diverse population of students considered average to struggling learners. Some have been diagnosed with learning disabilities. A fair percentage of my students have academic and behavioral files filled with IEPs and 504s and other interesting baggage from school years past.

No one expected "greatness" from most of my students—or even mediocrity in some cases, but here they were. *My* seventh graders were actually talking about authors and literature and writing styles and strategies. And they were doing it on their own by the end of the first week of school. Those aliterate kids whom Kyleen Beers (1998) would consider *dormant*, *uncommitted*, or *unmotivated readers* or whom Cris Tovani (2000) refers to as *resistive readers*—the ones who can read, but seem to have no time or interest—were suddenly . . . *interested*. Even my struggling readers, who would typically not feel confident enough in their ability to contribute in class discussions, were actively involved because they, too, had something to bring to the table.

> *As a kid, I also longed for a career that I didn't actually believe real people got to do. The far-out, only-in-your dreams career I wanted was to be an author. All the grown-ups I knew were farmers (like my dad) or nurses (like my mom), teachers or dentists, housewives or grocery store clerks, etc., etc. The only authors I'd ever heard of were, well, just in books.*
>
> —Margaret Peterson Haddix, author of the Missing series, the Shadow Children series, the Palace Chronicles series, and many other titles

A Magical Adventure

I am not going to pretend that the quotes kept our workshop motors running smoothly all year long (at least not yet). They did, however, generate excitement that helped get that year's writing workshop off the ground. The quotes, and the curiosity they engendered, also encouraged my aliterate readers to venture back into books for their nightly free reading. This one simple assignment provided a natural bridge between the worlds of reading and writing and got the kids talking about authors and authorship as if they are things that don't live just inside books.

The real magic didn't happen until June—that is, the *end* of June—when I began dismantling the infamous bulletin board. The quote cards had become tattered, their colors sun-faded. But, somehow, they still had a little magic left in them. Kelly and Amanda, two eighth graders, decided to come in during lunch one day to help me begin to break down my classroom for the summer. While I was refiling papers and overhead projector sheets in one corner of the room, they made fast work of clearing that wall.

When the girls finished, they handed me several separate, neatly aligned piles of index cards. They had not arranged the cards by author or class period or even by color. As I flipped through the stacks, I saw that the girls had arranged them by *topic*. One pile focused on prewriting and idea generation, another targeted writer's block, and one had cards about developing characters and setting. The last pile contained some random quotes about philosophies of writing that didn't seem to fit anywhere else, but they all had to do with the importance of reading to improve writing.

I guess the girls noticed my questioning eyebrows because Amanda quickly said, "Oh, I hope that's okay. We figured that's how you'd want them so you can use them again."

Then Kelly chimed in, "Yeah, they sort of matched up with all the stuff you taught us, so . . ."

I glanced down at the blue index card that sat on top of the first pile. It was a quote from Lois Lowry, author of *The Giver*. "Ideas come from your imagination," she said. "What triggers your imagination? Things that you read, see, overhear, dream, or wonder about. Anything that makes you think: 'What if . . . ?' is the start of a story."

What if . . . ? My thoughts were churning so fast that I could hardly contain myself. "You girls are awesome! Thank you for your help." They had no idea what they had just set in motion. I can't believe that I hadn't seen the light before. In the beginning, these quotes were just intended to be a collection of wise thoughts about writing. Yes, they had become a springboard to reading and a wonderful introduction to writing workshop. And occasionally, as a student was struggling with a particular topic, I might direct him or her to the wall for insight or inspiration. But beyond that, the quotes were just *ambiance*—a part of the scenery in our workshop environment. They were never intended to be the guiding force behind our workshop.

But what if I actually used these quotes as the *basis* for my lessons instead of the background? In this case, my *what if* wasn't the start of one story, but the start of thousands over the years. For me, this one leap of faith would initiate a whole new expedition into writing workshop—an expedition in which I would be plotting my own course into uncharted territory. I would still be able to meet all of my content requirements as designated by the district, but this one small change in my plans offered my students and me the validation and inspiration we needed to write for writing's sake.

Just as we do when planning any big trip, I knew I needed to consult travel agents to help me develop my itinerary. I went right to the experts: real authors would become our guides. These trip advisors could help us get the most mileage from our writing journey.

As I scrutinized the quote cards, looking for patterns, three major themes arose:

Successful authors read. They read for entertainment and for research, and in their reading, they form opinions about and find ideas for writing. They notice the craft, story structures, and nuance that make writing good. They fall in love with characters, with settings, and with words.

Successful authors write. This may seem like a no-brainer, but contemporary middle grade and YA authors have a lot to share about their writing experiences and the *wheres*, *whens*, and *hows* that make good writing happen. Not surprisingly, very few—if any—of their strategies appear in my middle school writing curriculums or textbooks. I am not sure why this is so, but in our classroom, this is about to change. We are going to focus on doing the work that real writers do.

Successful authors publish. Professional writers and authors publish their work and share their words with the world. Once writers publish, others can read their work and, in return, continue to fuel the writing of others. (See Figure 1.1.)

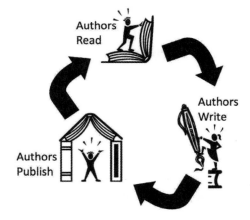

Figure 1.1 Publication provides the missing link in the reading-writing-publishing cycle.

Until now, the writing process for my students was just a one-way street that, in most cases, led only to a grade and a folder or an overstuffed locker and a trashcan. Read . . . get a grade. Write . . . get a grade. Nothing was connected. We were doing some good work, but not for reasons that mattered to my students, so I saw little growth. My students rarely got real satisfaction from what they wrote because the writing had no life beyond my written comments and checkmarks on a rubric.

The possibility of authentic publication that reaches beyond a grade book provides a real reason to read and write. And it presents all students with the opportunity to give back to the writing world—to be a part of it—to continue the cycle so that future writers can find inspiration for their own writing. This was exactly the framework I needed to keep my writing workshop alive with possibilities all year long.

> *One of the reasons I started writing is that I never felt I met children who were like me in the books I read . . . So I wanted to write about children like me.*
>
> —E. L. Konigsburg, author and illustrator of children's books and YA fiction, including *The View from Saturday, The Outcasts of 19 Schuyler Place, The Mysterious Edge of the Heroic World,* and many other titles

Of course, the scores earned on our classroom reading and writing assignments continue to provide the motivation for those students who are grade driven. There are many kids, however—like Bill—who are not motivated by grades because they have never felt successful in this content area. These kids need something more. The expectation of publication raises the bar for all students—for those who have had a history of success and for those who have not. Publication levels the field for all learners, and it gives each of them a reason to want to write. The external expectation of publication validates their efforts and makes students feel like the writing that they are doing matters.

Ralph Fletcher and JoAnn Portalupi know that "skilled writing teachers need to become resourceful and self-reliant and not rely on preprinted lesson materials" and that we need to learn to be "responsive to all of the unplanned teachable moments that arise during writing workshop" (1998, 1). So I started thinking:

What if we could have a structure in place to help facilitate those teachable moments in an organized way throughout the year?

What if we could return to and learn from the advice of the authors that my students selected to promote interest and involvement from September until June?

What if my students could develop their own unique road maps for becoming published authors themselves?

What if my students could find their voices and carve out a space for themselves in the real world?

> *I'm not sure why, but many people seem to think writing is different from any other talent. They think you just do it, and your skill level never changes. Nothing could be further from the truth. Writing is like basketball. Writing is like dancing. Writing is like playing the piano. You must practice, practice, practice. Write, write, write. Every time you do, you will improve.*
>
> —James Dashner, author of the Maze Runner series, the Mortality Doctrine series, the 13th Reality series, and other titles

This was going to be a gamble, letting my lessons ride on the student-found advice of authors, but these authors truly *are* the experts in the field of writing, and they have a lot to say. And most important, my students were willing to listen to them, so this was a gamble that I was willing to take.

Many of us have become well versed in the workshop approach and use mini-lessons as the primary vehicle for moving writing forward. But there still seems to be missed connections between the work that *authors* do and what *we* do in our classrooms.

Nancie Atwell believes that "middle school teaching should be organized so that it helps kids begin to understand and participate in adult reality" (1998, 54), and when middle school students have the ability to choose topics and purpose of writing, "their commitment to their ideas and purposes made them work hard; their hard work made significant writing happen" (14).

According to Ralph Fletcher and JoAnn Portalupi, "Kids in writing workshops *do* see themselves as writers. They develop a genuine feel for writing—its power and its purpose. They know what it means to write for themselves—in a writer's notebook, for example. But they also know what it means to write for an audience of interested readers. They understand the heavy lifting writing does in the real world" (2001, xi). I challenge you to raise the bar. Help students to truly *see* the writing that exists out in the world. Help them to seek authors whose published words *and* advice provide inspiration. Help them to make the connection between the writing they do in the classroom and the writing that is done by professionals in the field. As educators, we have the ability to do more than just develop proficient writers who can perform on an assessment. We can truly create authors who contribute their words to the world *and* have the confidence to tackle any test. By taking this approach, we are teaching adolescents to think for themselves and become aware of a larger audience. We are giving them the ability and experience to accept a challenge, to solve problems, and to use the tools and strategies they have learned through literacy lessons to craft memorable writing that will set them apart on the test and in the real world.

Our classrooms today are filled with diverse students and diverse voices longing to be heard. If our promise is to teach writing well, let's make it matter to our students—not just for grades, district ratings, or feathers in caps they won't ever wear. Let's develop empowering, memorable teaching that raises student voices in ways that reflect the authentic writing practices of the world.

If you want to be a writer, three main things are: (1) Read a lot because that is where you are going to get your inspiration and learn how other writers do a good job with their books. (2) Write a little every day. Writing is like exercise; it's like practicing for a sport: The more you do it, the stronger your writing muscles get, and if you don't practice, you don't get any better. (3) Don't give up. Everyone feels terrible when they get their first rejection note, but it happens to everybody, so just keep going, don't give up, believe in yourself and just keep trying.

—Rick Riordan, author of *Percy Jackson and the Olympians* series, the *Kane Chronicles* series, and other titles

Chapter 2

The Apprenticeship Approach: Understanding the Structure Behind the Strategy

Every well-written book is a light for me. When you write, you use other writers and their books as guides.

—Kate DiCamillo,
author of *The Tale of Despereaux, Because of Winn Dixie,
The Magician's Elephant,* and many other titles

*I*f you want to plan a trip across country or overseas, you would probably scan brochures, travel guides, and websites, seeking possible destinations, reviews, and advice for your spree. The journey to publication is no different. We begin the year scouring author websites and blog posts, searching for strategies and advice that will help us reach our destination: publication. This critical step fuels our travel to the key signposts in our itinerary: *Basecamp, Authors' Territory,* and *Becoming Word Travelers.* (For the complete Backstage Pass lesson on collecting author advice, see Chapter 3.)

Basecamp: What Do Authors Do? By design, students look to the middle grade and YA authors whom they are currently reading to draw inspiration for writing. Through our classroom "author research" we have discovered that *reading* is the number one piece of advice given by authors to young writers who want to know how to improve their writing! Reading serves as the natural basecamp for our journey—one that we will come back to time and time again. Students scrutinize the creative crafts and word choices in the spirit of Katie Wood Ray's *Wondrous Words* and Lynne Dorfman, and Rose Cappelli's *Mentor Texts*. We ask: What makes writing good, and how do we know when we see it? Students read to examine their favorite authors' writing processes and read like writers, collecting evidence of good work and using it as a model for their own writing.

Authors' Territory: How Do They Do It? In addition to seeking out luscious language in our mentor texts and then applying those traits to our writing, students and I also look to the authors for their advice on all stages of the writing process, creating a vicarious apprenticeship with the authors by following in their footsteps every step of the way. From idea generation to manuscript completion, authors have many writing lessons that they are just waiting to share with us on their websites and blogs about every stage of the writing process, for all kinds of writing. Authors even have advice for writer's block and procrastination! This writing advice serves as the foundation for our writer's notebook lessons. The writing from these lessons becomes the seeds for future publication. In addition to practicing true authors' crafts and strategies on the pages of their notebooks, students also build writing fluency and stamina by participating in *National Novel Writing Month*. After my students write their novels, they can tackle any writing assignment of any length with confidence and ease.

Becoming Word Travelers: How Can I Become a Published Author Too? Lastly, students transform from writers who complete their work just for a grade into authors who publish their work to share with a real audience. Yes, there are dozens of publishers who accept student writing and encourage submissions in their local and national anthologies, magazines, and contests. The students learn the process of writing for publication. This strand begins with writing for the reader's eye and addresses various stages of revision on the way to publication.

The lessons and activities in our writing workshop are not part of our traditional curriculum. Instead, they form enrichment lessons that help students gain an understanding of how professional writers work and that enable my young authors to apply the skills and strategies in the formal curriculum. Although the Common Core State Standards encourage a deep exploration of expository and argument writing, there is still a need for narrative writing in the middle grades. According to the 2011 National Assessment of Educational Programs (NAEP) Writing Framework, 30 percent of our middle school students' writing assignments should serve the purpose of "writing to convey experience." My current curriculum structure reflects very little narrative writing as compared to argument and expository writing. It is critical that we find authentic and organic ways to incorporate meaningful narrative writing into our curriculums. This workshop approach fills this need, and it also provides the narrative writing skills and strategies necessary to prepare students for the more sophisticated demands of imbedding narrative structures into argument and informational writing in other content areas.

There have been times in the past when I felt stuck between the requirements of the curriculum and the best practices of teaching writing well. I have no doubt that many teachers share my concerns. In order for students to write (or do anything) well, the assignment must be designed with three qualities in mind: *autonomy, mastery,* and *purpose.* The writing apprenticeship approach is not about writing in response to literature or a canned prompt. It is about providing an authentic writing experience—one that preserves writing for *writing's sake,* providing a space for students to write on self-selected topics that are important to them (autonomy). The lessons in the apprenticeship approach also transfer to curriculum-prescribed topics, increasing the overall quality of these responses (mastery). And the possibility of publication offers motivation that transcends the grade (purpose).

Securing student interest and autonomy with authentic learning experiences is time well spent. It actually decreases the time you must spend teaching or *re*teaching as the year goes on, because the students develop writerly habits and an eye for quality reading and writing on their own. This approach helps students learn to instinctively scrutinize what they read and form opinions about their reading. It also offers a platform for thoughtful conversations about literature as well as student-generated writing.

> *In telling my stories I could be all of those things I ever did and did not become . . .*
>
> —Jerry Spinelli, author of *Maniac Magee, Loser, Stargirl, Smiles to Go, Hokey Pokey,* and many other titles

The Structure and Management of the Writing Apprenticeship Approach

During inservice training workshops that I've presented, I have had many conversations with teachers who struggle year after year to complete all of their curriculum objectives, and they wonder how they could possibly have time to do all of this "extra stuff." The answer: frontloading. Fortifying the reading-writing diet earlier makes them healthier and stronger readers and writers in the long run. This conditions students for strength and endurance on the long road to publication.

Here's how it works: Our workshop is divided into two legs coinciding with our school-year semesters. Each semester consists of the three essential components reflected in our signposts: *reading, writing,* and *publishing* (see Figure 2.1).

Weekly Writing Assignment

	FIRST SEMESTER		SECOND SEMESTER	
	ACTIVITIES	WHAT'S GRADED?	ACTIVITIES	WHAT'S GRADED?
READING Authors read for inspiration, ideas, and research.	• Performing author studies to collect words of wisdom from famous YA authors • Learning to read like a writer and developing awareness of "good writing" • Discovering and collecting examples of craft, "cool words," and vocabulary	• Backstage Pass (completion grade only) • Weekly "Personal Vocabulary" (five words/wk. = thirty points/wk.) • Weekly Reading Journal	• Returning to author advice and mentor texts to develop writing • Continuing independent practice of "reading like a writer" and collecting examples of "good writing" and vocabulary • Applying newly acquired craft lessons and vocabulary in personal and graded writing	• Weekly "Personal Vocabulary" through 3rd marking period • End of year: five amazing quotes submitted (three from published authors; two from own writing) • Evidence of craft and vocabulary use in two checklist writing pieces
WRITING Authors keep track of their writing territories; they write frequently and for extended periods of time.	• Establishing a writing "home" in a writer's notebook • Establishing writing frequency via Weekly Writing Challenges • Establishing writing fluency and stamina via novel writing with NaNoWriMo	• Number of completed writer's notebook entries (WWCs) • Percentage of novel writing goal accomplished • Specific NaNoWriMo tasks completed and posted online	• Continuing to develop writing ideas and territories in writer's notebook • Self-selecting two entries from writer's notebook to bring through entire writing process to publication • Self-selecting one stand-alone scene from novel to revisit and revise time and time again to practice newly acquired grammar and conventions and to test out new craft ideas	• Two completed "Writer's Workshop Process Checklists" (number of items completed out of fifteen items on list; end percentage is weighted in 4th marking period gradebook) • Novel excerpt (percentage of list of items included from craft and grammar lessons; use of state scoring rubric to evaluate end product)
PUBLISHING Authors survey the writer's market and attempt publication multiple times by making multiple submissions of multiple pieces of writing to multiple publishers.	• Writing with an eye toward publication and the deliberate intent of making the words sound like literature • Participating in formal and informal writing conferences with diverse reading and writing partners	• Weight of *style* domain on state scoring rubric increases gradually as we learn to incorporate craft in curriculum writing assessments • Preparation for and participation in weekly conferences	• Surveying the young writer's market • Aligning writing to specific submission guidelines • Formatting manuscripts and writing letters to editors • Submitting a minimum of three original pieces of writing for publication: one poem from poetry unit and two personally selected pieces to take through checklist process	• Points for completion of Surveying the Writer's Market, Surveying the Reader's Market, and Project Planning Sheet • Points for correctly following publication formatting guidelines on letter, manuscript, and SASE • Quality of poem based on our poetry unit requirements • Quality of end products for two self-selected pieces taken through checklist process (graded using state scoring rubric)

Figure 2.1 Apprenticeship Approach Yearlong Overview

The first semester focuses on the direct instruction and modeling of what I like to call establishing "writerly habits." During this time, students develop an awareness of the impact that reading has on writing as they practice reading with a writer's eye. They begin to identify and collect examples of amazing word choices, craft, and vocabulary to serve as models and inspiration for their own writing.

In addition, during each week of the first semester, my students must try a different author-identified strategy (also known as Weekly Writing Challenges, or WWCs) at home. These practice sessions must include writing three separate entries for each week's WWC, with each entry requiring a minimum of twenty minutes per sitting. Although the strategies in the WWCs are explicit, the students have choice in what they want to write about, where and when they want to do their writing, and which prior techniques or crafts they would like to apply to these new entries. (See Figure 2.2 for a visual display of our WWCs.)

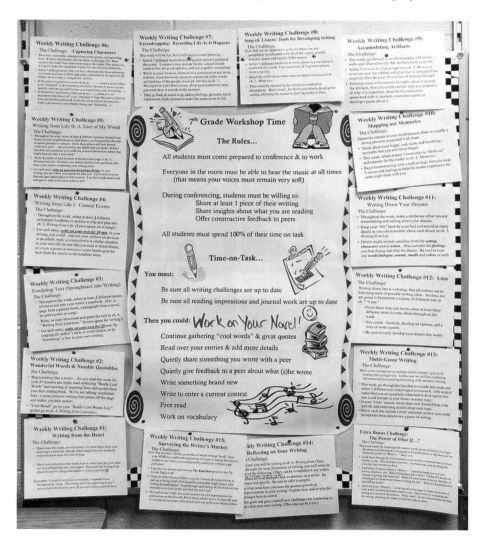

Figure 2.2 I decorate a bulletin board with reminders about the Weekly Writing Challenges.

During the second semester, students must select two entries from their writer's notebooks (or they can begin something new if they are so inspired) to bring through the entire writing process and expand into fully developed manuscripts. Students are still expected to write at home for a minimum of twenty minutes three times a week, but now they are doing so with the prospect of publication. The Writer's Workshop Process Checklist helps students keep track of all the steps. The final products must reflect the lessons learned earlier in the year as well as the submission guidelines and manuscript formatting extracted from lessons during the second semester.

My role during this phase is not to direct my students on what to write or how to write. Rather, I help them make the most effective and efficient use of the tools we've studied in order to get across their ideas clearly and concisely to their intended audience. This method of instruction produces fantastic results in terms of process confidence and product quality, and the bonus is that it falls in line with the Common Core State Standards for English and Language Arts (www.corestandards.org/ELA-Literacy). (See R.CCR.4-6 [Craft and Structure], 9 [Integration of Knowledge and Ideas]; W.CCR.1-3 [Types and Purposes], 4-6 [Production and Distribution of Writing], 8 [Research to Build Present Knowledge], 10 [Range of Writing]; SL.CCR.1 [Comprehension and Collaboration]; L.CCR.1-2 [Conventions of Standard English], 3 [Knowledge of Language], 5-6 [Vocabulary Acquisition and Use].)

In *Teaching Adolescent Writers*, Kelly Gallagher notes that students are simply not doing enough writing in school. He says: "To significantly improve their writing skills, our students need to swim in the writing pool much more frequently" (2006, 9). To this end, I loosely apply the business world's Pareto principle of management, or *80/20 Rule*, to our writing time to motivate my students to produce more writing. This principle suggests that 20 percent of our efforts produce or enhance the majority of our results or rewards. As Daniel Pink (2009) shares in *Drive: The Surprising Truth About What Motivates Us*, some of the most successful companies in the world offer employees 20 percent of their time to work on whatever they want, however they want, with whomever they want. The only stipulation is that at the end, employees have to produce something that demonstrates evidence of time well spent. It has been proven that these companies' best, most innovative ideas were developed during their employees "free time," and these innovations feed and sustain the other 80 percent of their workload. Very similar to the premise behind Genius Hour (www.geniushour.com), our workshop time is our subject-specific 20 percent "free time" that supports, inspires, and fuels the remaining 80 percent of class time that is spent on teaching curriculum.

According to Pink, "Autonomous people working toward mastery perform at very high levels. But those who do so in the service of some greater objective can achieve even more"

(2009, 133). Furthermore, "People need autonomy over task (what they do), time (when they do it), and technique (how they do it). Companies that offer autonomy, sometimes in radical doses, are outperforming their competitors" (2009, 207).

In my classroom, we write on a daily basis for a variety of reasons, including reading response, research, writing to learn, and the other "school writing" in our curriculum. *And* we proclaim one day a week as Workshop Day (my students tend to like Mondays for this purpose, and I have to admit it is a great way to start the week). This day is sacred; no matter what else is going on in our world, we workshop.

> *I got frustrated in school because there were always rules about what you were Supposed to Write: about your summer vacation, about Shakespeare. I wanted to be able to make everything up, even then.*
>
> —Sarah Dessen, author of *Lock and Key, Just Listen, The Truth About Forever*, and many other YA titles

We begin each workshop with "Writer's Wisdom"—author advice specifically selected from the myriad quotes the students have collected (and from quotes I've compiled over the years) to reinforce the day's lesson. Then I teach a mini-lesson. In the first semester, the lessons take the form of a Weekly Writing Challenge (WWC); in the second semester, this may be a lesson on a specific revision, editing, or publication strategy. After the lessons are presented and modeled, the students get to test out the new strategy and/or continue working on their own workshop checklist or on their novels, while I circulate through the room and confer. In effect, Workshop Day—and the accompanying WWC work—becomes their 20 percent free time, which again feeds the 80 percent curricular time.

Conferencing looks different in the first semester than it does in the second. For the first half of the year, I tend to do more small-group conferring to build my community of writers and to teach them how to properly offer and receive feedback to their peers. During this time, we discuss the students' writing experiences from the previous writing challenge— what worked and what didn't, the ease/difficulty of the task compared to previous challenges, and the quality of writing compared to the entries from the previous weeks. For example, for week two's WWC, Emulating Text, I might ask questions such as these: *What was special about the original piece of writing that you jotted down in your writer's notebook? How did you decide to emulate it? (Did you write off a line? Imitate the author's vivid word choices or style? Take the idea and make it your own?) Where did your ideas come from for your piece of writing? Do you think the snippet of text you wrote has the potential to be further developed into a full-length piece?* By the time we get to week eight, when we are working on setting in WWC 8: Stop (and Listen): Tools for Developing Setting, I am posing questions such as these: *Why did you select the settings that you chose to write about? Which senses were easiest to include in your writing? Which senses were the most difficult? How did using sensory details (i.e., imagery) help you to re-create the scene? What luscious language, crafts, or figures of speech from previous lessons did you find creeping into your writing? Did it seem easier to include these things in this WWC than in others?* (For a complete list of suggested writing conference questions, see Appendix A.)

During our small-group conferences, I take a moment to check for completion, and then everyone in the group is required to share one of their latest entries from their writer's notebook. After each share, all of the group's participants are expected to offer one specific reflection of *praise* (a genuine compliment about the writing) and a *push* (a piece of constructive criticism to help the author move his or her writing forward). These are jotted down on mini sticky notes by the listeners and posted directly on the author's entry for future reference.

Second-semester conferring is much more individualized, as the students become more autonomous. During this time, my conference groupings vary depending on the unique needs of the students in my class. For example, if one student is struggling with developing an idea specific to his or her own story, then I will meet one-on-one with him or her to explore avenues for idea development. Similarly, if a group of students are all working on figuring out the nuances of weaving internal and external dialogue into a narrative scene, I'll pull them all together around a mentor text so that we can work through it together. My goal for this portion of the year is to meet each student's needs on his or her way to publication. Many of these conferences are driven by student request and based on their Writer's Workshop Process Checklist (see Appendix B), where both the student and I must sign off for each phase of completion.

The upcoming chapters in this book will help you establish the Reading, Writing, and Publishing strands for the first and second semesters of the workshop through a variety of hands-on lessons and materials. Figure 2.3 shows a sample handout containing the Weekly Writing Challenge topics in the order I present them in my classroom. The list is based on the advice my students have collected from authors. The order and content of this list is subject to change from year to year, depending on my students' findings, curriculum tie-ins, and specific classroom needs. (Figure 2.1 includes the breakdown of information and what I will grade in each of the three areas.) The first fourteen lessons occur during the first half of the school year. I use the remainder to start the second semester workshop, in which the primary goal is to select two or more vignettes from their writer's notebooks to expand into fully developed manuscripts.

Each of the WWC topics and the correlating author strategies can be found in Chapters 3–8. Advice from authors is sprinkled throughout those chapters and at the beginning of all WWC lessons to make the connections between the writing work that authors do and the writing work that students will be doing more clear and to serve as a model for your class.

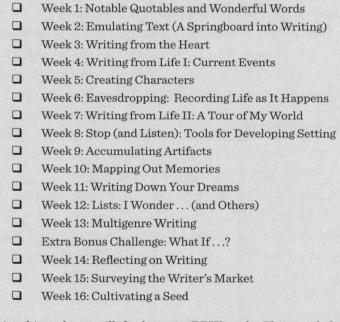

Mrs. M-K's Weekly Writing Challenges

For the first semester of this course, we will be exploring many of the different ways that authors use their writer's notebooks. Each week (or so), you will be asked to complete one of the writing challenges listed below on your own time at home. All tasks will be introduced in class prior to being assigned (so do not attempt to work ahead), and they should all be completed within your writer's notebook.

Progress on Weekly Writing Challenges will be monitored via in-class teacher-student conferences. So keep track of what you've done on your writing log and don't procrastinate . . . If you've found a challenge that you particularly enjoy, feel free to continue adding to it even after the week it's assigned. If you find that one of these tasks inspires you to take a piece of writing even further, go for it!

- ❑ Week 1: Notable Quotables and Wonderful Words
- ❑ Week 2: Emulating Text (A Springboard into Writing)
- ❑ Week 3: Writing from the Heart
- ❑ Week 4: Writing from Life I: Current Events
- ❑ Week 5: Creating Characters
- ❑ Week 6: Eavesdropping: Recording Life as It Happens
- ❑ Week 7: Writing from Life II: A Tour of My World
- ❑ Week 8: Stop (and Listen): Tools for Developing Setting
- ❑ Week 9: Accumulating Artifacts
- ❑ Week 10: Mapping Out Memories
- ❑ Week 11: Writing Down Your Dreams
- ❑ Week 12: Lists: I Wonder . . . (and Others)
- ❑ Week 13: Multigenre Writing
- ❑ Extra Bonus Challenge: What If . . .?
- ❑ Week 14: Reflecting on Writing
- ❑ Week 15: Surveying the Writer's Market
- ❑ Week 16: Cultivating a Seed

During this cycle, we will also have two **RRW** weeks. This stands for **Revisit & Revise Writing**. These weeks will fall during our first-semester holiday weeks. During such weeks, you could:

- ✒ *revisit* any of the strategies that you liked or found helpful to make new entries in your writer's notebook

  -or-

- ✒ *revise* any of the entries that you have already written to take them to the next level

Good Luck! Have fun & live like a writer!

Remember: Write . . . *As if each word could be the one that makes you famous!*

Figure 2.3 Detailed explanations of the Weekly Writing Challenges prepare students for the work ahead.

On his official website, children's author Andrew Clements writes, "Sometimes kids ask how I've been able to write so many books. The answer is simple: one word at a time. Which is a good lesson, I think. You don't have to do everything at once . . . You simply have to do that next good thing, and before you know it, you're living a good life."

Teaching writing well is the same. You don't have to do everything at once. From each lesson in this book, students will glean advice from mentor authors. You decide which elements will work best in your classroom now and which could be added on the future. Start small, and do that next good thing. Before you know it, as Andrew Clements says, you and your students will be living the good life.

Writer's Notebooks: Passport to an Authentic Writing Experience

In their book *Writing Workshop*, Ralph Fletcher and JoAnn Portalupi affirm the need to use a writer's notebook because "Many professionals consider a writer's notebook essential to their process of writing. It's an excellent tool for young writers as well" (2001, 26). I agree, with one caveat: impose an organizational strategy to make it easy for students and teachers to find a specific entry. As Kelly Gallagher (2006) does in his classroom, I have my students number the pages and set up a table of contents, but our writer's notebooks must have "permanent pages" that are reserved solely for the purpose of writing.

> *Before I begin to write I fill a notebook, jotting down everything that pops into my head about my characters and story—bits of dialogue, ideas for scenes, background information, descriptions of people and places, details and more details. But even with my notebook, I still don't know everything. For me, finding out is the best part of writing.*
>
> —Judy Blume, author of *Deenie; Are You There, God? It's Me, Margaret; As Long as We're Together*; and many other titles

When I first started teaching, I had my students keep grammar notes, examples of writing craft, and reading responses in their writer's notebooks, as well as all of their writing entries. Years later, I realized that this gave their notebooks a serious identity crisis. After all, how are you supposed to write freely and without judgment with all of those "lessons" staring you in the face? Now our notebooks are reserved strictly for writing—not note taking or analyzing literature. Those writing tasks have other homes in other notebooks.

Setting Up Writer's Notebooks

The day we create and organize our writer's notebooks is one of my favorite days of the school year. It takes nearly an entire class period to complete, but designating the time shows my students how significant this book will be in their lives that school year (and even beyond, for some). Note: I *know* this sounds like a task that surely any middle schooler could complete without such explicit instruction, but trust me when I say that the simplest tasks are the easiest to mess up.

Inside Organization

- Select an *enduring notebook,* such as a marble composition book with sewn-in pages, to help ensure that students' writing doesn't get lost and that they will have enough paper by the end of the year. Note: If some students insist on picking apart the seams (assuming you're using marble composition notebooks with sewn-in pages), apply a bead of hot glue directly on the stitches inside the front and back covers and along the center seam between the pages in the middle of the notebook, where the stitches are visible. That should do the trick! Some marble copy books have wide-ruled lines, which students might find too elementary. If so, tell them to be on the lookout for college-ruled notebooks—they do exist. Also, beware of the notebooks found in discount stores. In my experience, most of these books have fewer than one hundred pages, which is not sufficient for a full year of middle grades writing.)
- Ask students to take out a *pencil* (yes, this is an extremely important detail) and small sticky notes and open to the first page of the blank notebook. Then, one step at a time, tell them to do the following: Write the number 1 in the upper right-hand corner of the first page. Turn the page. In the upper left-hand corner of this page (the back of page one), write the number 2. Then go to the upper right-hand corner of the next page and write the number 3. Continue this meticulous process for a few more pages. Ask students what they notice about all the numbers on the left-hand pages (they are even). Ask them what they notice about the numbers on the right (they are odd). Then have students continue numbering on their own until they get to the sewn-in seam at the middle of the notebook. Ask them to raise a hand when they get to the middle of the notebook so you can check for accuracy.
- Once students get to the center of the notebook, the page numbers should be 100 and 101 (assuming a 200-page book). Some of your students will inevitably find that their numbering is off at this point. Here are some troubleshooting tips:
  - If the odd and even numbers are switched, have them go back and find the place where it happened. Erase and renumber.
  - If the odd and even numbers are in the right place, but the numbers are not 100 and 101, it is likely that they skipped numbers or missed pages that were stuck together. Have them go back and find the place where the error happened. Erase and renumber.

- If the odd and even numbers are in the right place, but the numbers are not 100 and 101, and they've already thoroughly checked and it is clear that they did not skip any numbers or miss any pages that were stuck together, it is possible that their book is just missing pages or has a few extras. You will know if this is the case if at the center sewn-in pages, their numbers are off by a multiple of *two* or if by the end, they are off by a multiple of *four*. If this is the case, simply hot-glue the extra pages into the seam at the back of the book.

- Once you have checked a student's numbering at the middle and made sure he or she is on track, the student is ready to finish numbering the rest of the book. Obviously, all students should arrive at 200 on the last page (except for those few who may be missing pages or have a few extra).

- The next step is to make the table of contents. I create chapters based on my needs and the overall themes of my writing workshop lessons (feel free to modify these, based on your classroom instruction). The table of contents is on page 1 of the notebooks. On page 1, have students write down chapter titles and page numbers that you specify. Here are the chapters I use:

Chapter 1:   Words of Wisdom   page 3
Where we keep track of our favorite author advice to stay motivated.

Chapter 2:   Memories   page 9
Where we gather our writing that stems from stories in our past.

Chapter 3:   Writing from Life   page 45
*Where we store our writing that stems from our current lives—from newspaper
    articles, from conversations we've overheard, from places we frequent.*

Chapter 4:   Writing from Literature   page 85
*Where we jot down amazing quotes (lines, sentences, or passages) from books, songs,
    and poems to inspire our writing, and where we emulate that text in our own words.*

Chapter 5:   Writing from ... Who Knows Where?   page 107
*Where we put all of the writing ideas that just come to us from, well ... who knows
    where?*

Chapter 6:   Writing from Class   page 133
*Where our in-class writing goes; this may be writing I have students do on specific
    topics, themes, or structures.*

Chapter 7:   Lists   page 179
Where we log our writing territories' "really cool words" and other personal inventories that feed our writing.

- Now we need to create the *dividers* that delineate the writer's notebook chapters. Have the kids open their notebooks flat on their desks and hold page 3/4 vertically up. Instruct them to fold the page in half toward the right so that the number 3 is visible when folded to the center seam. Have them lay the half page flat on top of page 5, then turn their notebooks sideways so they can write "Words of Wisdom" across the divider page. Repeat this process for each of the remaining chapters.
- The final step in organizing the inside of the notebook is creating *tabs* for the chapter dividers. (This is completely optional, but I find it helpful.) We use standard 3-by-3-inch sticky notes for the tabs. Have students peel off enough sticky notes so that they have one for each chapter. Ask them to spread them out on their desks with the sticky side facedown and the *bottom* edge stuck to the desk. Tell them to write one chapter title small at the *top* edge (this is the loose edge) of each sticky note. They need to make sure the title is written in the right place on the sticky note tab so that when it's attached to the inside of the corresponding folded divider, the title is visible sticking out from the top of the notebook. For a more finished look, students will want to open up the folded chapter divider and place the sticky note on the left-hand side of the inside of the divider page before folding it back over and moving on to the next tab. (For example, for the divider that is on page 3/4, students open up the folded page and place the sticky note at the top of page 4, to the left of the fold, so that the chapter title reaches past the top of the notebook. When they fold the divider back into place, the tab can be seen.)

Outside Cover Options

The outside cover is simple. I give each student an outline of large capital letters:

to decorate. The letters should be large enough to cover the entire front cover of their writer's notebooks, and there needs to be plenty of white space inside the letters to decorate however they want—with hand-drawn objects, clip art, photos, and so forth. The end result must represent the student author who will be writing in the notebook. Additionally, the student's name must appear somewhere on the cover, and the expectation is that the front cover will be carefully done and overall worthy of cover art.

When finished, students glue or tape the design onto the cover. I have also found that placing clear contact paper over the entire completed cover goes a long way toward preserving the cover art.

Mastering the Strokes: Filling the Pages of the Writer's Notebook

Now that we've talked about the design and organization of the writer's notebook, it is time to figure out how the students will use their creations. As mentioned earlier, our first semester is filled with writing tasks developed from strategies that our students have found on their favorite authors' websites. My next step is to sort through the quotes that the kids have collected, and then I either pin them to an existing writing strategy that I already teach or develop a new strategy lesson in order to connect the work that authors do with the work that my students are doing in their writer's notebooks. It is always best to highlight the author's advice first and then hop into the Weekly Writing Challenge mini-lesson.

The "category" that best suits the WWC determines the chapter where the writing is done in the notebook for each lesson. Entries for WWC 1: Notable Quotables and WWC 2: Emulating Text, for example, would be written in Chapter 4, "Writing from Literature," whereas WWC 3: Writing from the Heart may have entries that could be written in Chapter 2, "Memories," or Chapter 3, "Writing from Life," depending on whether the topic selected reflects a special moment from the past or a topic of current importance. It may sound complicated, but once you establish the habit of organizing entries with the students, it all falls into place and you will find that they will determine for themselves where entries belong. Ultimately, this system makes it far easier to locate and reference prior entries than notebooks that are only organized by date. The ability to locate specific entries becomes critical when it comes to preparing for novel writing and publication, as students will often seek "seeds" to plant and grow in later pieces.

> *[I]t's important to pay attention to your ideas and write them down. If you do, you'll start having more and more of them. It's almost as if your imagination suddenly realizes it's being taken seriously.*
>
> —Elise Broach, author of *Masterpiece, Desert Crossing,* and *Shakespeare's Secret*

In the following chapters, all of the Weekly Writing Challenges are described in detail and the corresponding author advice is revealed. I have also included additional materials and handouts that I use for the lessons, as well as simple how-to guides.

PART 2

Basecamp: What Do Authors Do?

Reading the advice of those who have traveled before us can open our eyes to the pitfalls and possibilities that are typically only known to native populations. Travel magazines and websites can inspire us with ideas for excursions we'd like to take and activities we'd like to try during our expeditions. The classroom is no different. Reading helps us understand the terrain of writing.

In this section, we start building a foundation that connects reading to writing. The focus is establishing authors as mentors and showing students how to self-select mentor texts. The Backstage Pass and the Weekly Writing Challenges presented here become the critical front-loading lessons that will lay the groundwork for all your workshop needs during a school year. As part of this apprenticeship approach, we get the most out of nightly "free reading" by connecting this writerly reading habit to advice from published authors. We describe how to help students learn to read through a writer's telescope, bringing into view interesting word choices, new personal vocabulary, and writer's crafts. Throughout the year students continue to scrutinize all the novels they read to build a collection of crafts and techniques that they can transfer into their own writing. These "go-to texts" can guide them as they are writing. When students feel uncertain about their writing, they can refer to an author, an expert in the field, and draw inspiration for writing that is more than just acceptable. This approach is so powerful because students are learning directly from the authors they admire.

Chapter 3

The Reading-Writing Connection

My main advice for kids who want to write would be to read a lot of books. I know everybody says that, but it really is true. . . . You should read the kinds of books you want to write. . . . And obviously, you should write all the time. . . . So much of writing is just sitting there and writing.

—Meg Cabot,
author of the Princess Diaries series, the All-American Girl series,
and many other titles

When I was in eighth grade, I stopped reading. I no longer read for school or pleasure. I learned that if you can't keep up with the pace of everyone else, then you must be dumb (even if slowing down meant visualizing and enjoying it more). I also *learned* that there was little point to reading if all I had to do was pay attention in class to earn respectable grades on the test. (I was no dummy; why put in the extra work if it wasn't necessary?)

I don't want my students leaving my classroom feeling the way I did in middle school. I know now that reading matters—not just for reading's sake, but also for writing's sake. When adolescents dislike reading, they can't grasp the importance of writing for an audience of readers because they transfer their negative attitudes about reading to anyone who may read their own writing. In addition, nonreaders usually have limited vocabulary development and often do not recognize the craft and structures that make for good writing. Such students also can't create or replicate good writing on their own, for high-stakes assessments, or outside the classroom. They never make the connection that reading can inform writing in ways that go far beyond traditional research or school assignments.

We need to give our students experiences that will help them to see these connections and fortify their writing toolboxes. As Katie Wood Ray recognizes in *Wondrous Words*, "Reading is the writer's way of visiting another craftperson's 'gallery' . . . And when readers read, they can't help but see writing possibilities in the texts they encounter" (1999, 13). When we can combine the reading of authors' published words with their advice and strategies for writing, as we do in a writing apprenticeship approach, we show students how reading relates to their own reading and writing lives. In *Reading Reasons,* Kelly Gallagher acknowledges that reluctant writing often stems from reluctant reading. He believes, "When we read, good writing is modeled for us. Seeing these models over a period of time makes us better writers" (2003, 66).

If you've ever traveled with teenagers, you know what a challenge it can be to keep spirits high and attitudes in check. From experience, I've learned one of the best ways to keep adolescents "on board" is to involve them in the planning process and let them help build the itinerary.

> *Read, find out what you like to read, and try to figure out what it is about it that makes you like it.*
> —Louis Sachar, author of *Holes, Fuzzy Mud, Small Steps, Card Turner*, and other titles

In the classroom, we must likewise involve students in their learning. When students can work together to share their insights (as real authors do), and when their discoveries help to guide the classroom instruction, they find validation for their assignments, which makes it worth the extra time we spent planning them. When our students are actively involved in deciding what advice we glean from published authors, what they will write about, and which writing pieces they will take through the entire writing process to publication, they become invested in their learning.

I recognize the need to *cover* the curriculum, but it is also critical that we keep one thing in perspective: Most of us did not get into teaching to teach a *curriculum*. We became teachers to teach *students*. As the experts in our field, we still need to be the authority in deciding how our students will best acquire that curricular knowledge, and that can change from year to year depending on our students as well as on innovations in our field. We need to listen to our students—their interests, their strengths, and their struggles. We need to be open to new ideas and ways of learning that will help students find success in the classroom and beyond. We need to recognize that, sometimes, the most effective lessons that we teach can come from the students themselves, but only if we give them the opportunity to contribute and participate in the process of their learning.

Let the Apprenticeship Begin!

Before our favorite authors were writers, they were readers. They had years of experience being entertained, deeply touched, or even scared by the writing of authors who came before them. They learned what they enjoyed about reading (and what they didn't). They discovered topics that moved and inspired them. They learned their craft, noticing details, word choices, and interesting uses of punctuation. As Kelly Gallagher shares in *Teaching Adolescent Writers*, "Students need the opportunity to read and study other authors" (2006, 13). The Backstage Pass assignment offers students this opportunity to study authors—their inspirations, strategies, and techniques for writing. In addition to giving me the basis for a new lesson or an extension for one of my tried-and-true lessons, tackling the Backstage Pass assignment also helps my students begin to think of themselves as writers. As they read the ideas and advice of their much-loved authors, they begin thinking, "Oh, yeah, that makes sense. I could try that!" Our students can feel as if they are developing their writing right alongside their mentors, imitating the processes, and testing out their strategies.

As I was writing this book, National Council of Teachers of English revised their 2004 "Beliefs About the Teaching of Writing" to reflect an updated perspective on writing as a process in a new statement entitled "Professional Knowledge for the Teaching of Writing." This updated version reflects and reinforces so many of the processes and practices that I use with my students. In it, NCTE shares the following:

> Often, when people think of writing, they think of texts—finished pieces of writing that stand alone. Understanding what writers do, however, involves thinking both about what texts look like when they are finished as well as thinking about what strategies writers might employ to produce those texts. . . . The procedural knowledge developed through reflective practice helps writers most when they encounter difficulty, or when they are in the middle of creating a piece of writing. How does someone get started? What do they do when they get stuck? How do they plan the overall process, each section of their work, and even the rest of the sentence they are writing right now? Research, theory, and practice in the teaching of writing has produced a rich understanding of what writers do, those who are proficient and professional as well as those who struggle. (NCTE 2016)

Nearly all YA and middle grade authors have websites or blogs where they share valuable advice and strategies with young readers and writers. Their books include wonderful examples of craft as well as interesting sentence structures and word choices made at every level, from picture books to complex novels. My young writers begin their apprenticeship by mining these resources for inspiration that will help them to be successful in their own writing throughout the year. Sharing authors' advice and practices helps build confidence and a sense of community in the classroom.

Approaching writing from one author to another also levels the playing field for all learners. The examples that come from books far below the seventh-grade reading level can be as valuable as the selections from books favored by our most advanced readers.

A few years ago, I had a student in my seventh-grade class named Kyle who was shy and socially awkward. He was also a lower-level reader according to his test scores. At the end of the second day of class, he slowly packed up his belongings, stalling, waiting for everyone else to leave before he approached me.

"Mrs. M-K . . . I think I'm in the wrong class," he said, without making eye contact.

I looked at him, puzzled, and asked, "Kyle, what makes you think that?"

"I don't know . . . I'm not good at any of this stuff. I don't like reading and I suck at writing. There's no way I can do this."

Prior to being in my heterogeneously grouped classroom, Kyle had been placed in the lowest language arts class (for "learning support" students). In those classrooms, the curriculum and/or the expectations were modified so that students with learning disabilities could feel successful by meeting these modified learning goals. No wonder he felt anxious and unsure of his abilities.

"Well, my friend, I do know one thing," I said, smiling. "If *I* didn't think you could do this, you wouldn't be in my class. You are just going to have to trust me on that!" But I could still see the uncertainty on his face. "My job is to help you see for yourself all of the potential that I already see in you. I *know* you can do this."

Kyle rolled his eyes and let out a sigh, looking more defeated than inspired. He knew he wasn't getting out of this class.

"Look, you like being on the computer, don't you?"

He nodded.

"This first assignment will be a piece of cake for you, then! Which author are you going to investigate?"

Kyle shrugged his shoulders. I reached over and pulled *The Kid Who Only Hit Homers* by Matt Christopher from his pile of notebooks and binders. "How about this?" Kyle had chosen this as his free reading book.

Kyle snatched it back. "I can't. It's a baby book."

"Really? Why don't you check out the author's website and see if you feel differently. I am sure that he will have some pretty good advice. He's been an author for a long time, you know."

With that, Kyle left. The next day, he came in with a different demeanor. When I asked the table groups to share the authorly advice they'd found online, Kyle listened as two other kids shared quotes from their authors' websites. Then he found the confidence to share his quote from Matt Christopher aloud:

> I had my own personal experiences, and I saw how other players reacted to plays, to teammates and fans' remarks and innuendoes, to managers' orders, etc. All these had a great influence on my writing . . . I've lived through a lot of problems many children live through, and I find these problems excellent examples to include in my books.

Kyle's tablemate, a high-achieving student named Sarah, sat up and commented, "Oh, that's cool. So he played sports as a kid, and then wrote stories about his experiences when he got older."

"Well," Kyle said, smiling, "actually, I think he started writing when he was like fourteen."

"Wow, *really*? I'm twelve now," Sarah said. "Can you imagine?"

"Oh, yeah, that is pretty cool. So, like, I could write about stuff that happened at one of my soccer tournaments, or something," said Marc, another student at the table.

"Yeah," said Kyle, "I mean, I think it can be anything, like sports or whatever you do— you can write about it."

I love Kyle's idea that you can write about anything—that whatever you do, you can write about it. It's so empowering. Suddenly, the boy who had very little confidence in socializing or writing was conversing with his classmates about strategies for developing writing ideas.

In the past, it was difficult to gain admission to an author's world of writing, but these days the Internet provides an all-access backstage pass for children of all levels and abilities. By exploring an author's official website and other resources, students can fill your bulletin boards and your classroom lessons with inspiration, advice, and insights about the writing process.

In *Wondrous Words* (1999), Katie Wood Ray writes, "It's not what a piece of writing is about, but how it is written that makes good writing *good*" (93). When Ray says *how*, she is referring to both *product* and *process*. Let's look at each of these in turn.

When teaching students about *product*, we refer to mentor texts. We may ask, "What's going on in this published piece of text that makes it so powerful?" We encourage our students to notice how the words work together to make the reader sit up and say *wow*. We examine the components of good writing in the hope that our students will begin to use them in their own writing.

But how did the author know what to write in the first place? This question leads to the discussion of *process*. Where do authors get their ideas? How do they develop topics for exploration, characters, and plots? We need to show our students how professional writers work to help them think of themselves as writers.

Author Quest: A Pursuit to Uncover the Creative Process

I have learned that I cannot simply assign the Backstage Pass with enthusiasm and expect tremendous results. So, in preparation for that assignment, we have a mini-reading-writing lesson about the writing process called Author Quest. I ask my students to imagine that they will have the opportunity to interview their favorite authors—*not* as readers, but as *writers*. I ask students to brainstorm a list of the questions they would ask, not only because they are curious about how the authors do their jobs but also because students want to learn how to advance their own writing. Ultimately, we want our students to get up close and personal with their favorite authors by searching for answers to any or all of their "interview" questions. They look for the answers to the interview questions in the form of quotes and actual advice directly from the author.

For the Author Quest activity, I prefer using a think-pair-share technique to open up the questioning possibilities for all: students who love the limelight, quietly thoughtful kids, and those who lack the background reading knowledge to even know which questions to ask. First, students take a few minutes to brainstorm questions on their own. Then, they discuss their ideas with a partner. Finally, partner pairs share ideas in a whole-class discussion. Student-generated interview question ideas generally include these:

- Do you have a special/regular writing place?
- When and how often do you write? How long does it take to complete a book?
- What inspires you? Where do you come up with your ideas for what to write about?
- Once you have a topic, how do you make it come to life and make it seem so real to the reader with details and descriptions?
- Do you have any prewriting or organizing habits or advice? (My students usually have a bunch of very specific questions related to this general one, including asking if "real" authors use note cards, outlines, plot roller coasters, four squares, or other tools that teachers often encourage student writers to use. Do you see where this is going? *"If real authors don't do this, then why should I?"* Already, students are comparing the habits of writers to their own.)
- Do you ever get writer's block? If so, how do you get past it?
- Who is your favorite author? Favorite book? Why? Do these influence your

writing in any way? (As a side note, I tell my kids to keep an eye out for answers to these question and possibly write down their findings in the *Lists* section of their writer's notebook for future reference. If they really like a particular author, students can discover additional enjoyable reading possibilities based on that author's recommendations—more reading that can serve to inform their writing.)

- Do you ever have to research historical, scientific, or other facts about which you want to be accurate? If so, when do you need to research and how do you do it?
- What specific advice do you have for . . .
  - developing characters/setting/plot/conflict?
  - revising and editing? (Students will learn that these are two very different things.)
  - creating realistic dialogue?

I encourage students to look for any advice that has to do with reading-writing connections, as well as for any other interesting insights about writing that their author has that the students hadn't thought to ask about. Taking time to brainstorm the inquiry possibilities expands students' collective knowledge base, builds excitement, and ensures that they will give quality responses.

Typically, I type students' interview questions into my computer and project them onto the board for the class to see as we discuss, and then I send the document to the printer. Before the end of class, I send a runner down to pick up the copies so that all of the students will have our compiled list of questions at their disposal. Alternatively, I can post the interview questions along with the upcoming Backstage Pass assignment on my school web page for easy access at home or from our media center if we choose to begin that assignment there.

> *Write the sort of thing you like to read and the sort of thing you want to write. And if it doesn't get published, try again.*
>
> —Philip Pullman, author of the fantasy trilogy *His Dark Materials* and other titles

The All-Access Backstage Pass: A Sneak Peek into an Author's World

I have my students complete the Backstage Pass activity one to three times during the school year (depending on the students that I have in class each year and their growth and development throughout the year). We always complete the activity during the first week of school in order to build interest, to secure student buy-in, and to get kids talking and thinking about authors, writing craft, and the way books are constructed. This also helps me to begin building a library of quotes from the authors who are important to *my students*. I use the author quotes as a rationale for and as a springboard into my reading and writing workshop lessons and for the rest of the curriculum. My friend Lois teaches in a smaller, private-school setting, so she already knows well in advance who her students will be for the following year. She designates the Backstage Pass as one of her "over-the-summer" language arts assignments so that her students will come in ready to share their discoveries and begin their own journeys into authorship from day one.

Some years I have chosen to begin each marking period with a Backstage Pass in order to refresh our writerly minds and to expose students to new authors and, therefore, to new opportunities for reading. The Backstage Pass assignment has additional bonuses for teachers: it helps you learn about the authors your students are reading throughout the year, including what these authors have to say about the process of writing. These are the lessons that will help to guide your writing workshop.

There is a beautiful synergy to this process. Your students do the footwork (and they *want* to because it involves technology and because they want a say in driving the classroom instruction), and then you develop the lessons or simply infuse the quotes into the lessons that you had already planned to teach to add an extra layer of affirmation for your students. My students love seeing the quotes and strategies they discovered up on the big screen as I introduce each new mini-lesson. They are proud of their contributions and feel a sense of ownership that makes them want to work harder on each lesson.

By helping our students discover how writers work, we are showing them that writing isn't just a *school thing;* writing is an important skill to learn for communicating ideas, passions, concerns, and creativity. Through the Backstage Pass activity, students begin to hear this message: Whether you are a student or an author, your ideas matter and your ability to share them effectively is what will help you to be successful in school and out in the world.

In *Study Driven: A Framework for Planning Units of Study in the Writing Workshop*, Katie Wood Ray encourages teachers to cultivate an inquiry approach to writing that will enable students to thrive when they leave the classroom. She writes that "if teachers eliminate the gray areas and give students a simple way to write something, not only is the teaching not true to product, it isn't true to process either. Outside of school, when faced with tasks that require composition, writers have to figure out how to write things. No one gives them a graphic organizer, and the struggle to organize and make everything work together is there anew every time they set out to write. This struggle is an essential part of the writing process, and if it's taken away, students develop a false sense of how real writing gets done" (2006, 27).

Creating this classroom inquiry environment does take some planning, but trust me when I say it's worth it. In this process, everyone wins because this one simple assignment provides the basis for an entire year's worth of learning opportunities!

Backstage Passes are very simple to create. I prefer to use colored, unlined 4-by-6-inch cards, designating a different color for each class. The first year I used the cards, I asked my students to write down the stems for the information to be recorded on the cards, but it looked very sloppy when I put them up on the bulletin board (and some students were missing pieces of the assignment because they hadn't copied the stems properly, or at all). I have learned that it is much easier for everyone if I type up a blank card on the computer, print it out, and make copies directly onto the cards.

There is also a place on the Backstage Pass (see Figure 3.1) where students can record interesting items beyond writing advice that they find out about their authors. Some students will be exhilarated by the opportunity to explore and share all the information they find on websites. On the other hand, you may have several students who cannot remember a book they *ever* liked, let alone an author whom they want to emulate. My advice is to direct them to www.slimekids.com. SLiMe is an acronym for **S**chool **Li**brary **Me**dia. The website was developed by teacher Andy Fine. From the SLiMe site, students can explore numerous reputable book review websites as well as book trailers and author sites to find a book or author worthy of investigation.

Here are four tips to help students find just the right author advice that will inform your classroom mini-lessons:

1. Locate the official author website by going to a search engine and typing in the author's name followed by *official website.* (This is important to tell them, because some kids will try to be clever and type "author quotes on writing" into the search bar. This obviously defeats the purpose, and it is unlikely that they will find a quote by a current YA author that they will be interested in anyway.)

2. As you navigate the website, look for tabs such as "Interviews," "FAQs," "Author Info," and so on. (Tell your students to be prepared to do some digging. Most sites won't have a tab entitled, "Here are my quotes about writing.")

3. If you do not find any noteworthy author advice anywhere in the site, go back to the search engine and type in your author's name followed by "interviews." (Again, students may need to poke around a bit while investigating various sites, but typically, something of value does pop up.* Prepare your students to expect transcripts of interviews, Q & A sessions in ezines, or audio/video interviews, which your students will need to transcribe.)

4. Regardless of where the information comes from, it is important always to record your sources.

Front of Note Card

VIP BACKSTAGE PASS

This pass entitles _____ (name) to an
All-ACCESS backstage tour of your favorite author's studio!

During your tour, pay close attention, so you will be able to record at least one really awesome & inspirational quote from your author about writing <u>on the back of your pass</u> (*think: a writing place; inspiration; idea generation; prewriting and organizing; writer's block; revising/editing; publishing; reading-writing connections; developing characters, setting, plot, and dialogue, etc.*)

Jot down other cool things you find out about your author below:

1.

2.

3.

Back of Note Card

Quote about writing:

From (author's name):

Author of (list books written by author):

http://

Figure 3.1 The all-access pass gives young writers the VIP treatment as they explore the background of their favorite authors.

*A note on using "unofficial" sites: Be wary of using sites that are not labeled as "the official website of . . ." Anyone can create and host a website these days; not all sources are reputable. If you need to find an alternative site that is valid, I suggest checking out Scholastic's website at www.scholastic.com (it also has wonderful video book talks and interviews broken down by topic for many of our favorite YA authors—a great addition to any mini-lesson!), Bookbrowse (www.bookbrowse. com), Bethany Roberts' Directory of Children's Book Authors and Illustrators (www.bethanyroberts.com/childrensbookauthorsA-Z), or the website of the author's publisher.

As students share the quotes and other interesting findings with their peers, they pique interest in new authors and promote peer recommendations. Often, authors use their websites to reveal their favorite books and authors, literary inspirations, and other authors or characters they would most like to meet. These nuggets can offer fabulous springboard opportunities for both the avid reader and the dormant reader. In essence, it can make reading more accessible to all.

Reading Through the Writer's Eyes

One gloomy Monday afternoon, as students were lackadaisically strolling into my room for my final language arts block of the day, Marisa came barreling in, waving a book adorned with a multitude of sticky notes poking out at arbitrary angles. "I will never be able to just *read* a book again, thanks to you!" she said in a snarky voice that any seventh-grade teacher would recognize.

> *Imagine what it would be like if every day you had to pay even just one penny for every word you use. Words are free, they can't be used up; they are ideas. They are what we use to dream with, and think with, and communicate good thoughts and bad thoughts, and dream and pray . . . and you know, they're pretty amazing things. I think the more kids become aware of that, the more they become aware of the power of words. That awareness makes us better thinkers, and it certainly makes us better writers and thinkers.*
>
> —Andrew Clements, author of *Frindle, Things Not Seen,* and other titles

"Um . . . *sorry?*" I replied, clearly not understanding the context here.

"Well, you *should* be," she admonished me. "Do you see my book? Do you see all of these little *things* sticking out of it? *And,* do you know why they are all there?" She leaned in with the best hairy eyeball she could muster. "Well, it's *not* because I had a lot of questions."

I couldn't help but laugh at her dramatics. "Okay, so, what happened?"

"I can't read just to read—just to *enjoy* reading—anymore. You know I love to read. You know I always have to have a book in my hand, right? Well, now, I have to have my book *and* my Post-its! I can't help myself. I can't stop reading like a writer. I can't stop Post-it-ing things!"

From Mentor Authors to Mentor Texts, Self-Selection Is Fundamental for Middle School Students

It seems simple enough—reading is the gateway to better writing. Once we can get kids reading (first, in class, and then on their own), most of them can quickly identify what they like about a book—from word choice and craft to plot development and characters. Although this intentional reading of the text is an obvious *reading* workshop lesson, it also helps kids to understand how a writer's craft move may influence their opinion or enjoyment of a book. With the right guidance from teachers this discovery, in turn, sets up a series of *writing* workshop lessons where the students learn to raise the quality of their own writing by mimicking the literature they are reading. If you are a middle school teacher, the idea of using mentor text or children's books (as presented in WWC 1, which follows this section) might be unfamiliar, whereas our elementary counterparts are likely well versed in using mentor texts. Either way, it's important that we begin with a consistent understanding of what we mean by *mentor texts*. Who better to turn to than Lynne Dorfman and Rose Cappelli, the women who wrote the book on it? In *Mentor Texts: Teaching Writing Through Children's Literature, K–6*, they explain:

- "Mentor texts are pieces of literature that we can turn to again and again as we help our young writers learn how to do what they may not yet be able to do on their own."
- "Mentor texts serve as snapshots into the future. They help students envision the kind of writer they can become; they help teachers move the whole writer, rather than each individual piece of writing, forward. Writers can imitate the mentor text and continue to find new ways to grow. In other words, mentor texts help students and teachers continually reinvent themselves as writers."
- "[Mentor texts] ignite the writer's imagination and determination to create high-quality text that mirrors the mentor text in many ways. Mentor texts help writers notice things about an author's work that is not like anything they may have done before, and empower them to try something new." (2007, 2–4)

Over the summer, I always pick up several new middle-level novels. Some I read right away, partly because my brain has been craving the time and space to sit down, uninterrupted, to just read something for pure pleasure, and partly because I want to have some new books to talk about and recommend when I return to school. However, I save a few novels to read during the school year. When I give my students free reading time, I also pull out one of my books and read to myself. Reading when students read shows them that you value reading as an *activity* (rather than an *assignment*), and it lets them get a view into your reading life—your facial expressions, your sticky note habits, your process. It is a great opportunity to share your firsthand experiences with a new book and to start making that reading-writing mentorship connection.

Because our students are writing with the expectation of future publication, they will need to examine texts to discover for themselves why these authors and their works were so successful. In elementary school, teachers typically select the mentor texts for the entire class to study and then return to these periodically throughout the year. In middle school, the responsibility for selection ultimately must transfer from teacher to student. Obviously, teachers will need to model the process. Depending on the level and experience your class has with reading like a writer, you may want to make this transition naturally by using the students' self-selected "free reading" novels as the basis of discovery, or you could take a more scaffolded approach by beginning with picture books and moving up to the more complex text in novels. Either way, Dorfman and Cappelli agree that "young writers should be introduced to mentor texts first as readers. They need to hear and appreciate the story and characters as well as the rhythms, words, and message" (2007, 5).

We want to start by reading narrative texts (picture books, short stories, novels), because the text structure is fairly predictable. Students know what to expect, so it is a natural place to seek new crafts, punctuation and grammar, and author-specific writing strategies. Next, they can easily experiment and test these in their own writing within their writer's notebooks, free from judgment and grading. They first discover new craft in the familiar—that is, in their own free reading and other in-class texts. Then they document the strategies that authors use in their writing. And if they have the opportunity to apply these new techniques in their own "free writing"—that is, in their own self-selected vignettes in writer's notebooks—then, in no time, they will build up their writing confidence and fluency. In addition, they will be able to transfer these newly acquired skills into any mode of writing, including "school writing" tasks and high-stakes tests.

The primary focus of Weekly Writing Challenge 1 is to train the eye and ear to linger over language and to model the thinking behind reading through a writer's lens. Weekly Writing Challenge 2 enables students to see a world of possibilities in their writing that they may never have imagined before.

Weekly Writing Challenge 1: Notable Quotables and Wonderful Words

Weekly Writing Challenge 1: Notable Quotables and Wonderful Words (see Figure 3.2) was inspired by authors Christopher Paolini, Rick Riordan, Lois Lowry, and Ann M. Martin (and I am certain that your students will find a few more authors to support this strategy). In this lesson, students start on their journey, learning to read like writers.

There are two different paths that you can take in preparing for this WWC. The picture-book version includes a scaffold for students (and teachers) who may need to break down the process and take it more slowly through multiple lessons, whereas the novel version lumps all of the skills together in one lesson. For either version, visit a bookstore or library ahead of time to select a novel or to collect an array of quality picture books, if you do not have enough in your classroom. Figure 3.3 shows the breakdown of lessons.

Taking the Novel Path to WWC 1

I stage the novel-path lesson as though the students are going to be "free reading" for twenty minutes. I make sure everyone has a free reading book out, and then I set the timer and select my own book as they begin reading to themselves. This day I choose *The 5th Wave* by Rick Yancey. Instead of using an excerpt from a novel, I use the inside flap, because at this point in the year, I am trying to get students invested in reading and demonstrate a new lens through which to view the text. First, I carefully look at the front and back cover, and then I flip to the inside flap that contains the summary/teaser.

"Oh, my gosh, you guys, I am so sorry for interrupting," I exclaim, "but my book sounds so good. I have to share this with you." I read the inside flap aloud to them: "'After the 1st Wave, only darkness remains. After the 2nd, only the lucky escape. And after the 3rd, only the *un*lucky survive. After the 4th Wave, just one rule applies: trust no one.'

"Can you feel the suspense? *I really can't wait to read this!*" I share with the class, and several heads nod in agreement. "It's only four sentences long—and they are short ones too. How did this author make me *have* to read this book from just the first four sentences of the flap?"

Amanda calls out, "It's just creepy. It makes you wonder what happened and what's going to happen."

"Yeah, but why?" I ask, prodding. "What did the author do to lure you in?" I put the text up under the document reader, so everyone can see it.

Stephen raises his hand. "I like how he used 'lucky' and then '*un*lucky.' It's almost like it didn't matter if you survived or not, 'cause there's no way you are gonna make it."

"Yeah, and the 'after' and 'after' and 'after' actually makes you want to know what is coming next," Josh added.

Weekly Writing Challenge 1

"Read a lot. But don't just read for enjoyment; take a book you know is well-written and study how the author constructs the sentences and paragraphs. Also examine how he or she gets readers emotionally involved—whether through use of an engaging style, the characters' situations, or a combination thereof."

—Christopher Paolini, author of *Eragon* and the rest of the the Inheritance Cycle series

"Read everything you can get your hands on. You will learn the craft of writing by immersing yourself in the voices, styles and structures of writers who have gone before you."

—Rick Riordan, author of the Percy Jackson and the Olympians series, the Kane Chronicles series, and many other titles

"Think about what you read: how the author made it interesting, or funny, or suspenseful. And write as much as you can, too. Keep a journal."

—Lois Lowry, author of the Giver Quartet, *Number the Stars,* and and many other titles

"Check out how your favorite authors have caught your attention on the first page of their stories. You are the best judge of what captures your interest and makes you want to continue reading."

—Ann M. Martin, author of *A Corner of the Universe, A Dog's Life*, and many other titles

Weekly Writing Challenge 1: Notable Quotables and Wonderful Words

THE CHALLENGE

- Begin reading like a *writer* . . . As you read this week for your twenty minutes per night, start collecting "Really Cool Words" and amazing or inspiring lines and quotes from your free reading book. We're not talking vocabulary here . . . I mean *fantastic* writing that jumps off the page and makes you take notice!

- "Cool Words" go on your "Really Cool Words List"; quotes go in Chapter 4, "Writing from Literature," in your ME book.

Figure 3.2 Weekly Writing Challenge 1 features wonderful words and notable quotes.

NOVEL PATH (One Class Period)	PICTURE BOOK PATH (Two to Three Class Periods)
Lesson 1. Teacher reads aloud an excerpt from a selected novel. 2. During class discussion of the text, students describe the attributes that make the writing luscious (deliberate word choices, author's craft, etc.). These concepts are written on the board for reference as the students work independently. 3. Students are asked to independently read their self-selected free reading novels for twenty minutes and to be on the lookout for writing that inspires and cool words as we did during our discussion above. The examples they find should be marked with sticky notes (this is great practice for their work this week with WWC 1; this in-class time allows me to check for understanding before they go it alone). 4. At the end of the free reading time, ask students to share what they found with a partner. 5. Students then select their favorite example and write it down on one of their sticky notes (or you can distribute index cards) along with an explanation of why the example is so powerful. 6. Students share their examples with the class and display their responses on a wall or on the board for inspiration (we have a bulletin board for "Luscious Language" in my classroom that we use for this purpose). 7. Introduce WWC 1. 8. Distribute and have students affix the handout *Really Cool Words (that I want to use in my writing someday)*, as students did in Figure 3.4, onto the last page and inside back cover of their ME books (writer's notebooks). 9. Distribute and have students affix the *Writing That Inspires* worksheet (Figure 3.5) into the "Writing from Literature" chapter of their ME books. 10. Homework: Have students continue finding and then recording really cool words in the back of their ME books and writing that inspires in the "Writing from Literature" chapter throughout the week as they complete their nightly reading and meet expectations of WWC 1.	**Lesson 1** 1. Distribute and have students affix the handout *Really Cool Words (that I want to use in my writing someday)* onto the last page and inside back cover of their ME books (writer's notebooks). Present a brief mini-lesson about listening for really cool words. 2. Teacher reads aloud a picture book and thinks aloud as he or she finds and records really cool words from the reading. 3. Homework: Students continue to collect really cool words during nightly free reading, as they did in Figure 3.4. **Lesson 2** 1. Distribute and have students affix the handout *Writing That Inspires* (Figure 3.5) into the "Writing from Literature" chapter of their ME books. 2. Provide a brief mini-lesson about writing that inspires using the sheet mentioned above. 3. Teacher reads aloud a picture book and thinks aloud as he or she finds and records writing that inspires. Ask students to write their favorite quote from the read-aloud in the box at the bottom of Figure 3.5. 4. Optional Homework: Students can continue to collect words and begin to look for writing that inspires in nightly free reading. **Lesson 3** 1. In small groups, students begin picture book exploration and collection of writing that inspires. In their groups, they are to be on the lookout for writing that inspires and cool words, as we did during our earlier lessons. The examples they find should be marked with sticky notes. At the end of each reading, students within the groups should discuss specifically what makes each selection of text "luscious." 2. Each student selects his or her favorite example to write on one of the sticky notes (or you can distribute index cards), along with an explanation of why it is so powerful. 3. In the large group, students share examples of writing that inspires and display their responses on a wall or on the board for inspiration (we have a bulletin board for "Luscious Language" in my classroom that we use for this purpose). 4. Introduce WWC 1. 5. Homework: Students continue collecting really cool words in the back of their ME books and writing that inspires in the "Writing from Literature" chapter throughout the week as they complete their nightly reading and meet the expectations of WWC 1.

Figure 3.3 This chart shows the breakdown of possible lessons to prepare students for Weekly Writing Challenge 1.

"I know, right?" I agreed. "I love how he used *repetition* to create *suspense* before I even read one page! Oh, hang on, that was a really amazing observation, Josh. Let's start a brain splash up on the board of the things we discover. Do you mind if I write it up on the board, so I don't forget that as I read? I'm curious to see if Rick Yancey does this again as I am reading."

Reinforcing the language of writing craft (*repetition, suspense*) in these early discussions is critical. In this way, I share clues about things that writers might notice and give them vocabulary for future discussions.

Several students want to know what the book is about, so I finish reading the inside flap to them:

> Now, it's the dawn of the 5th Wave, and on a lonely stretch of highway, Cassie runs from them. The beings who only look human, who roam the countryside killing anyone they see. Who have scattered earth's last survivors. To stay alone is to stay alive, Cassie believes, until she meets Evan Walker. Beguiling and mysterious, Evan may be Cassie's only hope for rescuing her brother—or even saving herself. But Cassie must choose: between trust and despair, between defiance and surrender, between life and death. To give up or to get up.

Colin's hand shoots into the air. "So what are they? Zombies? Aliens?"

"They're aliens, I think, from what I can tell so far," I say. "To be honest, I'm not generally drawn to science fiction, but when I picked it up and read this part at the bookstore, I decided that I just had to give it a try. Does it sound like a book you would want to read?"

A chorus of "Yeah!" and "Sure!" reverberates through the classroom.

"Okay, so what made you want to read it? In other words, what did the *author* do to make you want to read on?" I place the book back under the document reader so everyone can see the text.

"Well, he did it again! That repetition thing," Josh says. "Look! He says *who* three times!"

"Do you feel like it creates suspense this time?"

"Yeah," Josh answers. "Definitely."

"Nadia, you look like you wanted to say something," I encourage her.

"Well, I like that word *beguiling*. It sounds cool but I don't know what it means."

"I really like it too," I agree. "That word stuck out to me as I was reading as well. Do any of you know what beguiling means?" No takers. "Okay, Nadia, you are not alone. It's definitely a cool word, and I'd like to know what it means so that I can use it in my own writing sometime. Do you mind looking it up? You may need to look under *beguile*, the root word." While Nadia looks up the meaning of the word, we continue the discussion, noticing more craft moves.

"Okay, did anyone else notice any authorly moves to get you to want to read the book?"

MacKennzie raises her hand and then leans back in her seat and cocks her head, thinking out loud, "I think it's neat how at the end he goes back and forth, and back and forth . . . I can tell that the girl is really going to have to make some big decisions, so I guess that kind of builds suspense too."

"I know what you mean," I say, "and I think it does build suspense. Those are actually called seesaw sentences, and MacKennzie is right. Authors use them to create tension to emphasize the stress a character may be feeling. This will also help to develop the conflict in the plot of a story." I jot "seesaw sentences = internal conflict" on the board.

By that time, Nadia was ready with our definition: "Well, it seems like it means he's charming, but the definition also has synonyms like *cheat, swindle,* and *distract,* so . . . I'm not sure if it's a good thing or a bad thing."

MacKennzie says, "Wait a minute. Isn't that the point? We just said that the girl will have some big decisions to make . . . she's got some . . . conflicts. She doesn't even know if she should trust him or not, so maybe that's the point—that we aren't supposed to know if he's good or bad yet, right? We will probably find out as we read."

I can see the mental light bulbs illuminating above the rest of the class.

"Excellent conclusion!" I say. "What I think I hear you saying is that that deliberate word choice, *beguiling,* was the perfect word in that situation. It makes the reader stop and think. It's an intriguing word . . . it almost sounds like *smiling* . . . like I want to trust it, but, wait . . . I'm not sure if I should. Deliberately choosing that just-right word is something authors do all the time. They make very deliberate word choices to reveal things about the character, setting, or situation—this helps to create the mood." I add "deliberate 'just-right' word choices to create mood" to our collection.

I mention that I also noticed some interesting punctuation decisions—punctuation marks that we don't think to use often in our writing. This class doesn't have much experience with punctuation, so my goal early on is to build their awareness of stylistic techniques to serve as a memory marker for later conventions lessons. I add a colon and a dash to our brain splash and note that they highlight what's important. Then I recap the lesson:

"We just learned four things in the past ten minutes. Pretty impressive: (1) authors use *repetition* to create *suspense,* (2) sometimes authors also use a cool little trick called a *seesaw sentence* to show *conflict* and to further *suspense,* (3) authors select *deliberate word choices* to develop *mood,* and (4) authors use unique punctuation to highlight big ideas. Now, we are actually going to read for twenty minutes, and I want you to be on the lookout for these four author strategies in the book you're reading."

I answer a few questions, and then everyone reads silently and jots down noticeable craft moves on sticky notes.

After twenty minutes, I give the students their next task. "Now that we have practiced reading like a writer, I would like you to skim back through everything that you noticed. Pick your favorite one—the one that you feel is the best example."

Considering this was a very early lesson—our first attempt of the year to focus on this kind of reading—I have to say that the results were surprisingly on point. I had the students post their sticky notes on the whiteboard so that they could serve as inspiration for the entire class. Then I introduced the WWC by sharing the author advice accompanying the writing challenge. The students and I glued the Really Cool Words sheet into the back of our writer's notebooks. For this lesson, we also added the word *beguiling,* because it sounded "cool." Writing down cool words is a great idea—in theory. However, I have found that simply writing the words down, even in the writer's notebook, is of very little use if my young writers want to go back and find a word to use in their writing. As a result, we created the Really Cool Words (that I hope to use in my writing someday) organizer, which consists of a table of boxes arranged alphabetically. Students can navigate the list fairly easily to find just the *write* word. (See Figure 3.4 for a sample.)

> *I had benefited enormously from writers who'd laid their gleaned bits of wisdom on the table for me to pick through.*
>
> —Sue Monk Kidd, author of *The Secret Life of Bees*

Taking the Picture-Book Path to WWC 1

If jumping into novels seems to be too big of a leap for your students, or if you have reluctant or resistive readers, try introducing this lesson with picture books. Because these authors have learned to use words efficiently and effectively to capture the essence of the scene on every page, this genre is rich with language. The words in picture books also have to be both visual (in terms of word choice) and rhythmically interesting (in terms of sentence structure and punctuation) since the books were designed to be read aloud. Many students will not have looked at picture books since they were little, and the shorter stories enable them to move through several books and view myriad examples of author craft in a class session. Picture books have a way of reigniting an adolescent's interest in reading. They take students back to the time when they fell in love with words.

Here are some of my favorite picture books for this lesson:

My House Has Stars by Megan McDonald

My Mamma Had a Dancing Heart by Libba Moore Gray

Singing Down the Rain; *Mrs. Goodstory* by Joy Cowley

Tigress by Nick Dawson

Snow Moon by Nicholas Brunelle

I Walk at Night by Lois Duncan

Sky Tree; *Water Dance*; *Mountain Dance* by Thomas Locker

Listen to the Rain; *The Turning of the Year* by Bill Martin

Night in the Country; *Long Night Moon*; *Snow*; *In November* by Cynthia Rylant

Really Cool Words
(that I want to use in my writing someday)

Aa	Bb	Cc
auspicious	beguile	charming
atrocious	battered	coiling
antagonize	beaming	chief
apologize	bail	chaotic
ambiguous	brazen	crinkled
alone	belittle	crimminally
		critical
		compress

Dd	Ee	Ff
desensitized	errant	fizzle
defer	erratic	frantic
dread	exaltation	foolhardy
decend	exuberant	faze
dredged	erroneous	

Gg	Hh	Ii
grim	kind	illustrious
glint	harped	intoxicated
garment	hazy	impossible
gleaming	hankering	
grated		

Jj	Kk	Ll
jet-lagged	know	leached
	killjoy	linger
		leaked

Really Cool Words
(that I want to use in my writing someday)

Mm	Nn	Oo
miffed	noxious	obvious
manifestos	never	omen
mutter		
murmur		

Pp/Qq	Rr	Ss
query	rolled	skulk
prophetorial	recede	snucker
procrastinate	revoke	spatter
perverse	remain	sinuous
pure	refined	stunted
quaint	ressurect	simper
quarrel	ransacked	

Tt	Uu	Vv
training	utter	vexed
transfixed	unbelievable	vague
time	uber	vague
tidal		ventures
terror		virtuous
tremble		

Ww	Xx/Yy/Zz	
wheeze	yankee	Use this grid to record and keep track of the cool words that you find as you read. Then refer to this list as you write to spice up your word choices.
whisper	zealous	
whimper	zesty	
wisened	zombiefied	
waterlogged		
wanton		

Figure 3.4 From their reading, students collect really cool words they'd like to use in their writing.

Sun Up; Hide and Seek Fog by Alvin Tresselt

Come on, Rain by Karen Hesse

Owl Moon; Moon Ball; Before the Storm; Harvest Home by Jane Yolen

The Night the Moon Blew Kisses by Lynn Manuel

My Life with the Wave by Catherine Cowan

Sun Song by Jean Marzollo

Night Is Coming by W. Nicola-Lisa

Hoops by Robert Burleigh

To Be Like the Sun by Susan Marie Swanson

Canoe Days by Gary Paulsen

Winter Is the Warmest Season by Lauren Stringer

Poet and teacher Georgia Heard knows that teachers need to figure out a way to "foster an awareness, an appreciation, and a love of words—both their meaning and their sound" (1999, 8). On the first day of the picture-book lesson, as I read our first picture book aloud, I ask my students to do as Heard suggests, "to listen for words that make a picture in their mind; are an unusual or surprising way of expressing something; give a strong feeling; or evoke a memory" (8).

The picture-book path is similar to the novel approach, except that it is more directed. For example, at the beginning of this lesson, I give students copies of the Really Cool Words organizer and have them glue the sheets in the back of their writer's notebooks, as I did with the other class, but I let them know exactly what kinds of words they are looking for right up front. (Tip: Ralph Fletcher [2003] has a great lesson on keeping track of favorite words in Chapter 7 of *A Writer's Notebook*.)

On the second day of the lesson, we continue to collect words that make an impression on our tongues and our ears. We also make the transition to longer phrases and sentences that just knock our socks off, using our Writing That Inspires sheet as an example and a jumping-off point (see Figure 3.5). As I do in the novel path, I start with a read-aloud and a similar discussion to cultivate the practice of seeking out luscious language—interesting uses of word choice, crafts, sentence structures, figurative language, imagery, and punctuation—in the text. While reading an entire picture book aloud to the class, I model the process of marking cool words and language with sticky notes as we discuss noteworthy snippets that we discover.

> *Think about what you read: how the author made it interesting, or funny, or suspenseful. And write as much as you can, too. Keep a journal. Get together with friends who enjoy writing, and read things aloud to each other and talk about them.*
>
> —Lois Lowry, author of the Giver Quartet, *Number the Stars*, and many other titles

Following our discussion, I break the kids up into small groups of three to five students and send them with their pencils to predetermined book stations, where numerous picture books and sticky notes are waiting in baskets. Students are given fifteen to twenty minutes to read through the picture books in their group one at a time. While one student is reading aloud, his or her teammates are instructed to use sticky notes to mark examples of luscious language, so as not to interrupt the flow of reading and for ease of reference later on. After each book is completed, the groups must select no more than three examples to record in "Chapter 4: Writing from Literature" in their ME books (writer's notebooks). This evokes some great conversations within groups, and I expect them to be able to justify and defend their choices. I try to rotate students through two to three book groups during this lesson, and I find that I can give less time for the second and third rotations. In the end, students within each group select their favorite quotes from among all of the books that they've read, and they write them down on sticky notes or index cards that they share and then put up around the room for inspiration.

Depending on the length of your class, this group activity may take place on day two or three of the lesson. It may sound like a lot of time is dedicated to this activity, but the ultimate goal is for students to identify cool "writerly moves" in their reading and later begin to emulate these stylistic choices as they write with readers in mind.

I thoroughly enjoy seeing my students' passion and love of books and words reignited as they dive into the picture books and begin harvesting wonderful bits of language from their nightly reading. Through this process, my students have discovered cool words such as *absentmindedly*, *clutching*, *gnarled*, and *zealous*. These words are not what we would consider *vocabulary words,* studied for meaning and understanding; rather, they are powerful because in their *sounds* and *connotations* they hold meaning. In *Falling in Love with Close Reading*, Lehman and Roberts (2014) acknowledge that "our students read words all day long, but often times they (and perhaps we) use them mostly as tools for understanding. A close reading ritual for word choice shifts this, making words both something to gather meaning from and also something to admire the craft of and to interpret. In a sense, we ask students to make the writers of those texts come to life, to imagine actual authors and journalists poring over their drafts thinking, 'Should I use this phrase or this other one?' and making those choices with a purpose" (34–35).

These early lessons will help students extract both explicit and implicit meanings from all genres of texts, which in turn leads to better reading comprehension. My students cover our classroom "Luscious Language" wall with found craft and beautiful language from the novels that they are reading. They also post examples that they find inspirational along with their craft analysis on our classroom blog, which promotes community and accountability (see Figure 3.6).

Writing That Inspires

Authors learn from authors. Period.

Consider yourself an author.

Consider these authors your peers.

Read the quotes below. Then, as you read, watch for sentences that really inspire you. Write one of your favorites in the space at the bottom of this page, and be ready to share what you like about it.

"I'd slip-swish behind Mama through the newly green grass. And afterward we'd read rain poems and drink sassafras tea with lemoncurls floating."
—Libba Moore Gray, *My Mama Had a Dancing Heart*

"The shadows were the darkest things I had ever seen. They stained the white snow."
—Jane Yolen, *Owl Moon*

"Sometimes in the dark she shimmered like a rainbow. To touch her then was like touching a piece of night tattooed with fire." —Catherine Cowan, *My Life with the Wave*

"Night is coming, creeping through the forest, slipping through the valley, silencing the day."
—W. Nikola-Lisa, *Night Is Coming*

Special quote:

Figure 3.5 I want students to become inspired by luscious language and descriptions they read.

Hey! Here's a great example of a really good response that I created using my book, *The Rules of Survival*, by Nancy Werlin. (Yes, I know this is the same book as last week. I am soooo close to finishing, I can taste it!) On a scale of 1–10, I would rate this book about a 4 on the luscious language scale. For the most part it is written pretty plainly with ordinary language, but every now and again, I come across something spectacular that really blows me away like this quote from page 3:

> "That particular night in August, it was over a hundred degrees, and so humid that <u>each breath felt like inhaling sweat</u>. It was the fourth day of a heat wave in Boston, and over those days, our apartment on the third floor of the house in Southie had become <u>like the inside of an oven</u>. However, it was date night for our mother—Saturday—so we'd been locked in . . .

> " . . . Not that the key mattered. Once Callie and I heard you snoring—a soft little sound that was almost like a sigh—we <u>slipped</u> out a window onto the back deck, <u>climbed</u> down the fire escape, and <u>went</u> one block over to the <u>Cumberland Farms</u> store. We wanted a breath of air-conditioning, and we were thinking also about popsicles. *Red ones*."

Okay, so here's why this passage is so awesome:

1. I love the 2 **similes**—super creative! I can totally *feel* the heat and humidity. This is the perfect way to describe it! (solid underline)
2. Gotta love the **commentary dash**—so fulfilling! It interrupts the train of thought and adds in important details that might normally be left out (dotted underline)
3. OMG! The **power of three** (dashed underline) really adds anticipation and suspense to the scene: "slipped . . . climbed . . . went . . ." Makes it sound sneaky!
4. This one might not seem very important now, but it is a key tool that authors use to connect with their audience: **powerful proper nouns** (grey). They just sprinkle in a few proper nouns—places, products—that everyone is familiar with to draw the reader into the story.
5. Wait. Did you see that? The author wrote an incomplete sentence. An incomplete sentence. In a published novel? Yup. How cool is that? In this case, the **incomplete sentence** (*italics*) serves to highlight a specific detail: the *red* popsicles. To me, this seems deliberate to show how young the kids are at the beginning of the novel. I mean, they were locked in their apartment all alone on a sweltering night with no A.C., and all they can think about is red popsicles? It really shows their age and level of maturity here, which ends up changing monumentally as the book continues, and the kids begin to really see how horrible their lives are.

Now, that's how you do it. Obviously I picked this passage because it is chock full of amazing writer's crafts. I don't expect all of you to find passages with quite as much in one chunk as this one, but I wanted to show you all of the possibilities! Good luck with yours ☺ —M-K

Figure 3.6 Here I notice and note writing craft, punctuation, and figurative language that make this excerpt luscious.

If you do not already have a classroom blog for these kinds of assignments, I suggest choosing a free, education-specific blog site for your classroom. We use TeacherLingo primarily because it is easy to set up, maintain, and monitor. I receive e-mails when students respond and I can easily post and unpost weekly assignments, replies, and threads. This was also one of the few sites not blocked by our school's firewalls. Before deciding on a site, check your school's firewalls to be sure you will have accessibility.

Sweat Equity Extra: Personal Reading-Writing Vocabulary

Have you ever noticed the interesting vocabulary choices many contemporary middle-level and YA authors include in their books? It seems to me that they lure readers into the text with their intriguing characters and lifelike action, and then all of a sudden—*WHAMMO!*— the writers pop in an unfamiliar vocabulary word. As a teacher and a writer, I have no doubt that this is a deliberate word choice, intentionally designed to move the reader up to the next level by broadening his or her vocabulary. And I think that we have the obligation to help our students make this jump—not only in their reading vocabulary, but also in their writing vocabulary. According to Ralph Fletcher (1993), "A rich vocabulary allows a writer to get a richness of thought onto the paper" (38). With a personal resource of self-selected vocabulary words, all students can enrich their writing vocabulary.

In many districts, vocabulary is a prescribed course, complete with a textbook and tests, whereas other districts focus on developing content-area vocabulary. Either way, a student's reading, writing, and speaking vocabulary can directly impact his or her future success. In *Reading Reasons: Motivational Mini-Lessons for Middle and High School*, Kelly Gallagher (2003) makes two critical points that are worth mentioning as we explore our vocabulary practices.

1. "Reading broadens a student's vocabulary. A broadened vocabulary makes the student a better writer" (68).
2. "By reading regularly, students expose themselves to unfamiliar vocabulary in meaningful context and, in doing so, build mature vocabularies" (56).

I have noticed that even our strongest readers tend to gloss right over the unfamiliar vocabulary words they encounter in their nightly reading without fully understanding the meaning or seeing the possibility of adding such new words into their own written vocabulary. Because my students are reading for one hundred minutes or more each week, and I am teaching them how to look more closely at word choices, I seize the opportunity to notice and acquire new vocabulary in a context that makes sense for them. As Gallagher says, "The best 'bang for the buck' in acquiring vocabulary comes from regular reading, but only if we embrace unfamiliar words by examining the context around them" (2003, 56).

My curriculum does not include a prescribed vocabulary program, so I have developed a weekly vocabulary assignment that my students complete in conjunction with their nightly reading (see Figure 3.7 for the format). For this assignment, students are required to pinpoint five unfamiliar words from their nightly free reading that they would like to add to their personal vocabulary list each week. The only rules that I enforce for this assignment are that textbooks and dictionaries are not appropriate choices for "nightly free reading" and that proper nouns are not appropriate vocabulary words. As Brenda J. Overturf suggests in *Vocabularians* (Overturf, Montgomery, and Smith 2015), my students use the following word-learning strategies as part of their vocabulary acquisition process: context clues, word parts, and reference materials. During this process, students make their best guess at a definition for each of the five words selected based on context clues, and they break each word down into prefixes, roots, and suffixes before heading to the dictionary. This reinforces reading comprehension skills and word-learning strategies that will help them find success in all of their subject areas, while developing a unique list of vocabulary words that they can later use in their writing. Because "the writer's real pleasure comes not from using an exotic word but from using the right word in a sentence" (Fletcher 1993, 38), the purpose of our vocabulary collection is to ultimately create a personal resource of words that my students can refer to during the second semester when they are revising their own writing pieces for publication or any time they are simply looking for a more specific word.

Weekly Writing Challenge 2: Emulating Text (A Springboard into Writing)

Weekly Writing Challenge 2: Emulating Text (A Springboard into Writing) picks up right where WWC 1 left off. Students move from *recognizing* luscious language to *creating* some of their own (see Figure 3.8). This challenge was inspired by some of my students' favorite authors: Natasha Friend, Jordan Sonnenblick, Christopher Paolini, and Shannon Hale. The lessons that accompany this writing challenge are designed to set the bar for the quality of writing that will be expected throughout the year as well as establish students' at-home BIC time (aka "Butt in Chair," coined by author Alyson Noël).

During this week's lesson, the students will be reading nightly at home while we continue exploring avenues of writing-from-reading inspiration in class. Along the road to developing distinct writing voices of their own, I am asking my students to "try on" an author's words or style to see how it feels. Ellis and Marsh recognize that "As students read and write at the same time, they naturally borrow the voices of the authors of the books they are reading without realizing it" (2007, 52–53). To this end, I am asking the students to pay attention to the words and language that make them sit up and take note, and then to make a deliberate choice toward writing well by emulating that text.

Personal Vocabulary

Name _____   Week _____

Period _____   Date _____

While you are reading for your nightly twenty minutes, you are to find five challenge words to add to your personal vocabulary list by the end of each week. Because these are designed to boost your reading comprehension and writing vocabulary, proper nouns are not permitted.

Word _____   Book _____   Page _____

Word parts   root word(s) _____   prefix(es) _____   suffix(es) _____

Sentence from book _____

_____

Best guess definition _____

Part of speech (circle one)   noun   verb   adjective   adverb   preposition

Dictionary definition

_____

Your own sentence using the word

_____

_____

Figure 3.7 Each week, students select five challenge words from their nightly free reading to add to their personal vocabulary lists. These words later become part of their writing vocabulary. This figure shows the form students complete for each one of the new words.

My students and I are always amazed at the writing that comes out of the lessons I describe in the following sections. Many of the pieces are extremely powerful because of the word choices or personal connections that my students discover. Every time I teach WWC 2 to students in the classroom or teachers in a workshop, I am blown away with the results.

I think from reading. My favorite authors became my heroes, and I wanted to be like them.

—Louis Sachar, author of *Holes, Fuzzy Mud, Small Steps*, and other titles, on why he became a writer

"The formula for me was read, read, read. Read everything. Read books you think are good. Read books you think are bad . . . You have to read a ton of wide stuff to discover yourself in the words. You have to just be a funnel—open up a funnel into your brain and pour in every word you can find. And then hopefully, you'll fill up your brain with enough stuff that it will go through the blender of your brain and come out as new stuff."

—Jordan Sonnenblick, author of *Drums, Girls & Dangerous Pie*;
Curveball: The Year I Lost My Grip; and many other titles

"Flip through your chosen books and read the first sentences and paragraphs of chapters 2–6. Notice how the author is drawing you into the action or introducing a new topic with powerful images or intriguing dialogue. Do you notice patterns? Do some styles appeal to you more than others? Think about how you can apply what appeals to you in your writing."

—Christopher Paolini, author of *Eragon* and the rest of the Inheritance Cycle series

"Often when I begin to write I don't know exactly where I'm going; I just start with something that intrigues me—a phrase or a character—and see where it leads me."

—Natasha Friend, author of *Perfect, Bounce, For Keeps*, and many other titles

"Don't be afraid to imitate. Don't worry, eventually all your ideas will be original, but when starting out, it's OK to imitate your favorite authors . . ."

—Shannon Hale, author of the Princess Academy series and many other titles

Weekly Writing Challenge 2: Emulating Text (A Springboard into Writing)

THE CHALLENGE

- Throughout the week, select at least *three* different pieces of text to put into your ME book. (Ex: a page from a picture book, a paragraph from a novel, an entire poem or song)

- Write or copy/download and paste the text into Ch. 4, "Writing from Literature." (Leave space for writing!)

- For each entry, *write on your own for at least twenty minutes* by copying the author's style or word choice, or by "borrowing" a line for use in your own writing.

Figure 3.8 The second writing challenge encourages students to create their own luscious language by emulating their favorite authors.

Lesson 1: Emulating Text by Modeling a Scene

I always begin with the lesson's author advice as inspiration for our writing before sharing Weekly Writing Challenge 2. I also make an explicit connection between this week's challenge and last week's, noting that last week we were *identifying* luscious language and wonderful word choices, and this week we will be continuing to notice amazing literature—but, as writers, we're taking it one step further. This week we will be *applying* the style of the text or individual word choices to our own writing. This challenge is broken up into two lessons: Modeling a Scene and Borrowing a Line. If you have a lengthy language arts block, you could do both lessons in one day. That said, as long as my regular curricular schedule allows, I prefer to do the lessons on two separate days to give the kids time to play with each one in isolation.

To begin the first lesson for emulating text, I hand out the Weekly Writing Challenge 2: Emulating Text worksheet (see Figure 3.9), and I have students turn to the side for Emulating Paragraphs. I read aloud and project on the document reader the excerpt from *Maniac Magee*. The passage includes author Jerry Spinelli's vivid description of a setting. As a class, we discuss how the author uses the setting to develop mood and characterization.

Next, I show students how I emulated Spinelli's style in describing a setting for one of my own characters (see Figure 3.9). Again, we discuss what we know about the characters based on the details in the setting.

Now, it's their turn: I ask my students to select a setting that is meaningful to them and evokes a strong memory. I explain that choosing a familiar setting is important if they are going to write by emulating Spinelli's style as I had done, so that they can really dig down to flesh out the details and capture the essence of the place. Then, I suggest that they all take a minute to close their eyes and picture the setting—every crack, every corner, and every detail. Finally, I unleash my writers. Most of them take this first actual writing assignment very seriously and jump right in. While they are writing, I too sit and write. Occasionally I will break the studious silence by suggesting places to look for details: the lighting in the room, the time of day as evidenced by the windows, the temperature/humidity, the particles or smells in the air, and so on. After about fifteen minutes, I have them wrap up this first vignette. Some classes are just getting in the writing groove at the fifteen-minute mark and want to continue writing. If this is the case, how can I say no? I'll add another three to five minutes of writing time. When finished, I encourage students to share their writing with one another and then ask if anyone heard anything that should be heard by all.

In doing this exercise, Karen shared that she started with the intention of describing an area of her own house, and then suddenly it took an unexpected twist. She was willing to let me put her work under the document reader so that everyone could see as she read aloud:

Weekly Writing Challenge 2: Emulating Text

Part 1: Throughout the week, select at least three pieces of text to put into Ch. 4, "Writing from Literature," in your writer's notebook.

Examples include these:

❑   a page or two from a picture book

❑   a paragraph from a novel

❑   an entire poem

❑   lyrics to a song

You could . . .

- photocopy, then cut and paste it in
- download from Internet, print and paste it in
- write it in by hand

Part 2: Below or next to each piece of text that you have selected, you get to do some writing of your own based upon the text that you have selected. Here are some options for emulating text:

You could . . .

❑   copy the author's format, plugging in your own words

❑   copy or imitate the author's word choices in your own writing

❑   emulate the author's style (sentence structures, interesting use of language)

❑   pick one line or sentence to use as a springboard for your writing

❑   find a connection between the text and you, then write about a similar topic

For part 2, **think about *how* you want to write**. Will it be a quick freewrite, full of your internal thoughts and reflections? Will it read like a finished poem or narrative description, with specific details that make it read like literature? Whatever you decide, make a conscious effort toward writing well. **Find a special place** that will help you focus on your thoughts and your writing this week. This kind of writing can't be rushed. Dig that hole in your life to make the time, and let's see what crawls inside!

Figure 3.9 I share my process of emulating a text.

Emulating a Few Paragraphs from a Novel

"Maniac had seen some amazing things in his lifetime, but nothing as amazing as that house. From the smell of it, he knew this wasn't the first time an animal had relieved itself on the rugless floor. In fact, in another corner, he spotted another form of relief that could not be soaked up by newspapers.

Cans and bottles lay all over, along with crusts, peelings, cores, scraps, rinds, wrappers–everything you would normally find in a garbage can. And everywhere there were raisins.

He ran a hand along one wall. The peeling paint came off like cornflakes.

Nothing could be worse than the living and dining rooms, yet the kitchen was. A jar of peanut butter had crashed to the floor; someone had gotten a running start, jumped onto it, and skied a brown one-footed track to the stove. On the table were what appeared to be the remains of an autopsy performed upon a large bird, possibly a crow. The refrigerator contained two food groups: mustard and beer. The raisins were even more abundant. He spotted several of them moving. They weren't raisins; they were roaches."

—from Maniac Magee, by Jerry Spinelli (pp. 131–132)

Okay, from a reader's point of view, the descriptions that Spinelli gives of the rooms in the bully's trailer are amazing! I can totally see every last corner and can easily create a picture in my head. Beyond that, the word choices and details that he reveals give the reader a real sense of the mood. Within this setting, we also learn a great deal about the character who lives there.

This passage inspired me to bring to life one of the settings from a novel that I am currently working on entitled Perfect. *Below is my emulated passage that brings to life the childhood bedroom of the main character and her little sister. Notice that my topic is completely different, but I have emulated his detailed style and ability to create mood. (Both of them are basically just descriptions of rooms.) What can you tell about the lives of these girls based upon the details given? What mood am I trying to create based upon my word choices?*

Emulated text:

" . . . It was loud and wild—no contrast to the mind-bending parties that often took place long into the night right outside our filmy windows. Wall-to-wall carpeting was a luxury we could not afford. Instead, my bedroom floor was a minefield of shag carpet squares—red, pink, mauve—not one of them quite matching another. Above the bristly carpet fingers, four sleepless walls stared. One red, two pink and one covered in immense daisy petal eyes, hypnotized by the darkness. The gaping hole in the fiery red wall was a doorless closet—an empty throat— yearning for Polly Flinders hand-smocked dresses, shiny Mary Janes. There was no toy box—no Cabbage Patch or Barbie; only dirty, second-hand dolls with matted, wiry hair who went to bed each night shivering without any clothes."

—from Perfect, by Mrs. M-K

Figure 3.9 (continued) I share my process of emulating a text.

> I sauntered down a cascading wooden staircase, gliding my hand down the freshly-polished railing, making my way toward the kitchen, searching for a snack. For some unknown reason, I pause and turn to look into the dimly lit dining room. Suddenly, I feel a draft on my neck—it feels like a gentle cool breeze or maybe more like the soft touch of a cold hand. And then, I froze, eyes glued to an object set in the middle of the room. What was I looking at? Nothing. It was just that "new" antique rocking chair—the one with the fine, ornate carvings that ran up the back and the rounded arms worn down from years, if not centuries, of use—the one that my mother *had* to have. And there, in front of the window it rested. No, it rocked. Back and forth, back and forth. Not a soul was there. Or, was there? All of a sudden, I caught my breath. It was caught in my chest, and my spine tingled. I let out a scream. My parents ran down to see what had happened. My mother comforted me and I just stood, pointing. My father approached the chair. He touched the seat. It was warm.

It was fun to see Karen playing with punctuation and really concentrating on her word choices. She also held true to the challenge by developing a mood through her writing moves that captivated the reader with its creepiness.

Lesson 2: Emulating Text by Borrowing a Line

This second lesson could be done immediately after the first emulated text lesson or the next day. Either way, at the start of this lesson, I explain that this time we will be *stealing* a single line from a piece of text—it could be crafty and luscious, but it doesn't have to be. (By the way, no need to worry about copyright infringement for just a phrase.) The important thing here is that the chosen phrase has to speak to them and offer a springboard into writing. I have selected a song to model the process, because, well, it's fun, and the words are designed to evoke emotion. A few weeks prior to the lesson, I start tuning in to the popular music stations and really listening for quality lyrics that I can bring in and use in my classroom. In general, I listen for lyrics that are school appropriate (based on topic and word choices). I like to try to pick a style of music that fits the personality of my classroom. Linkin Park is a great go-to band that most boys can connect with because of its edgier style. I have also used everything from Katy Perry to Grandmaster Flash, so feel free to have fun with your music selections. For today I select "Let You Go" by Ashley Parker Angel.

For this lesson, I project the lyrics up on the board and distribute copies that the students can highlight and write on. I explain that while we are listening to the song, they are to read along with the lyrics and highlight any phrase or line that "speaks" to them in some way. The line does not need to be particularly luscious; it just needs to strike a chord. Once we listen through the first time, I show them how I pulled a phrase ("broken promises") as inspiration for writing my little snippet. I explain that I liked the idea of a promise literally broken and shattered on the floor, so I made up a character and a situation (see Figure 3.10). *"Broken promises* lay shattered on the cold, gray concrete at Jesse's feet. His entire life had been blown to pieces, his whole world based on lies. He stood frozen, statue-still. Afraid to move, afraid to breathe, afraid to think; his mind was swimming—no, drowning—in the darkness." Obviously, this is not a finished piece, and there is a lot of ambiguity, but it gives me a seed that might sprout into a longer piece.

Now that the students have an idea of what they're looking for, and how their selected phrase or line can be used, I play the song again, giving them the opportunity to look more closely at the lyrics. Next, students select one of their highlighted lines to spring them into writing. Before they begin, I tell students that they are to incorporate the selected line somewhere in their writing. I remind them that the borrowed line does not need to come first in their writing; it can be imbedded anywhere. (Many will simply mimic what I did in the example if I don't mention this.) I only give about ten minutes for the writing of this one, so that we have time to share and potentially move on to another song. If they beg for additional time, however, I am happy to give more!

Let U Go
by Ashley Parker Angel

<u>Broken promises</u>
But you don't really mind
It's not the first time
And you know it, don't you know
Tell me why it is you only smile inside
But when you break me into nothing
Don't you know

It's not like I haven't tried
Over and over again
Stupid fights
Wrong or right
Goodbye . . .

<u>Broken promises</u> lay shattered on the cold, gray concrete at Jesse's feet. His entire life had just been blown to pieces, his whole world based on lies. He stood frozen, statue-still. Afraid to move, afraid to breathe, afraid to think; his mind was swimming—no, drowning—in the darkness.

Mrs. M-K

Figure 3.10 Using the lyrics from a popular tune, I show students how I used a line to inspire my own writing.

Throughout the week, students complete three emulated text entries on their own to meet the guidelines in the WWC. This is one of my favorite writing challenges, because you never know what you are going to get. Some kids really enjoy working in the narrative mode (some personal and some completely made up), developing their details and creating mood, whereas others prefer to take these vignettes into a more persuasive realm, discussing issues that genuinely concern them. None of the pieces that the kids write this week will be polished, but now they see that they have the ability to create language that sounds like literature.

During our writing conferences and my "drive-by" eavesdropping missions during workshop time, I get to see a staggering variety of writing from these two lessons and students' work on WWC 2. The kids surprise even themselves at what they've come up with. One class period, Erin and Quinn were talking about their WWC entries. Each one had a slightly different take on the assignment.

When I buzzed by, Quinn was sharing writing inspired by a line borrowed from Taylor Swift's song "I Wish You Would":

> *It's 2 a.m. in my room. Headlights pass my windowpane.* Lying there awake in bed, I try to get my mind off of you. Wondering. Thinking. Asking out loud, to myself, "why did you look at me like that?" Do you hate me? Do you really think I'm that cruel? You are my mother. Aren't you supposed to love me unconditionally? I feel like I'm dying inside. My tears burn my eyes and my thoughts, staining my mind. Why wouldn't you just say something? Anything? Instead, you just walked away, leaving me with your disappointment.

She started laughing before she finished, "This piece is so funny to me!"

"Why? Oh my God, it's sooo good," Erin said. "I really like the end—like you had to figure out how to deal because your mom wasn't gonna let you fight back. I hate that, when parents just give you the look, and you know they're disappointed."

Quinn replied: "Well, my mom and I did have a fight, but it wasn't like this. It was over something totally stupid. It wasn't even a big deal, but that's what I was thinking about when I wrote this. My mom refused to speak to me. It was so dumb. But this sounds like it was such a big deal, it's funny!

"Okay, well . . . read me yours."

Erin seemed embarrassed about her entry; she was reluctant to share what she had written based on Shel Silverstein's *Where the Sidewalk Ends*, but eventually Quinn talked Erin into reading her piece aloud:

> *There is a place where the sidewalk ends and where the street begins.* The roads and streets are a dangerous place for not only kids, but for everyone. One wrong step can cause injury or even death. Staying safe and alert in your surroundings is an important matter . . .

Erin stopped mid-sentence.

"C'mon," Quinn prompted. "Just finish it."

"I can't. It's stupid. It doesn't sound right."

At that point, I interjected, "Erin, I hope you don't mind me overhearing your conversation with Quinn, but I was wondering why you stopped?"

"It's just not good. It sounds like a news article, not like anything . . . *good.*"

"Okay, so what if it sounds like a news article? Why can't it be a *good* news article? Actually, I think it sounds like the beginning of a really great article. Can you tell me what you were thinking?

"Well, on the news, they are always talking about texting and driving. I don't drive, but I think it's just as dangerous to text and *walk,*" Erin said, laughing. "People are always bumping into things or tripping because they're trying to text and walk at the same time."

"Oh, my God, I know!" Quinn interrupted. "My sister walked right into the doorway of her bedroom! She's got a huge lump on the side of her forehead! It cracks me up!"

"I can see how that would be funny," I jumped in to refocus the discussion. "But, can you see how you really have something here? I mean, what if someone literally walked off the sidewalk and right into traffic? I'll bet it happens all the time in the city."

Erin agreed that perhaps she had an idea worth cultivating. She returned to her piece during one of our RRW weeks (These are the *Revisit and Revise Writing* weeks that are assigned over our longer breaks to keep the students writing; see Figure 2.3 for details). She did a little research and ended up turning this seed into a darn good argument proposing public safety laws for cell phone use.

> *Write for readers. Maybe you understand what you have written, but the writer's job is to have the reader understand it. Keep in mind: writers don't write writing, they write reading.*
>
> —Avi, author of *Catch You Later, Traitor*; *Nothing but the Truth*; *Sometimes I Think I Hear My Name*, and many other titles

Basecamp: Returning to Nightly Reading

My middle school students continue to return to nightly reading as a basecamp to replenish their supplies and refresh their minds and eyes throughout the school year. They self-select many of their own mentor texts, keep track of the books they have read, and share the craft, "cool words," and vocabulary that they have discovered and collected. In addition, as my students learn to write their way through their own tough spots, each can go back to his or her own mentor texts to find out how their go-to authors handle similar developments in their writing.

During writing conferences, I may direct my students' attention to specific chapters in certain books that I keep on my shelf, but in many cases I ask my students to refer to their own free-reading memory banks—to return to their own novels and authors for guidance. Frequently, if they can't find what they are looking for within the text, I encourage them to speak to classmates who have tackled similar issues or who may be able to guide them to an author who has. In some cases, it may make more sense to go right to the source and e-mail an author directly or post a question on his or her blog site.

Framing the workshop in the author apprenticeship approach creates a crazy-wonderful ripple effect. Just as immersing yourself in a new culture can transform your outlook, students enter a metamorphosis stage by seeing themselves differently from the inside out. As they begin to distinguish themselves as authors' apprentices, some fascinating changes occur:

Students become more resourceful throughout the year. In time, they discover that these authors and their writings provide a wealth of knowledge for figuring out how to write through their own tough spots.

Students develop problem-solving skills as they begin to think about how authors write, seeking answers for their own writing questions.

Students learn to take risks and try out multiple ways of attacking an assignment because they learn that struggle is part of the writing process for authors.

Students create a classroom community with their fellow readers and writers. They learn to share with and learn from each other. Working together, they also expose the group to a larger collection of literature, craft, and strategies than a single classroom teacher or textbook series alone could possibly provide.

Students explore a global community of writers as they use technology to seek answers and share their findings. Through the author websites, students learn that they can e-mail an author directly for answers to specific questions that may not have been answered in the FAQ section of their web page. And through our own weekly blog, students have the opportunity to post questions about their reading or writing, and they share some of the best writing that I have ever seen. They also begin to realize that through this process they will be developing texts that will be read by the world beyond our classroom. Later on, they learn that there are even more opportunities to expand our global community by communicating with classrooms around the world during National Novel Writing Month (see Chapter 5)!

Obviously, to cultivate this consciousness for our students that they are truly part of a global writing community, we need to deliberately scaffold assignments that not only represent the work of professional writers but also are grounded in sound educational practices. It is our job to guide our students in ways that develop a writerly mind-set and turn those activities into habits that can impact students' reading and writing long after they've left our classrooms.

Because our Weekly Writing Challenges are based on the author advice amassed from our Backstage Pass assignment and are organized to represent the stages in our Reading-Writing-Publishing cycle (see Chapter 1), students get to experience what it means to read with an eye toward writing, and to write with the goal of publication. These first lessons, Weekly Writing Challenges 1 and 2, are essential for setting high expectations throughout the year.

PART 3

Authors' Territory: How Do They Do It?

This section is about doing what authors do best: write. This is where students begin road-testing all of the strategies that our vicarious author-mentors use when they put the pencil to the paper and make some magic. Our exploration ranges from idea generating via our Weekly Writing Challenges to developing fluency and a fearless attitude as students are guided through the process of writing an entire novel in one month. That is: one novel, per kid, in one month. It sounds insane, but that's what National Novel Writing Month is all about. And we *love* it! This is the single most amazing experience for solidifying our class as a true community of writers who learn to develop plot, character, and setting on the fly, who support each other through writer's block, and who celebrate amazing word-count milestones together in class and online.

Once they've written a novel, your students will be able to approach any writing assignment with confidence. The activities in this chapter serve to warm up and condition their writing muscles so that students feel prepared for the most incredible and rewarding writing challenge imaginable.

Chapter 4

Exploring Writing Territories

If you wanted to play basketball, and you couldn't hit a free throw to save your life, what's the coach gonna do? He'll put you on the line, you take a lot of free throws, you get better. It's the same thing with writing: See what works, see what doesn't work, you make adjustments just like an athlete makes adjustments, and you improve as a writer.

—Gordon Korman,
author of the Swindle series, *Schooled*, *Ungifted*, and many other titles

When I was thirteen years old, Tricia Burns was one of my best friends. We had a lot in common: We both loved clothes and hair, we were in most classes together, and we had crushes on many of the same boys. One thing we did not have in common was athletic talent. She was an amazing, state-recognized tennis player. I was a good recreational athlete in most sports. But tennis? Forget it. I was never any good—unless I was playing with Tricia.

When I was in Tricia's territory, I could play. She had a way of lobbing the ball just right, so that I could hit it. She made it easy for me to find my rhythm and get a great volley going. No matter where I sent that ball sailing on her side of the court, she was able to make contact. With her racket, she'd always find a way to bounce it gently back to me so that I could give it another go. Though she was only thirteen, Tricia was a pro in my book, and in many ways, a tennis mentor. When I played with her, I got better. Tricia wasn't trying to coach me, and she certainly wasn't judging me in any way. We were just two friends having fun. Because Tricia spent so much time on the courts, I wanted to share in this activity she loved, and because we were such close friends, she didn't mind. Eventually, after watching her form, getting a feel for her style and rhythm, and heeding her advice, I developed techniques that worked for me. Because we played frequently in her territory, I gained both confidence and skill that I could use no matter what court I was playing on or with whom I was playing. Don't get me wrong; I did not go on to become a state champ as Tricia did, but I could certainly hold my own at camp!

Learning to play the game required me to be on the court, in the same territory as someone who could serve as a model (and who had a model serve). That's what the Weekly Writing Challenges do for students. They enable young adolescents to step into unfamiliar writing territories with a guide and a mentor ready to show the way. Students will discover things that they never knew they had inside them.

In Chapter 3, I described how my students discussed and selected mentor authors and some mentor texts, but we hadn't yet discussed writing territories. The Weekly Writing Challenges in this chapter help students discover previously untapped writing opportunities, regardless of the writing mode. Traditionally, we have been programmed to think of writing territories as linear lists of *things* we can write about someday. Authors have a more expansive perspective, and it is this imaginative view that we must share with students.

By studying their favorite authors and "interviewing them" to see how they work, students have learned that there is more to being a writer than simply sitting and writing. This is quite an eye-opening understanding, because most kids have been taught to do only those two things in school during writing time: Sit. Write. Although authors do plenty of *sitting* and *writing* during the drafting phase, prior to that they are "Swiffer-ing" their world, grabbing on to bits and pieces of anything that has the possibility of finding its way into a future draft. A sweet exchange overheard between a mother and child; a newspaper article; an old, abandoned house; a grainy photo that evokes special memories . . . writers spend their lives collecting this kind of auditory and visual sensory material for future writing.

Just as we train our budding authors to look at *text* with a writer's eye, we also must train them to look at their world through that same lens. With guidance from their favorite author-mentors, my students discover myriad writing opportunities. Because of the personal investment we've established in the beginning of the school year and because the mentor authors have set the precedent, the students buy in to the process and produce higher-quality writing than they ever did with traditional writing territory lists.

Don't be mistaken; these Weekly Writing Challenges are not journal *prompts*. I do not distribute sheets of writing topics for students to explore. These are the real, idea-generating *strategies* that authors use. In my classroom, all students test strategies to discover which will give them the best personal writing results.

Although authors knowingly seek inspiration from writers who have come before them, most students have never been explicitly instructed to do so. Katie Wood Ray refers to learning from writers as "office work." In *Wondrous Words*, she shares, "Studying office work crafting helps us to imagine how to live our working lives as writers . . . We need to study the ways in which writers engage in the craft of office work so we can see possibilities for our own writing office work" (1999, 27).

When we can give students both a platform and a process for sharing what matters to them, their attitudes toward writing become more positive. As a result, they are willing to take greater risks and begin to see more growth in their writing overall. Every year I find that several students get emotional during our writing exercises. For many, I think it is the first time they put into words their feelings about their parents' divorce, or an uncle dying so young from cancer, or a father who abandoned the family and left to be with another one, or some other personal pain. According to Barry Lane, "When we write from the heart, we return to the past and bring with us all the knowledge we have gained since . . . We can understand the events of our lives by reentering them with our current wisdom in our pockets. We can discover hidden secrets; heal painful memories; unleash joyful thoughts and visions; destroy outdated patterns of thought and behavior that cloud our thinking; create new ways of seeing ourselves, our families, our country, our world. Writing is a form of verbal medicine. Used wisely, it can initiate self-discovery and healing" (2008, 1–2).

> *There are only three places an author can find things to write about. The first is his or her own life. The second is stories told by others. The last is total imagination.*
>
> —Jordan Sonnenblick, author of *Drums, Girls, & Dangerous Pie*; *Curveball: The Year I Lost My Grip;* and many other titles

I remember one of my seventh graders; she was named Tori. Her older sister had committed suicide several years earlier. Because this event had such a huge impact on her life, Tori's notebook was filled with entries about her sister. Some were extremely personal and expressed sadness and regret, whereas others celebrated her sister's life. Tori included lists, stories, poems, and even drawings. After several writing conferences, Tori and I decided that this was an acceptable and necessary part of the healing process as well as a way to practice the writerly life. Although she focused on the same topic each week, she used it to explore every author strategy from our Weekly Writing Challenges.

For example, in her "What If" writing challenge, the obvious heartbreaking questions were "What if my sister hadn't died?" and "What if I could have helped her before it happened?" These questions led Tori to rewrite part of her life and develop a fictional character who was able to save her sister. From her "Lists" and "Multigenre" writing challenges, Tori discovered that she had an interest in finding ways to help other girls who had lost loved ones. She wanted to learn more about the warning signs of suicide and ways to help families and friends recognize and act on these signs before it is too late.

Although Tori's experiences are unique to her life, her methods of exploring them through writing are not. Authors use proven methods of extracting writing material from their hearts, minds, and lives. This means there is no need for teachers to reinvent the wheel for workshop lessons.

The learning doesn't end with the entries. Because we have established high expectations of our writing from the beginning of the year by investigating and emulating the language of literature in our first two WWCs, and we continue to highlight and surround ourselves with luscious language as we unearth it in our nightly free reading, the writing bar remains high throughout the year. I strive for greatness in my classroom, just as Nancie Atwell shares in her book *In the Middle*: "Right from the start, I hope for rich, authentic, adult-like experiences for my students. I want them to use writing to know themselves and the world and to discover what writing is good for . . . And I expect them to try to make literature every time they write, to never be killing time by 'doing another piece for the folder'" (1998, 111).

The Weekly Writing Challenges in this chapter provide small, manageable writing exercises that help to boost writing confidence while building writing fluency and frequency.

During the first semester, we take time to develop our writing territories, compiling items in our notebooks and sampling from the buffet of ideas, strategies, and craft that our author-mentors have graciously laid out before us. From this virtual smorgasbord, we gain confidence as writers, and we begin our journey toward authorship.

Binoculars: Noticing the World Within and the World Beyond (An Introduction to WWCs 3 and 4)

Middle schoolers are thoughtful, curious, and reflective, yet rarely get to write about what interests them because it doesn't "fit" into the curriculum agenda. The author strategies for idea development in Weekly Writing Challenges 3 and 4 give students permission to tap into their deep thoughts. These are designed to train students in the concept of mining for seed ideas and help them to recognize the potential for writing that comes from within as well as developing an eye toward writing when they look out at the world.

Weekly Writing Challenge 3: Writing from the Heart

In *Awakening the Heart: Exploring Poetry in Elementary and Middle School* (1999), Georgia Heard coined the term "heart mapping," or writing from the heart. Wendelin Van Draanen, Judy Blume, Ann M. Martin, Neal Shusterman, and countless other published YA and middle grade authors have used their hearts and innermost experiences and feelings to guide their writing. After years of teaching and using this strategy in my classroom, I have found it to be the easiest way to get kids started on their writing journey. Adolescents love to *talk* about themselves, so it is a natural transition to have them *write* about themselves.

Although there are kids who will simply write about their pets or their hobbies, many choose to write about more deeply emotional topics and find these writing exercises freeing and cathartic, because this is the first time they have been permitted and encouraged to write freely and without judgment on something that matters uniquely to them. For my students, writing from the heart is the first step to feeling empowered by writing.

> *The golden rule of writing is to write about what you care about. If you care about your topic, you'll do your best writing, and then you stand the best chance of really touching a reader in some way.*
>
> —Jerry Spinelli, author of *Maniac Magee, Loser, Stargirl, Smiles to Go, Hokey Pokey,* and many other titles

In order to encourage deep writing that matters, we have to provide a scaffold first. I spread the in-class instruction that prepares students for WWC 3 over two days. Day one follows this general format, which introduces the heart map and scaffolding for the lessons to come:

1. Read aloud the questions from the heart-mapping list one number at a time and have students jot down their responses (see page 80 for heart-mapping questions).
2. Show example of and explain your own heart map (mine is shown in Figure 4.1).
3. Ask students to begin sketching their own heart maps on a blank sheet.
4. Homework: Students complete their heart maps.

Figure 4.1 Using my heart map as an example, I show students how to mine their emotions for writing territories.

I use Georgia Heard's heart-mapping lesson from *Awakening the Heart* as a model for my approach. She believes that "creating heart maps helped [her students] visualize and make concrete what they really cared about, and helped them sharpen their inner vision . . . Drawing a map of our hearts helps make order out of what often feels like chaos and reveals the meanings behind the confusing emotions. And these meanings shine like gems that have been long buried" (1999, 109). Although Heard uses heart mapping primarily as a vehicle for teaching deep and meaningful poetry writing, I broaden the scope to help kids begin to identify important writing territories in the form of memories, hopes, fears, questions—anything that might spark a great jumping-off point for writing exploration.

To begin, we dim the lights and make a promise to one another to write openly and honestly and not to peek at each other's lists or share until it is time. Students are to stay focused and quiet through the entire exercise. I have them turn to the "Lists" section in their writer's notebooks and select a page to title *Heart-Mapping List*. Based on Heard's suggestions, I have compiled these nine heart-mapping questions (feel free to add or modify for your classroom):

1. What is a symbol that would represent you? (draw it or write it in words)
2. What are some things or people that are important to you?
3. What are some experiences or events that you will never forget? (happy, sad, embarrassing, etc.)
4. What small objects are really important to you? (I'm not talking video games or iPods here; in other words, if there was an emergency and you had to leave and never return, what small things would you *have* to take with you?)
5. If you could have one wish, what would you wish for? ("more wishes" isn't acceptable!)
6. What are some activities you could not live without?
7. What things stir up intense emotions in your soul? What truly makes you happy? Sad? Angry? Fearful?
8. What personal beliefs or social/global issues are you truly passionate about?
9. Finish this sentence after choosing "do" or "do not": I do/do not believe in magic because . . . (For this one, I tell students that they can think about magician magic, or they can substitute the word *miracles* for *magic* to dig a little deeper.)

I read each of these questions, one at a time, and give my students time to get as many of their ideas down as possible before the next question. Along the way, I may prompt them or offer examples to trigger a memory. After going through the list once with them, I review each question a little more quickly to give them a chance to add to or change anything they have written.

From this heart-mapping list, we develop our heart maps. Because the kids potentially can use their heart maps all year long as a resource for writing, I want to see a high-quality product. Modeling is critical in this step. I never ask my students to do anything that I haven't done myself already or that I am not willing to do myself right by their sides. This approach helps us to build and reinforce our sense of writing community. To ensure that they understand how to create a heart map from their list of responses to the questions, I take the time to demonstrate an appropriate use of words, drawings, color, layers, and "compartments." I begin by putting my heart map under the document reader to serve as an example.

As with any first-time writing experience, it is important for me to model the process so that the students can not only see what a quality product looks like but also understand my thought process. As I walk them through my heart map, I explain how my two boys are at the center of my heart. No matter what happens in life, they keep me going, so they also serve as the life-source that pumps through my heart. I point out that my next layer has two compartments: family and friends. Although I do not list specific names of friends or family members, I show my students how I use color to signify each: my friends are "true blue," and therefore colored blue, whereas my family members are natural, so I color them green like the features in nature. I also point out the pencil that shoots straight through my heart, which indicates how I draw from my life when I write. I walk my students through several of my hobbies and other important objects inside my heart map. And then I mention some of the things outside my heart, but not separated from it completely. I explain that although I would like to remove these negative things from my heart, I know they are part of what makes me who I am today, so they deserve to be present on my heart map.

After answering any questions, I distribute blank heart map templates. Before allowing my students to unleash their creativity, I take the time to go over the questions on the side of the template: Will you use pictures? Words? Color? Should some things be *outside* of the heart instead of inside? Should there be more than one layer? What will be at the center of your heart? Will colors represent different emotions? Will there be a source that flows through it, keeping it pumping?

Typically, we have some time in class for students to get their creative juices flowing, but I expect them to complete the rest of their heart maps at home so they will be ready to go for the next day's lesson. What my students don't initially realize is that this one activity marks the first step in their journey to becoming published authors. As I have learned over the years through the collection of author advice during our Backstage Pass research, many authors let their own lives—their memories of events, people, and places; their experiences; the things they value; the things they love, hate, or miss—guide their writing. Often, they will write from what they know until a character makes an experience his or her own. Much of the detail work in narrative and expressive writing comes from writing about one's own life. It is also from here that potential research topics and opinion pieces arise for professional authors and for my students alike. These initial writings often develop into themes or scenes in their novels or later become the foundation for publication projects.

The next day, students come in with their completed heart maps, ready to begin exploring their memories and what they hold dear. To facilitate this freewriting process, I format our class in this lesson to look something like this:

1. Have students cut out and glue heart map to the inside front cover of their ME book. (We place it on the *inside* of the front cover, where others will have to be invited to get to see what lives inside a student's heart. Conversely, the decorated ME on the *outside* of the front cover shows the sides of the students the world is allowed to see about them.

2. Have students share their heart maps with a partner, but tell them they only need to reveal the details they feel comfortable divulging.

3. Read aloud Writing from the Heart examples (WWC 3) from previous years. (If you do not have any student samples available, share an entry that you have written as a model.)

4. Show students the author quotes from WWC 3 (Figure 4.2) for motivation and inspiration.

5. Have students select one item from their heart map that they would like to explore through an in-class freewrite. Set a timer for twenty minutes. (Twenty minutes is important because it sets the stage for the writing work that students will be doing at home each week. It also gives you an idea of how much each student can write in that time frame.) Let students know that they *will* be writing for all twenty minutes. Let them know that they may find, as writers often do, that it is tough to sit and write on the same topic for that length of time, so they should try to add as many details, feelings, and emotions as possible. They should consider adding in dialogue if it seems appropriate. Tell students not to be afraid to jump around inside of their memory or to abandon one topic and begin another. That's what authors do.

6. Go over Weekly Writing Challenge 3: Writing from the Heart and explain the expectation that all students will complete three entries that look like they took twenty minutes to write. (Now that they've done the first one in class, you have a true measure of how much writing each student can complete in a concentrated, twenty-minute chunk of time!)

Weekly Writing Challenge 3

"The best books come from someplace deep inside . . . Become emotionally involved. If you don't care about your characters, your readers won't either."

—Judy Blume, author of *Deenie*; *Are You There, God? It's Me, Margaret*; *Iggy's House*; *Blubber*; and many other titles

"Through writing, I open up my heart and soul in ways I never could in everyday life."

—Wendelin Van Draanen, author of *Flipped*, *the Running Dream*, and many other titles

"There has to be not just a story to tell, but a reason to tell it. There has to be something about that story that just is screaming to be told."

"There has to be something about it that connects with you and something that you know will connect it to the readers."

—Neal Shusterman, author of the Skinjacker trilogy, the Unwind series, and many other titles

"Enjoy it! Write about something that interests you."

—Ann M. Martin, author of *A Corner of the Universe*, *A Dog's Life*, and many other titles

Weekly Writing Challenge 3: Writing from the Heart

THE CHALLENGE

- Three times this week, you will select one or more topics from your heart map to freewrite about. Decide which chapter in your ME book makes the most sense for your writing.

- This week the writing is all about you and the things that matter to you in your life. Focus on getting your ideas out of your head and onto your paper. And if you want to try to sprinkle in a little luscious language, go for it! ☺

- Remember: You are to write for twenty minutes, three separate times throughout the week. That means that I am expecting to see three entries and that each entry looks like you spent twenty minutes writing it.

Figure 4.2 Details from students' heart maps become fodder for regular freewriting exercises.

Sydney, a cute, bubbly girl, had ringlets of chestnut hair that actually bounced as she spoke. She was the quintessential cheerleader, both in and outside class, always keeping everyone's spirits up. Because of her positive attitude and energy, one would never expect that she was in remission from cancer (for the second time). The Writing from the Heart WWC allowed her to pay tribute to her experience with this terrible disease and put it in the context of the rest of her life. Sydney seemed to realize that there was so much more to her than her disease. Her cancer only appeared as a tiny little blip on the outside of her heart, whereas the inside was filled with the things she truly held dear. In her entire writer's notebook, this was the only entry that even mentioned her cancer:

Every year since I was six years old, my grandfather has given me a pearl to put on my necklace. It seems weird that a twelve-year-old girl would even care about getting a pearl. (They are so old-fashioned.) Most kids would probably put on a fake smile and say, "Oh, thanks . . ." and not really mean it, like we all do with most of the presents old people give you. But this pearl is precious to me, and so are the other seven that now dangle from my silver chain. My grandpa gave me the first one when I first found out that I had cancer. I was only six years old, and I was so scared because I thought that meant that I was going to die. I can remember him coming into my hospital room at CHoP. He put the necklace around my neck and told me, "We are going to beat this thing," and then he kissed me on my forehead. He told me about how a pearl is just a piece of sand that gets inside of a clam (or is it an oyster? I'm not sure.). Anyway, while it's inside, it really hurts the soft tissue of the clam, scratching it up. So—as a defense mechanism—the clam wraps it up and makes something beautiful out of a terrible situation. He said this is like what the cancer was doing to me. It got into my body and was hurting my tissue. I could let it hurt me—but I didn't have to. I could just wrap it up and make something beautiful instead. I remember my Grandpa said to me, "Let's make some pearls, kiddo." And that's just what I did. I got better. (I did relapse once, when I was eight, but I got through it and the chemo wasn't too bad. I mostly just missed my dog!) I now have seven pearls on my necklace, one for every year since. I keep it in a special glass jewelry box so that I can see it. It will always remind me that I am stronger than cancer. I didn't let it kill me. I just made pearls.

Sydney's piece was both innocent and powerful at the same time. I love that she was able to be honest in her fear of death, but she didn't focus on that. She didn't make herself a victim. She chose to focus on her pearls—the positive lesson that she took from the experience. It was as if she just needed to acknowledge it, front and center, on the first page of her "Memories" chapter, and then she just moved on without another word. And just like that, her cancer was only a memory, nothing more.

Weekly Writing Challenge 4: Writing from Life

Most kids genuinely enjoy having the freedom and opportunity to flesh out thoughts and feelings they have been harboring deep inside. I find that many kids are pleasantly surprised by what ends up on paper, even if they choose not to share the details of the writing with me (which is okay). All in all, week three of our Weekly Writing Challenges is generally a deep time, producing tremendous results. So as not to burn them out too quickly in week four, I allow my students to come up for air. In Writing from Life I: Current Events (see Figure 4.3.), our fourth Weekly Writing Challenge, students have the opportunity to continue writing about topics of interest, but this time the focus is on the world beyond them instead of inside of them.

> *Many ideas come straight from my inner 13-year-old girl. Some come from the lives of my friends, or from articles and books I've read. Often I begin with a seed—just the beginning of an idea, or a first sentence—and from there a plot begins to develop.*
>
> —Natasha Friend, author of *Perfect, Bounce, For Keeps,* and many other titles

Using current events as inspiration as a writing strategy is brought to your students by some heavy hitters in the YA world, including Suzanne Collins, Gordon Korman, and Laurie Halse Anderson. All have used some aspect of this strategy to develop ideas for some of their most famous novels. The beauty of this particular lesson is that by simply looking at the newspaper, we can find so many options. Kids could express an opinion, make a connection, or write something completely creative. The writing could be based on the facts in an article, an opinion in an editorial, or a headline alone. This WWC gives students a window for looking at the world with a new eye, noticing local, national, and global events.

About a week in advance of the class where I introduce the strategy of launching writing from current events, I contact my local newspaper and request a class set of newspapers (or however many they are willing to part with for free, and we make do). Not coincidentally, this writing strategy aligns with our *reading* study of newspapers and article layout, so the kids are already familiar with the sections and general format of the pages and articles. Because our world is increasingly becoming paperless, I also have an online class subscription through the Newspapers in Education program (NIE) so that all of my students can log on anywhere for a variety of purposes throughout the school year. The website nieonline.com is a good place to get started with all kinds of newspaper-related teacher

Weekly Writing Challenge 4

"One night, I was lying in bed, and I was channel surfing between reality TV programs and actual war coverage. On one channel, there's a group of young people competing for I don't even know; and on the next, there's a group of young people fighting in an actual war. I was really tired, and the lines between these stories started to blur in a very unsettling way. That's the moment when Katniss's story came to me."

—Suzanne Collins, author of the Hunger Games trilogy, the Underland Chronicles, and many other titles

"You can also find ideas in the newspaper, from a Youtube video, or a comment that you hear on the subway. Ideas are everywhere, just waiting for you to pay attention."

—Laurie Halse Anderson, author of *The Impossible Knife of Memory*, *Wintergirls*, *Twisted*, and many other titles

"I always start out with something real but then I use my imagination to make it funnier, more interesting and a better story."

—Gordon Korman, author of the Swindle series, *Schooled*, *Ungifted*, and many other titles

Weekly Writing Challenge 4: Writing from Life I: Current Events

THE CHALLENGE

- Throughout the week, select at least **three** different newspaper headlines or articles to clip and glue into Ch. 3 of your ME book, "Writing from Life." (Leave space for writing!)

- For each entry, **write on your own for twenty minutes**. In your writing, you could: *express your opinion* on an issue in an article, *make a connection* to a similar situation in your own life (or one that you read or heard about), or *create a poem* or *narrative scene* based upon the facts from the article or the headline alone.

Figure 4.3 Current events are great for finding ideas for writing.

resources. You should also consider a free digital educational membership with your local newspaper.

There is no special format for the rollout of this WWC. I display the author quotes on the WWC as motivation, and then I present the actual writing challenge. I pass out newspapers and scissors or ask students to log into our NIE account. Students first skim through articles (print or online), select one they feel will inspire them, and then either cut out the article (from print newspapers) or print the article (from NIE site). They glue the article into their ME books in their "Writing from Life" chapter. I set the timer for twenty minutes, and we see what kind of tracks we make in this writing territory.

> *My ideas come from experience, newspapers, listening to others, observation. It's all around us. Everything has a story if you take the time to listen and look for it.*
>
> —Ridley Pearson, author of the Kingdom Keepers series, the Starcatcher series, the Neverland series, and many other titles

In our area of the country, the Falcons and the Firebirds are two powerhouse high school football teams. The article that Cameron selected for his newspaper inspiration came from the local sports section. Although Cameron was not interested in sports, the title caught his attention because the game between the football rivals had ended in a tie. Cameron decided to shift lenses and read through the article with his writer's eye, looking for something that he could work with as a *writer*. At the time, Cameron was a big science fiction/mythology fan, knee-deep in reading *The Throne of Fire* (book two in Riordan's Kane Chronicles). It's easy to see the influence of Cameron's reading interests in his entry (see Figure 4.4).

Jackie, on the other hand, decided to take one of her WWC 4 entries in an entirely different direction. She also had been flipping through the sports section and came across a sports brief about a jockey and horse heading off to the Juddmonte Spinster Stakes (a thoroughbred horse race that was to be run in early October). Jackie was an avid horseback rider who had earned several ribbons in competitions, so she was naturally drawn to the story. In her writing, she decided to take a more opinionated approach, focusing on the treatment of the horses (see Figure 4.5).

Through this one writing exercise, kids can write in a genre that feels comfortable to them or experiment in a new mode of writing without the pressure of being right or wrong. They can share their opinions or express their creativity.

Figure 4.4 Cameron used a headline from the sports section to inspire his writing.

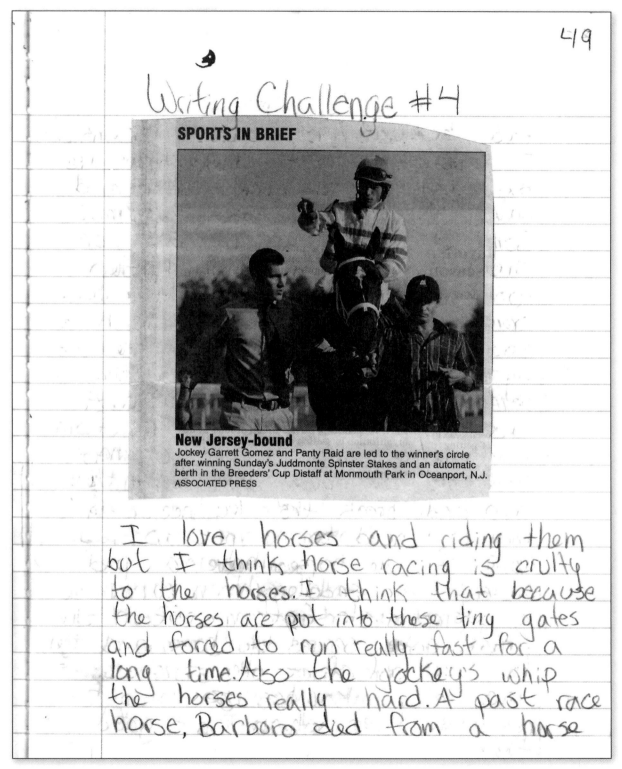

Writing Challenge #4

49

SPORTS IN BRIEF

New Jersey-bound
Jockey Garrett Gomez and Panty Raid are led to the winner's circle after winning Sunday's Juddmonte Spinster Stakes and an automatic berth in the Breeders' Cup Distaff at Monmouth Park in Oceanport, N.J.
ASSOCIATED PRESS

I love horses and riding them but I think horse racing is crulty to the horses. I think that because the horses are put into these tiny gates and forced to run really fast for a long time. Also the jockey's whip the horses really hard. A past race horse, Barboro died from a horse

Figure 4.5 A sports brief about horses inspired Jackie to write about the ethical treatment of horses.

50

race because he broke his ankle. I also think that horses that are ex-race horses are very hyper and have injuries from running so much. Some of the horses are put on drugs and steroids to make them run fast that can hurt the horse. Some horses once they retire have trouble finding homes because they are hyper and spook really easily from being on the track so much. A race horse can also get sick from running so much. A lot of horses can die from racing because if they trip and break their leg, knee, or ankle they will need to be put to sleep. None of the horses have a pad under their saddle which can cause a cut or blister. Getting put in the small gate scares the horse and then they bolt out of it when it opens. The horse also has to gallop for a long time which isn't good for them.

Figure 4.5 (continued) A sports brief about horses inspired Jackie to write about the ethical treatment of horses.

Chapter 5

Writing Novels: The NaNoWriMo Experience

My teacher was completely important in terms of encouraging my writing. If it hadn't been for that seventh-grade English project, I would not have sat down and tried to write a book.

—Gordon Korman,
author who published his seventh-grade English project
when he was only a freshman in high school

By this point in the year, it is nearing October and we have had four glorious weeks of building authorly habits of writing frequently in our ME books and sharing our Weekly Writing Challenge entries. This means two things: (1) I am likely gearing up for my short story genre study for the reading portion of my curriculum, and (2) I am equally likely to be having a *holy crap!* moment as I realize that we start writing novels in nearly a month.

Yes. Novels.

Novel writing is a key component in the apprenticeship experience. It combines all the literary elements that we learn about in our short story reading unit, and it functions as a playground for trying out all the new grammar, punctuation, and writing craft that we will learn throughout the year. During November, we abandon our regular Weekly Writing Challenges to plunge into Lake NaNo for the month. It's sink-or-swim time as students select their own writing goals and set out to reach them by November 30.

Participating in NaNoWriMo presents obvious benefits for our students by connecting the writing work that authors do in the real world with the writing work that we do within our classrooms. It provides validation and a wonderfully authentic opportunity to apply the short story elements of characterization, plot, setting, and conflict from our reading genre study to their own writing. All students also practice using literary devices such as flashback, symbolism, imagery, and irony throughout the month in the same way that real authors do.

Something unexpected occurs inside every student who takes part in this insane challenge. After writing novels, students will never read another story or novel without knowing the work that went into developing each character and his or her actions. They will no longer casually breeze by vivid details, deliberate word choices, or imbedded symbols. Learning the skills and then fearlessly creating and applying them in their own writing make an impression. This synthesis of knowledge bridges the gap between reading and writing and brings new meaning and a heightened awareness into their everyday reading lives.

"Writing my novel has helped me so much with my reading," says Tara, a seventh grader and published author. "I have learned how to really appreciate the crafts and style that these authors have put into their books. When I first started out this year, I would read really fast and I would not recognize all of the detail in the book, and by writing my novel and by seeing how much they really add, I have slowed down my reading and I now enjoy it a lot more."

Donalyn Miller, teacher and author of *The Book Whisperer*, writes of her NaNoWriMo experiences with her own sixth-grade language arts class in a blog: "Kids who love to write enjoy the challenge of it, while kids who are reluctant to write discover that they can write more than they ever thought possible" (2011).

Novel writing is both messy and empowering. Through the process, students develop writing fluency and stamina, and the ability to produce higher-quality on-demand writing. Jeff Anderson refers to this phenomenon as *motion*. In *10 Things Every Writer Needs to Know*, he explains, "Writing is not magic. It's work. Splashing the words on the page or across the screen is much easier than fretting about whether what we have to say is good enough. Start writing, and the rest comes. Most of what students hate (and writers for that matter) is the struggle, the procrastination, the pain of being stuck . . . If you write it, more ideas will come. When the pen hits the page or the fingers tap the keys, words flow. Indeed, they won't all be perfect. But knowing that is freedom" (2011, 2). This is the one opportunity in their school career for your students to write unapologetically, to write fiercely about whatever they want without the fear of their words being imperfect. They suddenly look forward to our language arts period and beg me for writing time. Really. How awesome is that?

The very first year that I introduced NaNoWriMo as a classroom writing activity, my students were not overly excited. That year I did not have any designated honors classes in my schedule, or any honors-level students on my class list. I had taught students classified as gifted for a number of years, and although I do agree that they deserve a more intense curriculum that digs a little deeper and pushes them a little further, all in all, I feel that all kids need to have the opportunity to be challenged and to feel "smart." Students considered *average* and *lower ability* are entitled to the same quality of instruction that will push them to be even better than they were when they walked into our classrooms in the fall. National Novel Writing Month shows our students that we believe in them, even when they think that what we are asking is impossible.

> *Write your adolescent fingers off. Write so much your family thinks you're turning into a recluse. (Mine did!)*
> —Veronica Roth, author of the Divergent series

My students' excitement levels rose exponentially, however, when those "smart kids" from Mr. Hohman's honors class across the hall caught wind of what we were doing in my classroom, and they wanted in on the action. Kids started casually wandering into my room between periods or during their "trips to the bathroom" to ask if they would be allowed to write a novel too.

Allowed to write a novel? Absolutely. Every year, closet writers come out of the woodwork to join our class in this endeavor. They write their novels in their spare time in addition to all of their other schoolwork. I ask these students from other classes to come in for a few minutes during study hall so that I can give them all the information they need to get started, and I add them to our virtual classroom so that they can be a part of our online writing classroom, even if they can't be here physically for class. The kids who join on their own are the serious writers who yearn for the motivation, inspiration, or the excuse to get their books written. Bobby, one of Mr. Hohman's honors students who joined us the first year, wrote more than 60,000 words in thirty days—on top of all of his regular school work and extracurricular activities. That's dedication.

Now, here's where it got interesting . . . year two. I teach both seventh and eighth grades. Roughly one-third of the previous year's seventh graders loop with me up to eighth grade. I don't get to select them; there are three eighth-grade teams, so it is truly the luck of the draw. I wanted to mention this, because it isn't as if all of the "great writers" get placed with me for another year of writing bliss, nor is it that I get to pick the "keepers." With only forty-three minutes in our eighth-grade English classes (compared to the ninety-minute seventh-grade language arts blocks I am blessed to have), I don't have time to worry about who is in or who's out. We have a lot of hard-core curriculum to get through in eighth grade,

> *Sometimes . . . the characters do something totally different from what you expected. And I tend to follow them then and try to figure out what is the truth behind what just happened . . . because the moment that they do something that you didn't expect, they have come alive.*
>
> —Cornelia Funke, author of *The Thief Lord*, the Inkheart trilogy, and many other titles

and very little time for anything extra.

Or so I thought.

One afternoon in mid-October, my eighth graders looked around the classroom in wonder, noticing the seventh-grade NaNoWriMo assignments and paraphernalia posted around the room. Jordyn, a student who had not experienced NaNo with me the past year, asked, "What is all of this Na-No-Wri-Mo stuff?"

Before I had a second to take a breath to answer, Marissa chimed in, "*NaNoWriMo?* Oh, my *GOD*! It's the best! Last year we got to write like an entire novel in a month. About whatever we want. It's so cool. Well . . . wait," she paused, reflecting on her experience last year. "I didn't actually *finish* my novel yet. And *actually* you won't really write your entire novel anyway—like the one you think you are going to write—your characters will come to life and take over and they will pretty much write the rest for you."

Wait . . . what?" Jordyn looked at Marissa like she was crazy.

Kasey, who had been listening in and who had already experienced novel writing with us, supported Marissa, "No, it's true. I know it sounds weird, but your characters do come to life and start to make their own decisions for your story. You don't believe what's happening until you realize that it's their story anyway, and they are helping you meet your word-count goal, so you just let them go with it."

Jordyn was laughing now. "Wait . . . *what?*"

"Or you could be like me," Greg sheepishly admitted, "and just not really do it at all. I think I got . . . what? Like 3,000 words total. I sucked so bad!"

"I know, I can't believe you did that!" scoffed Marissa.

"Well, whatever . . . I learned that procrastination is not my friend! I don't know, at the end, I kind of felt bad not doing it, because everyone else was so excited to finish theirs. The party was great though."

"Oh, yeah!" yelled Enid. "Are we going to get to do that this year too?"

I knew where this was going, and we simply didn't have time. With only three weeks to go before the November 1 start date, I had to nip this in the bud. "Sorry, guys," I said. "It's just not part of what we do in eighth grade."

To my surprise, the students groaned with disappointment.

"Well, that's not fair!" Melissa protested. "None of these guys have *ever* had the chance to write a novel. Are you going to *deprive* them of that?"

"I'm not depriving them of anything," I said. "It is a really cool opportunity, and I would encourage you to go online and sign up."

"You know it wouldn't be any fun if we just did it on our own, right?" said Enid, the eternal voice of reason. "C'mon, we'd never finish without each other."

He was right. That elusive "community of writers" is actually attainable. How could I deprive them of that experience?

Reluctantly, I sucked in my breath and made them an offer, "Okay, here's the deal: You have until tomorrow to decide—as an entire class—if we are writing novels in here or if we are not. If you choose *not* to, we simply move on with our regular curriculum, and those of you who would still like to do it can sign up on your own. I'll give you whatever information you need. If, as an entire class, you decide that we are going to write novels, we are *still* moving on with our regular curriculum in class. I will promise to give up one class period before November to give you all of the materials that you need for a successful month of noveling and to sign your contracts, set your goals, and give you directions for joining our virtual classroom online. *During* the month of November, you will all be responsible for meeting your word-count goals and completing all related assignments at home, on your own time. No excuses. You will be graded on your completion of your goal as well as the completion of a few novel-related assignments given throughout the month. I will also agree to scale back the regular homework. *After* November, you will be using an excerpt from your novel as the basis of the remainder of our grammar study throughout the year."

The next day, they unanimously agreed to take on this assignment outside of school, and it was the most fun I've ever had at that time of year! We'd find each other online, usually between 9:00 and 10:30 p.m., check in and offer support, compare the snacks of choice for the evening, or challenge each other to figure out how to work a secret item (like green Jello) into a scene. It was so comforting to know that even though we were writing on our own, we were never alone. And that made all of the difference.

My students, both seventh- and eighth-grade, decided that year that there was no reason that we should contain our novel writing enthusiasm to our classroom. Before we set up our virtual noveling world, we marched across the hall each and every class period for a week to lay down the gauntlet for Mr. Hohman's classes to compete against ours in novel writing. (Mr. Hohman is a coach and athlete at heart, so I knew he'd crack under the temptation of competition.) That year, I gave Mr. Hohman all of my lessons week by week to ease him into this experiment. We got our two classes together frequently for more formal lessons and allowed the kids to mix it up and work together during our prewriting and drafting sessions. It was actually really cool to see my veteran NaNo eighth graders sharing their experiences and giving advice to the seventh- and eighth-grade NaNo first-timers.

Keeping in the spirit of healthy competition between our classrooms, it was always a

Figure 5.1 Dozens of young writers decide to write a novel in a month.

race to see who would get to use the computers in the lab instead of in the media center (our computer lab had newer, faster laptops at the time), and once we were all down there typing (in whatever room we ended up in), Mr. Hohman would call me or I'd phone him and right on cue we'd set our timers to see which class could produce the highest word count in twenty minutes. It doesn't matter who wins when you are competing for the glory of word count. That year, Mr. Hohman and I each had three classes participating (two language arts blocks, plus a single, forty-three-minute class apiece). We also had one mom, a couple of cousins, a student teacher, and a dozen or more stray kids from around the school who participated. Together, we wrote 1,913,945 words (see Figure 5.1).

Without realizing it, Mr. Hohman and I were already preparing our students for future Partnership for 21st Century Learning (P21) initiatives that call for creativity, collaboration, and communication in addition to the technology skills that our students would be developing throughout the month. (See www.p21.org for more information). Participating in NaNoWriMo's Young Writers Program establishes a genuine writing community within the classroom as students share a common writing experience, help one another to succeed, and engage in healthy competition among peers.

Because the total word-count goals are individual to each child, everyone has an equal chance of reaching their targets. And the best part is that while a specific word count is a personal goal, we strive as a class to meet milestones. Whether a child's 10 percent milestone is 500 or 5,000 words, all students can celebrate their accomplishments. For writers of all ability levels, taking on this challenge suddenly makes the impossible possible—in writing as well as other areas of their lives. It boosts confidence and erases blank-page fear for every assignment that comes *after* November. My students look at me and laugh when I assign essay responses that need only be a typed page or two, asking, "Really? That's *it*?!" Or, as

"I never liked writing, but when we started [NaNo] it became really fun. I did a story about a girl my age . . . if something funny or interesting happened at lunch that day, I could go and add it to my story, and I could make things happen to her that I would love or *hate* to happen to me. It was like I was in control of her life. I worked really hard to make her come alive and once I did I read it through and said, WOW. I had never written something that long or good before. That is when my writing life changed."

> —Tara, grade 7

"I never in a million years thought I was going to write a novel. I was wrong. Our whole class wrote novels. We incorporated all of our strategies into this novel . . . This is where everything we've learned comes together."

> —Philip, grade 7

"[Writing a novel] was incredibly hard, but fun. The most frustrating thing was not knowing what to write, but I kept on writing, and now that I look back, I think I wrote a pretty good novel. I think it will be really fun to go back and revise it to make it even better. The most surprising moment for me was when I wrote 20 percent in under an hour! I think that any other writing assignments I have to do in the future will be easy after doing NaNoWriMo."

> —Corey, grade 7

"I am sad that NaNoWriMo is over. I never knew that I could actually write like the way I did this past month. The best thing about participating in NaNoWriMo is that I know I can write a thousand page essay if I have to! And that will definitely come in handy for high school and college!"

> —Lydia, grade 7

"The most surprising moment was when I realized it wasn't really me telling the story anymore; it was the characters I had created. I was just typing it all down for them! . . . After two years of doing NaNoWriMo, I think I can handle anything after all that I have accomplished. Even if it sounds crazy, I may actually do it again next year!"

> —Kasey, grade 8

"I LOVE NaNoWriMo! It is absolutely the highlight of my entire school year (no joke). I learned a lot about myself as a writer. For example, I typed my entire novel in first person, only to find that I prefer writing in third person. And, no matter how much I want to write in present tense, I naturally type in past. (I now have about 150 pages of mixed tenses that I know I am going to have

Figure 5.2 Students share some thoughts about writing a novel in a month.

to go back and revise!) Either way, I LOVE my novel! With some SERIOUS editing, revising, re-writing and RESEARCH as well as reading other novels for help, it will be pretty decent."

—Marissa, grade 8

"I thought this experience was crazy at first, like *yeah, no way I'm writing a novel in a month—impossible!!!* Once I got into it, it became a lot of fun for me and my mom because it was the only thing at school that really ever made her truly proud of me."

—Matthew, grade 7

"I actually wish that NaNoWriMo wasn't over because I like it a lot more than a lot of the other work we have to do. I like that in our novels we get to actually apply what we learn and it's a way more enjoyable way of doing it. Believe it or not, this was the first homework assignment that I would look forward to coming home and doing . . . I think that now that I have written a novel in 30 days, I will be able to put my ideas together better and faster on other timed writing assignments and tests."

—Abby, grade 8

Figure 5.2 (continued) Students share some thoughts about writing a novel in a month.

Marissa put it, "Once you write a novel, ask me to do any five-paragraph essay. Phfffft! I've got it. Piece of cake!" (For more student reflections on noveling experiences, see Figure 5.2.)

Through NaNoWriMo, students are encouraged to express themselves and explore their stories without worrying about red correction marks. They build sentence fluency and writing confidence by going with the flow of their story and playing with words and phrases. Grant Faulkner, the executive director of NaNoWriMo, explained in an e-mail interview that, like many students, he did not have positive writing experiences in school. "I grew up in classrooms where writing was a punishment (writing "I will not chew gum" fifty times on the blackboard) or something that seemed easier to get wrong than right because I associated writing with red pencil marks."

Faulkner says that the NaNoWriMo achievement for students is akin to completing a marathon, and it "breeds the type of academic confidence that crosses over into other academic subjects. Because they know they can accomplish such a task, a five-paragraph essay looks like a piece of cake, and when they're daunted by their next research paper, they know they can just jump in and write a draft. The best writers, whether they're writing business memos or scientific reports, know the joy of writing and understand how to critically play with words and put their visions and thoughts into language."

The ripple effect doesn't end there. Students develop an appreciation of the role that editing and revising play in good writing. This burst of confidence and newfound

> ### A Note on Test Writing
> *Test writing is a territory unto itself. My students now know how to tackle writing-test anxiety, and they can easily overcome blank-page fear. And after writing a novel during NaNoWriMo, developing quantity and voice in their writing is no longer an issue. Students learn to use specific details, interesting leads and closings, and myriad craft techniques, and by the time the spring testing period rolls around, they've also learned from the authors the importance of context, revision, and editing. Getting kids to view testing as just another form of publication will go far in making positive results possible. After all, when they are under a deadline, they must produce their best work under a specific set of submission guidelines, and they are sending off their writing outside of the classroom. (That sounds a lot like publication to me!)*

appreciation of the writing process is reflected in all kinds of writing for all audiences and purposes, including high-stakes testing.

Exploring National Novel Writing Month

National Novel Writing Month was started in 1999. Founder Chris Baty, author of *No Plot, No Problem: A Low-Stress, High-Velocity Guide to Writing a Novel in 30 Days* and *Ready, Set, NOVEL!,* and a few friends challenged each other to write a novel in thirty days. The writing marathon has exploded since then, gaining writers in nearly every corner of the globe. The Young Writers Program (YWP) of NaNoWriMo took root in 2005 after a huge demand to bring novel writing into the classroom.

National Novel Writing Month is a nonprofit organization in Berkeley, California, that is passionate in supporting all children and adults in finding "the inspiration, encouragement, and structure they need to achieve their creative potential" (http://www.guidestar.org/profile/65-1282653).

Both NaNoWriMo and its Young Writers Program are run by some of the most amazingly creative, literary, and educationally minded folks I've ever met. Chris Angotti, COO of the Young Writers Program, believes in the potential of creative writing as a tool for adolescent enrichment and achievement, and, along with his staff, has made it easy for educators to incorporate the YWP into their classrooms. At www.ywp.nanowrimo.org you will find everything—and I mean *everything*—that you will need to set up your classroom for a month of noveling bliss (or insanity). The Young Writers Program staff has gone to great lengths to put valuable resources right at teachers' fingertips. You can order a free classroom noveling kit, complete with the "Triumphant Chart of Noveling Progress," progress stickers, and reward buttons from the website. In addition, they also provide "100% Awesome, Non-Lame" Young Novelist Workbooks filled with reproducibles and motivating ideas that you can download and print from PDFs or order in their finished bound form. They also have downloadable teacher lesson plans that they have taken the time to explicitly align with the Common Core State Standards for English and Language Arts at every grade level, and a platform for creating a virtual classroom community and a hub for communication.

Teachers can customize their virtual classrooms with photos, announcements, and links to helpful websites. They can also post blog streams and send NaNoMail to students across the hall or on the other side of the globe. Through the virtual classroom directory, teachers can choose to link up with other participating classrooms in their own school and around the world. We've become NaNo buddies with English language classrooms in Japan and England, as well as with schools a town or two away.

On the YWP website, students create individual profiles about their reading and writing lives and link them to our classroom page. My students have used the classroom blog post feature to help them decide a character's fate, figure out how to make a relationship seem more real without being too wordy, and seek motivation to keep going.

> *I love the freedom of writing badly. Perfectionism kills the spirit of writing faster than anything I know of. It's best to just stop all that self-conscious struggling for instant excellence and begin. After a while, the bad writing will start to flip over into something much better, possibly even wonderful.*
> —Sue Monk Kidd, author of *The Secret Life of Bees*

Throughout the month, you will not be able to contain the excitement as students open their inboxes to find motivational letters and writing advice from the authors that they know and love. Past "pep talkers" include John Green, Lemony Snickett, Laurie Halse Anderson, Markus Zusak, and many more. Students will also hear from fellow young writers. Because of the way the NaNoWriMo group organizes these pep talks, the advice seems to come exactly when my students need inspiration.

All students who meet their writing goals and document them online receive a celebration video courtesy of the NaNoWriMo staff, a printable winner's certificate, and web badges. In December, students receive a code for a free bound proof copy of their books that they can redeem any time between December and June. This schedule gives them time to finish their stories and perform the necessary revisions. The folks at NaNoWriMo sure know how to celebrate a job well done.

And so do we.

The first week of December, we host our annual "I Survived NaNoWriMo" party. All students who participated get to attend, regardless of the number of words that they logged for the month. We celebrate becoming novelists together.

An Introduction to WWCs 5–8

You are probably asking yourself how you can possibly make the time for something of this magnitude within your already packed curriculum. If you can answer yes to any one of these questions, NaNoWriMo can work for you:

- Is *reading* novels part of your curriculum?
- Is *reading* short stories part of your curriculum?
- Are *elements of fiction (characterization, plot structure, conflict, foreshadowing, flashback, setting, mood, and so on.)* part of your curriculum?
- How about *grammar* and *revision*? Is that part of your curriculum?

All of these things are addressed through novel writing. It *is* curriculum, between the lines and in the cracks. After all, your students already *read* the curriculum in a book or classroom anthology. They already *study* the curriculum in context. So, why just *test* the learning when students could *apply* the curriculum in writing?

Of course, as with any large-scale writing assignment, proper preparation and scaffolding are necessary for success. We turn to the mentor authors once again to discover their strategies for developing the key components of our novels. Weekly Writing Challenges 5–8 are adapted from the advice of Jordan Sonnenblick, Rick Riordan, John Green, Stephenie Meyer, Ellen Hopkins, Sarah Dessen, Judy Blume, Lisi Harrison, Cassandra Clare, Anthony Horowitz, Jay Asher, and Sue Monk Kidd. I use their insights throughout the month of October to prepare my students for the expedition that is *a November to remember*.

Weekly Writing Challenges 5–8 stimulate potential ideas, but they will likely not be fully developed stories. Because authors know that great writing lives in the details, we cannot let our kids pass up opportunities for noticing and collecting these gems. With time and instruction, they will take notice of their world the way published authors do, and they will learn to write from snapshots and incorporate them to breathe life into their stories, particularly when we consciously integrate these this set of WWCs and the noveling lessons into the existing curriculum.

Each individual writing challenge described in this chapter correlates with the NaNoWriMo YWP lessons and workbook pages. Each writing challenge also complements a particular short story that we work on in our reading curriculum by focusing the writing on a related literary element. For example, WWC 5 emphasizes the development of characters, so in our NaNo workbooks, we work on "Creating Interesting Characters" and the "Character Questionnaire" during the same week. For our literature study during the same time frame, we focus on characterization as we read the short story *Charles* by Shirley Jackson.

As you get familiar with all that NaNoWriMo has to offer, you will undoubtedly find natural connections to your existing curriculum. In time you may find that your month with NaNoWriMo's Young Writers Program establishes momentum to keep your students' writing humming all year long.

Four to Five Weeks Prior to Starting NaNoWriMo

Because my students learn about characterization techniques and point of view in our literature study at this point in our curriculum, this lesson forms a natural bridge between the reading we are involved with and the writing that we will be creating. As part of this lesson, I emphasize that traits reveal a lot about a person. I ask my students to consider the following examples: Does a messy room mean the character is a lazy slob, or is it a sign that she is so busy with school and sports that she has no time to clean up after herself? Or is there an evil little brother or a bored and lonely dog destroying the room once the protagonist leaves the scene? When a stepmom sings in the car while you are riding with your friends, is she trying to embarrass you, or is she just fun loving and superconfident? This assignment helps kids to notice people's quirks and qualities.

> *If you read, read, read and study the way various authors make characters come to life on the page you will see that working both with the five senses and internal thoughts can really help. My advice is to read the character descriptions in the books you love and to especially pay attention to how they speak and what they say as that is what shapes people's impressions*
>
> —Ridley Pearson, author of the Kingdom Keepers series, the Starcatchers series, and many other titles

Weekly Writing Challenge 5: Creating Characters

I have to give all of the credit to author Jordan Sonnenblick (and to my student Audrey for finding his lesson!) for Weekly Writing Challenge 5: Creating Characters (see Figure 5.3). In the back of *Drums, Girls & Dangerous Pie*, Sonnenblick has added an amazing writing lesson called Now *That's* a Sandwich! How to Make Your Characters into *Characters*. In this lesson, he describes his strategy for developing characters, and we use this as a model for our own character exploration.

Students learn two lessons from this week's challenge. The first is that characters come first. It may seem strange to begin with characters instead of plot, but well-developed characters make the story. The second lesson is that we all have quirks, and we need to learn to appreciate them when we see them in others and laugh at ourselves when we recognize them on the inside!

Weekly Writing Challenge 5

> "Try to brainstorm a list of people you know and their really odd habits or characteristics."
>
> —Jordan Sonnenblick, author of *Drums, Girls, & Dangerous Pie*; *Curveball: The Year I Lost My Grip*; and many other titles

> "Define a character through action, first. Through dialogue and description, second. Through explanation, never."
>
> —Rick Riordan, author of the Percy Jackson and the Olympians series, the Kane Chronicles series, and many other titles

> " . . . all fiction is an attempt at empathy: When I write, I'm trying to imagine what it's like to be someone else more than I'm trying to express what it's like to be me. So in that sense, it's very helpful for me to write from the perspectives of characters who are at least a little different from me."
>
> —John Green, author of *The Fault in Our Stars*, *Paper Towns*, *Looking for Alaska*, and many other titles

> "I feel the best way to write believable characters is to really believe in them yourself. When you hear a song on the radio, you should know how your character feels about it—which songs your character would relate to, which songs she hates. Hear the conversations that your characters would have when they're not doing anything exciting; let them talk in your head, get to know them. Know their favorite colors and their opinions on current events, their birthdays and their flaws. None of this goes in the book, it's just to help you get a rounded feel to them."
>
> —Stephenie Meyer, author of the Twilight series, *The Host*, *Life and Death*, and other titles

Weekly Writing Challenge 5: Creating Characters

THE CHALLENGE

Most truly memorable characters have some quirky or distinguishing traits and habits that breathe life into them on the page. These nuances make them seem more real to the reader. This week you will get to make the characters in your life into lifelike characters in Chapter 2, "Memories," or in Chapter 3, "Writing from Life."

- Select three *different* people whom you have observed to have interesting or unusual qualities or habits and make a detailed list for each one (be honest, but it is okay to exaggerate—a little).
- If the person's quirkiness comes out as an *action*, create a scene where your "character" is demonstrating this action. Be sure to focus on your specific verb choices and the tone you want (funny, sad, frustrating, etc.).
- If the person's quirkiness comes out as a *trait*, create a vivid description. Be sure to focus on your detailed descriptions and word choices as well as the tone you want to get across to your reader (funny, sad, frustrating, etc.).

Figure 5.3 Noting quirky and distinguishing traits can help writers create memorable characters.

Weekly Writing Challenge 6: Eavesdropping: Recording Life as It Happens

> *Begin with great characters. Let the plot grow/flow from who your characters are, rather than try to force them into situations unnatural to them. As you write, listen to your characters. If they insist a story should move in a certain direction, consider it. (I know it sounds schizo, but my characters talk to me all the time.)*
>
> — Ellen Hopkins, author of *Crank, Glass, Traffick,* and many other YA titles

Conversations are a part of our world. If we listen, whether we're in the food court of the local mall or at a cocktail party, we can hear exchanges that lead us to story ideas. Spoken words—*how* they are spoken—reveal a level of truth beneath a character's exterior. Taking a few moments to record life as it happens, as we do in Weekly Writing Challenge 6, teaches our young writers the difference between how we perceive dialogue and how it naturally occurs. See Figure 5.4.

When we take time to jot down conversation word for word, three things become very clear:

1. **People rarely complete a thought.** Sometimes it's because another person interrupts them, sometimes it's because their eyes or gestures provide the rest of the story, and sometimes it's because they expect the other person to complete their thought. It's good to be aware of these possibilities as we begin to draft dialogue in our novels. At this time, I usually introduce writing conventions such as commentary (em) dashes, ellipses, and other punctuation marks so my students will understand how they support dialogue in writing.

2. **We all make judgments about people based on how they speak (and we are going to use this to our advantage in our writing).** In some of our narrative close-reading lessons, I have asked kids to notice the dialogue and make assumptions about characters and their situations—their level of education, their ethnicity, whether they come from a poor or rich neighborhood, their level of confidence. (To this end, we use Langston Hughes's short story "Thank You, M'am" as a close-reading lesson to highlight dialogue's impact on our perception of character.) In November, I will be asking students to apply this knowledge as they develop their own characters. I will expect them to integrate dialogue as a device for *showing* more about their characters, in order to give characterization clues to their readers, rather than *telling*.

3. **Writing authentic dialogue is hard.** People often communicate their ideas and change the direction of a conversation very quickly. We don't want students to add random, meaningless conversations into their novels, but the eavesdropping exercise

Weekly Writing Challenge 6

"Record great outfits, horrendous outfits, conversations, annoying habits, rude behavior, goofy walks . . . sprinkle these details into your writing like a chef with salt. They will make your work come alive."

—Lisi Harrison, author of the Clique series, the Alphas series, the Monster High series, and many other titles

"I keep my ears out for funny conversations my friends have and often adapt aspects of them for my books."

"One key to figuring out your dialogue is reading it out loud. Does it sound like something someone would actually *say*?"

—Cassandra Clare, author of the Shadowhunter Chronicles (the Mortal Instruments series) and other titles

"My friend, the author Lee Smith, once said that she considered sitting at the mall watching people go by as research, and I agree. There are so many stories out there waiting to be told. You just have to keep your eyes open."

—Sarah Dessen, author of *Lock and Key, Just Listen, The Truth About Forever,* and other titles

Weekly Writing Challenge 6: Eavesdropping: Recording Life as It Happens

THE CHALLENGE

This week will be fun, but it will require some planning.

- Select three *different* locations to bring your ME book this week. Locations may include: home, school (lunch room or bus are good options), and out in public somewhere.
- While in each location, listen in on a conversation and write it down, word for word, trying to capture all of the words and feelings of the people involved. Write the conversations in Ch. 3, "Writing from Life," in your ME book. Don't worry about punctuation for now; just write how it sounds.
- Later, go back and touch up each recorded conversation, adding feelings, gestures, facial expressions, body posture, and so on, to make the scene come to life.

Figure 5.4 Listening to real conversations can help young writers write authentic dialogue.

in WWC 6 does show them that monologues in real life are rare (unless, of course, a parent is talking to a teenager!), and that people do occasionally stop to think or pick their noses or bite their lips or roll their eyes and take big sighs while they are talking, and it's these tiny details that can reveal so much about character.

Admittedly, the listening in required by WWC 6 can be a little controversial. The purpose is to get kids to tune in to the world around them, listening for potential characters and story ideas. As both a teacher and a parent I certainly do not want to promote secretly "spying" on family members or to create "stalkers" out of our impressionable tweens and teens. But authors do frequently people watch (and listen) in their daily lives. They bring notebooks and pencils or tablets with them when they are eating out or attending their children's soccer games. It's part of their writing process. The scenes that they bear witness to can add depth and realism to their stories and characters. For families who may object, I offer two alternatives: (1) their children can watch a TV show or movie and plan to transcribe a conversation between two characters, or (2) they can skip the assignment. I look at this exercise as an enrichment assignment that only serves to build on our classroom characterization lessons associated with WWC 5.

Three Weeks Prior to Starting NaNoWriMo

The instructional focus for this week is conflict and plot. Or is it plot and conflict? It's the age-old question of which comes first. Our main characters have to grow and change in order to keep our reader's interest, but how do we as writers make that happen? It is a conundrum. Conflict within a character or between characters can advance the plot. But, on the other hand, a great plot can lead to conflict among or within characters. So where do we begin? Whereas the chicken-and-egg paradox can be answered definitively by science, we have to explore both sides of this enigma to see which approach will work the best for each young writer.

Weekly Writing Challenge 7: Writing from Life II: A Tour of My World

In order to bridge our reading and writing for this experience, I select a story for our in-class literature study that has an easily identifiable exposition and inciting incident, well-defined rising action events, a definitive climax, and brief falling action and resolution. "Rikki–Tikki-Tavi" by Rudyard Kipling is in our curriculum and has a fairly predictable plot structure to reinforce the components, so this is an easy choice for me. As we read the story, we take note of the plot points and explore conflict and motivation of the characters as background knowledge for the characters students are developing for their novels. (See Figure 5.5.)

Weekly Writing Challenge 7

"I once took an audiotour of a mock-up of King Tut's tomb. Once the tour was over, I went searching for a story to tell in a similar format, with one narrator being a recorded voice and the other being the thoughts of the person listening. Around that same time, a close relative of mine attempted suicide. Several years went by before both events clicked together, and I knew the pairing worked well. The audiorecordings weren't just a cute gimmick, but actually enhanced the story. It also allowed me to talk from the point-of-view of a suicidal character while also getting another person's perspective on the events being discussed."

—Jay Asher, author of *13 Reasons Why* and other titles

"The fact is, ideas come from all around you, from everything you experience every day. You see a light on in an abandoned building and you think 'I wonder who's in there and what they're doing?' The answer to that is an idea for a story. Whether it's a good story or not is up to you."

—Cassandra Clare, author of the Shadowhunter Chronicles (the Mortal Instruments series)

"I got ideas for gadgets in Alex Rider from my son's room."

-Anthony Horowitz, author of the Power of Five series, the Alex Rider series, and other titles

"Sometimes as a writing exercise, I walk around practicing paying attention. I try to really see the thing before me with new eyes, to find a fresh meaning for it, or a unique way to describe it. It helps if I pretend I'm brand new to planet earth, like I just stepped off the space craft."

—Sue Monk Kidd, author of *The Secret Life of Bees*

Weekly Writing Challenge 7: Writing from Life II: A Tour of My World

THE CHALLENGE

- Throughout the week, select at least three *different* locations (around your house, in your neighborhood, or other places you frequent, like the mall or sports practices or school). I want you to go to these places and look around "with new eyes." Do you notice any details that you hadn't before? Are there any questions you could ask yourself about those details that might lead you into a story idea?
- Write the name of each location at the top of a new page in Ch. 3 of your ME book, "Writing from Life." Jot down your details and list your questions, then draw a line before completing your writing entry.
- In your writing, just see where your questions take you. Try to write a scene that may have taken place in that location. Feel free to add details and dialogue to make your scene come to life!

Figure 5.5 This Weekly Writing Challenge helps students notice details in their surroundings.

> *I don't know the story before I begin. I only have a vague image in my mind of a character and a place. Then I write in order to find out what the story is. I want to know why the character is in this place and what is happening now, what happened before, and what will happen later.*
>
> —Sharon Creech, author of *Heartbeat*, *Love That Dog*, *Absolutely Normal Chaos*, and many other titles

Meanwhile, at home, the kids are working to develop settings that evoke potential conflict. Just a warning . . . Many of these entries will end up being a little morbid, as the kids' thoughts wander into some pretty dark places. I suppose that is what naturally makes for good conflict, and therefore a good plot line.

For one of her entries, Aleysha noticed an old house that seemed to be abandoned in a far-off corner of the community fields where she was playing lacrosse. She hadn't noticed this house before the assignment, and it's no wonder, because it sat half buried under vines of ivy and weeds on the edge of the woods. She came up with a short list of questions that had conflict potential, and from her list of questions she developed a narrative scene full of suspenseful details that showed us how introducing one setting can intrigue a character enough to derail a plot and take it into a completely different direction (see Figure 5.6).

Riley, on the other hand, was in the car with his mom on a typical evening, driving the same route home that they always do, when he passed by a serious accident. From the passenger window of his mom's car, he could see an ambulance and two completely mangled cars, and he just couldn't let go of that image (see Figure 5.7). He commented in our writing conference, "Oh, man! There was so much wreckage. I couldn't see any of the bodies, but I figured they had to be pretty messed up. I never saw that kind of accident that close up before. The cars were so smashed! I don't know how anyone could have survived. I wasn't planning on using that for my WWC, but I just couldn't stop thinking about it and seeing it my mind, so I figured, *why not?*"

In his case, Riley became the character in the crash struggling to remain conscious of his surroundings (and his limbs!). Although his text is graphic (boy writers tend to lean in that direction if granted permission), he did a fantastic job incorporating a simile and an out-of-place verb. In this setting his character died, but as our writing conversation continued, I mentioned that this piece could make for an interesting segue into a novel idea, with the accident serving as the beginning of the tale (where the conflict drives the plot). Then he could take it in one of two directions: (1) The rest of the novel could be a flashback that led to this moment, where the reader discovers what led to the crash, what kind of life this character led, and whether it was his or her fault. Or, (2), although this is the end of the character in earthly form, maybe he or she becomes a ghost or spirit trying to find his or her way in this new world, as the characters do in Neal Shusterman's Skinjacker trilogy, which Riley had read.

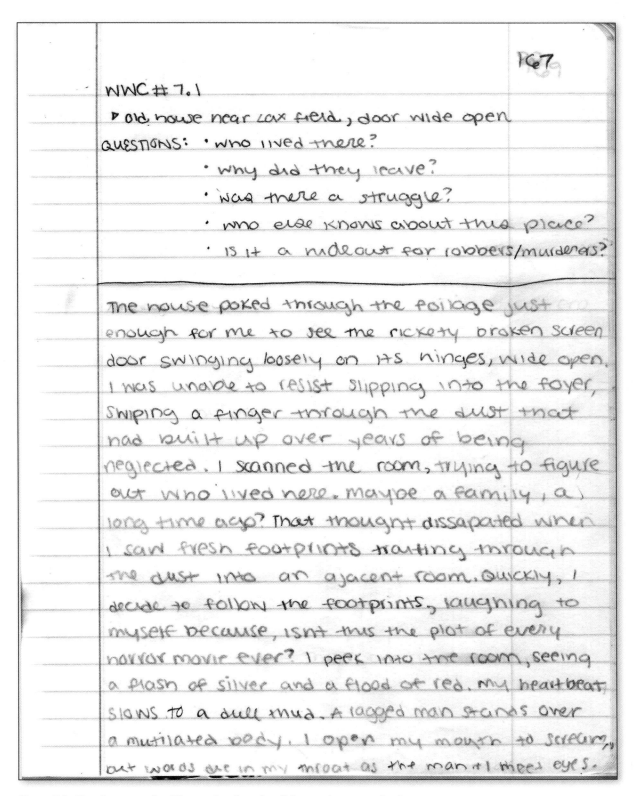

WWC # 7.1

▸ old howe near lax field, door wide open

QUESTIONS: • who lived there?

• why did they leave?

• was there a struggle?

• who else knows about this place?

• is it a hideout for robbers/murderers?

The house poked through the foilage just enough for me to see the rickety broken screen door swinging loosely on its hinges, wide open. I was unable to resist slipping into the foyer, swiping a finger through the dust that had built up over years of being neglected. I scanned the room, trying to figure out who lived here. maybe a family, a long time ago? That thought dissapated when I saw fresh footprints trailing through the dust into an ajacent room. Quickly, I decide to follow the footprints, laughing to myself because, isnt this the plot of every horror movie ever? I peek into the room, seeing a flash of silver and a flood of red. my heartbeat slows to a dull thud. A ragged man stands over a mutilated body. I open my mouth to scream, but words die in my throat as the man + I meet eyes.

Figure 5.6 Aleysha uses a familiar setting from her life to write a sample plot.

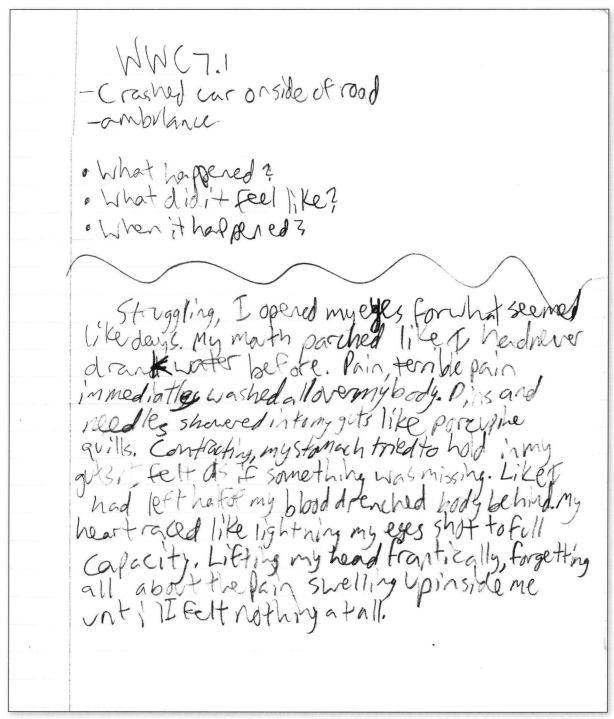

WWC7.1
- Crashed car on side of road
- ambulance

- What happened?
- What did it feel like?
- When it happened?

Struggling, I opened my eyes for what seemed like days. My math parched like I had never drank water before. Pain, terrible pain immediately washed all over my body. Pins and needles showered into my guts like porcupine quills. Contracting, my stomach tried to hold in my guts, it felt as if something was missing. Like I had left half of my blood drenched body behind. My heart raced like lightning, my eyes shot to full capacity. Lifting my head frantically, forgetting all about the pain swelling up inside me until I felt nothing at all.

Figure 5.7 Riley was so affected by seeing the scene of a car crash up close, he wrote in first person, as if he were a victim in the crash.

After completing Weekly Writing Challenge 7, the kids are ready to create plots, with the key events that will make up the exposition, inciting incident (the introduction of initial conflict), rising action, climax, falling action, and resolution. With so many ideas brewing, the students are excited to be at this stage.

Two Weeks Prior to NaNoWriMo

Now that we are approaching the final scrimmage before the big game, it is time to focus on developing the details, because during the month of November, the word count is in the details. According to Jeff Anderson, "With well-selected detail, writing transforms from the page to a movie in the reader's mind . . . It moves an idea from an abstraction to a concrete, well-drawn person, place, or thing, which readers can connect to their experiences in the world" (2011, 61). And there is no better place to capitalize on word count than in the deepest, darkest, dustiest corners of the setting. Because we are getting so close to Halloween, it should be fairly easy to select stories for your literature study that can really show readers how fantastic setting development can create suspense and reinforce characters and their motives. Because "Three Skeleton Key" by George G. Toudouze is already in our curriculum, I pair it with the setting development that we are studying through Weekly Writing Challenge 8. (Almost anything by Poe will also fit the bill.) This is also the ideal time to introduce or reinforce the concept of denotation versus connotation, as well as literary elements such as imagery, irony, symbolism, and foreshadowing, because these kinds of creepy and suspenseful stories are chock-full of examples!

In the case of "Three Skeleton Key," we use the rats in the story to discuss the difference between denotation and connotation. Technically, a rat is a long-tailed rodent, fairly intelligent and able to solve problems (denotation); but many people consider rats to be sneaky vermin (connotation) because of historical and literary references.

To transfer ideas about denotation and connotation from reading to writing, we have a conversation about setting and word choice. For example, if the time of day is *sunset*, and the *shadows* of the trees stretch long and far *dividing* the field in two, the three italicized word choices hold a deeper meaning for the reader beyond their dictionary definitions. Sunset comes at the end of every day, right before dusk and nightfall, but in the context of well-written literature, it holds much more meaning. My students have already learned that light often symbolizes life (whether it is in the form of a candle's flame or the sun); therefore, the *setting* sun could lead us to believe that there is an end of life approaching, especially when it is coupled with words like *shadows* and *dividing* (both negative connotations). Now let's flip the same scene: It's *sunrise*, and the trees and flowers *open* wide to *bask* in the *warmth* of the sun, their shadows *kissing* their stems and trunks. Other than the time of day, we still have the same basic concept—light on a field with trees and shadows—but this time, the entire mood shifts to something much more positive and uplifting. The students can easily see that deliberate word choices can change the mood of a particular setting. And when the setting is significant to characters, readers can better understand the characters' perspective on the world and their motivation.

Weekly Writing Challenge 8: Stop (and Listen): Tools for Developing Setting

As we approach the end of October, we are inundated with all of the sights, sounds, and smells that breathe fall. Weekly Writing Challenge 8: Stop (and Listen): Tools for Developing Setting (Figure 5.8) is designed to capitalize on all of the sensory details in our surroundings. With the leaves and weather changing and the smell and taste of pumpkin everywhere, most kids find it fairly easy to develop a quick scene involving their immediate environment.

Jake's family has a cabin in the woods that they visit almost every weekend during the fall. He used this opportunity to write about a setting that was very important to his family. With a deliberate eye (and ear), he described the details that make it a special place. Through our conference, Jake revealed that his favorite time of day at the cabin was the morning before everyone got up. He liked to enjoy the view from his upper deck without anyone watching or bothering him. The writing lens of his entry zooms in on his morning experience (see Figure 5.9). Notice how his word choices capture the quiet calm of the morning inside the cabin, contrasting with the bright sun of a new day outside.

Some students, however, don't enjoy the fall. As Lizzy put it when I dared to suggest that she write about all of the colors and smells of autumn during one of our writing conferences: "What's to love about dying leaves?" So for this writing challenge, she decided to mentally go to a better place filled with, as she put it, "more positive life energy." She chose *the beach*. Lizzy describes the sights and sounds of her ideal day on the beach (see Figure 5.10). It's not a sleepy, relaxing beach day that might bring a visitor peace, but it's also not packed with people and with seagulls squawking and attacking visitors for their food. Through her word choices, Lizzy captures that positive energy she spoke of and brings an appealing vibe to her scene at the beach.

One Week Before NaNoWriMo

Weekly Writing Challenges 5 through 8, which we've completed over the preceding several weeks, set us up for the final lessons before we begin our writing on November 1. For our literature lessons, we return to personal books and reinforce all that we've learned thus far by reading like a writer and noting characterization techniques, conflicts, setting details,

Weekly Writing Challenge 8

"My only advice [on becoming a good writer] is to stay aware, listen carefully, and yell for help if you need it."

—Judy Blume, author of *Deenie*; *Are You There, God? It's Me, Margaret*; *As Long as We're Together*, and many other titles

"Imagery is the heart of poetry, which is about painting pictures with words, so readers can see what you see. (Not just with your eyes, but with all of your senses.)"

—Ellen Hopkins, author of *Crank*, *Glass*, *Traffick*, and many other titles

Weekly Writing Challenge 8: Stop (and Listen): Tools for Developing Setting

THE CHALLENGE

Now that we are approaching the holidays, we are completely bombarded with all of the sights, sounds, textures, tastes, and smells of the season.

- Select three *different* locations to write about in your ME book this week. Use memories of important places from your life.
- Begin by *webbing* as many sensory details as you can in Chapter 2 of your ME book, "Memories."
- Then write by re-creating the setting in a narrative description. Write small . . . let the tiniest details develop the setting, allowing the reader to feel like she or he is there.

Figure 5.8 This Weekly Writing Challenge helps students notice details in their surroundings.

literary elements, and anything else that will serve as inspiration for the month ahead. For our writing lessons, we focus on developing narrative leads. The NaNo workbooks provide an excellent exercise, Back to the Beginning, which encourages young novelists to experiment with various starting places: at the beginning, at the inciting incident, in the middle of some major rising action, at the climax, or at the end. Once they have completed the written portion of the activity, I encourage my students to test their practice beginnings with a partner or small group to see which version resonates best with the audience.

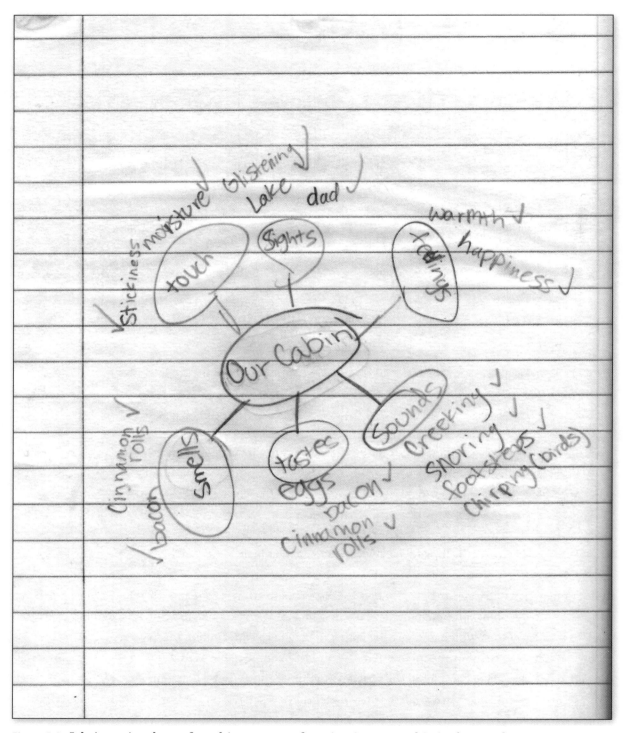

Figure 5.9 Jake's setting draws from his memory of a quiet time at a cabin in the woods.

WWC 8.1

(59)

Our Cabin

I dragged my body to the window, flung open the curtains. The sun's warmth burst through the window, wrapping me up like a blanket, warming me and my spirit. I wiped the moisture off the window and peered down at the lake. It was glistening from the early morning ~~sun's~~ rays. I crept to my parent's room, feet sticking to the wooden floor with every step, trying very hard not to wake my soundly-sleeping family. I slowly pushed the door open, and it creeks with every inch of movement. I take a quick peek inside. My dad sleeping like a hibernating bear, snoring like a steam engine roaring off into the distance. Closing the door, I become aware of ~~light~~ footsteps downstairs moving through the kitchen. One sniff of fresh baked cinnamon rolls and crispy, juicy, sizzling bacon calling my name, and I smile, knowing it's mom

Figure 5.9 (continued) Jake's setting draws from his memory of a quiet time at a cabin in the woods.

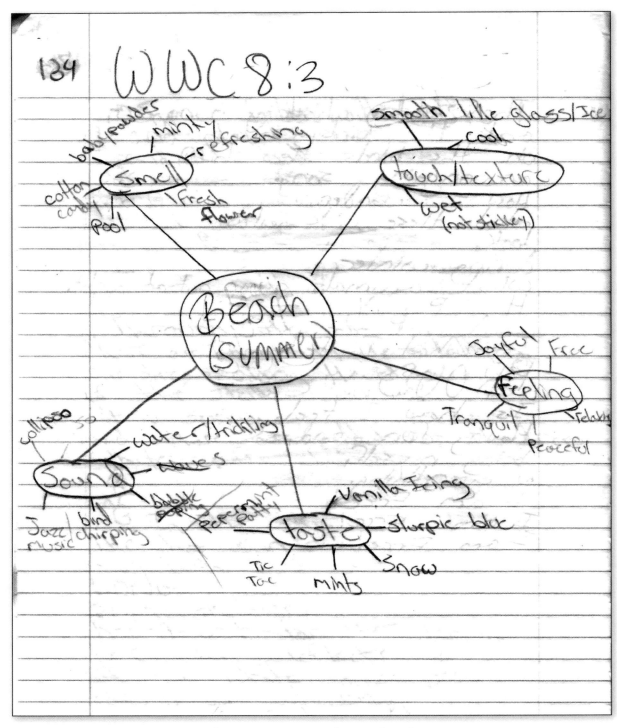

Figure 5.10 Lizzy's setting draws on her interpretation of a noisy beach scene.

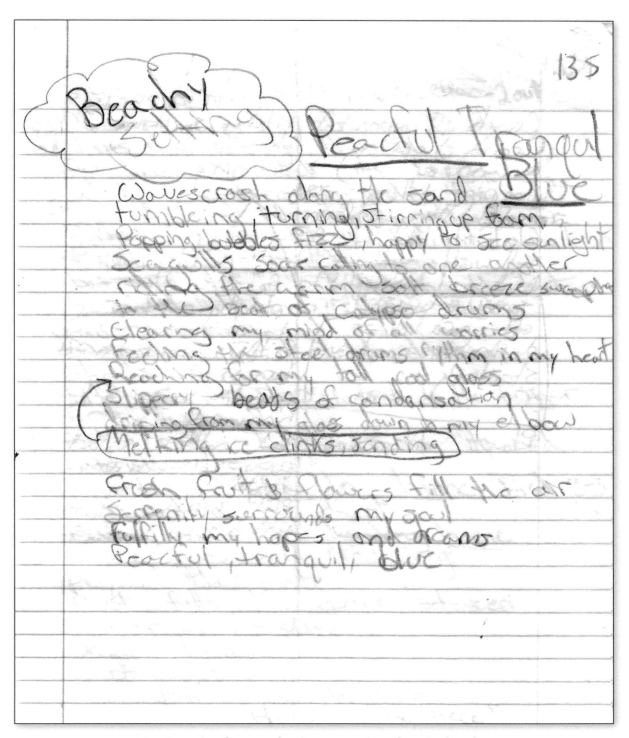

Figure 5.10 (continued) Lizzy's setting draws on her interpretation of a noisy beach scene.

Beyond the actual writing, we have a few other "housekeeping items" that we have to take care of. These items, which can be completed at any point prior to November, include setting personal word-count goals, signing the official NaNoWriMo contract, and filling out two copies of the Personal Chart of Noveling Progress (one for their own records, and one that I keep in class to track the dates when they meet their milestone or to kick them in the pants when they need a little motivation). I also take the time to create custom classroom calendars in Microsoft Publisher, marking days off and dates for milestone percentage completion to help them break this daunting task into manageable chunks.

> *I know this isn't very fun advice, but try to keep this in mind: how hard you work, unlike random inborn talent, is entirely up to you. If you work hard and complete your work, you're ahead of 99% of people who want to write a book.*
>
> Cassandra Clare, author of the Shadowhunter Chronicles (the Mortal Instruments series)

The final step of preparation is getting the kids online in our YWP virtual classroom and teaching them all the features of the website. The day before I take them on the virtual tour online, I assign my Getting Ready for NaNoWriMo worksheet (see Appendix C). Once completed, this worksheet keeps my students focused on inputting their information on their individual My NaNo pages online. Pages 3 and 4 give explicit directions for linking to our virtual classroom. (Please note that I modify this worksheet annually to correspond to updates on the NaNoWriMo YWP website.) After students have created their personalized page and have linked up to our virtual classroom, they can use the remainder of our class time in the computer lab to poke around the website to investigate the resources and create some classroom NaNo writing buddies who will help them to get through the month.

Now What?

By writing a novel, students have earned knowledge they can carry with them throughout their academic careers and beyond. That's fantastic, but now that we are finished, what do we do with the novels?

If students want to reach beyond the assignment, I direct them to a web page within the NaNoWriMo YWP site, titled "The 'Now What?' Months" (http://ywp.nanowrimo.org/now-what) and to "The Landing Page" for adult and young writers on NaNoWriMo's main site (http://nanowrimo.org/now-what). The folks at NaNoWriMo provide tips for editing and revising, connections for cultivating a virtual community of like-minded writers, and dozens of resources for acquiring an agent and publishing.

For the purposes of our class, the journey matters more than the destination. We experience being part of a community of writers, set and accomplish long-term writing

Here's What to Expect While Noveling During NaNoWriMo

Week 1: Life is good. You've been bragging to your friends about your endeavor. You've got some momentum and ideas are flowing. Until . . .

Week 2: Stormy seas. You begin to wonder why you told so many people about taking on this ridiculous challenge. Although you poke and prod your characters, you can't get them to move. You seriously consider leaving town and abandoning writing forever. Until . . .

Week 3: Wonderful, yet bizarre things begin to happen. Your characters have staged a mutiny. They have taken on a life of their own and hijacked your plot. They have no intention of turning back. Until . . .

Week 4: The deadline looms. Between your lollygagging during week 2 and abandoning your writing for Black Friday sales, you have suddenly realized that you are running out of time to reach your word-count goal. Strong cups of coffee and leftover Halloween candy quickly become your new best friends. Until . . .

THE END.

Teamwork

Student and adult writers are all in the same boat during the month of November. It will not all be smooth sailing! But working together, you can make it through. Figure 5.11 shows all the lessons and activities that will help you and your class plan for the month ahead.

Focus	Characterization (Four Weeks Prior to November)
Reading	Short stories with strong characterization, such as: "Charles" by Shirley Jackson and "Thank You, M'am" by Langston Hughes
Literature Lessons	• Character Terms: protagonist/antagonist, dynamic/static, round/flat • Characterization Techniques • Literary Point of View
Writing Lessons	• Jordan Sonnenblick's Lesson: Now *That's* a Sandwich: How to Make Your Characters into *Characters* (Bonus feature in *Drums, Girls & Dangerous Pie*, 2004) • WWC 5: Creating Characters • WWC 6: Eavesdropping: Recording Life as It Happens (optional)
Application: NaNoWriMo Connections	• Workbook lesson: Creating Interesting Characters • Workbook Lesson: Character Questionnaire • Workbook Lesson: Character Interviews on NaNo TV (optional)

Figure 5.11 Sample NaNoWriMo Curriculum Integration for the Month of October

Focus	Plot and Conflict (Three Weeks Prior to November)
Reading	Short stories with strong, predictable plot structure, such as: "Rikki-Tikki-Tavi" by Rudyard Kipling
Literature Lessons	• Conflict: Internal vs. External • Plot Diagram
Writing Lessons	• WWC 7: Writing from Life II: A Tour of My World
Application: NaNoWriMo Connections	• Workbook Lesson: Creating Conflict • Workbook Lesson: Outlining Your Plot • Students work on completing their own plot roller coaster for their future novels.

Focus	Setting and Literary Elements (Two Weeks Prior to November)
Reading	Short stories with strong setting and exemplary literary elements, such as: "Three Skeleton Key" by George G. Toudouze
Literature Lessons	• Denotation and Connotation • Literary Elements (symbolism, imagery, irony, flashback, foreshadowing)
Writing Lessons	• WWC 8: Stop (and Listen): A Tool for Developing Setting
Application: NaNoWriMo Connections	• Workbook Lesson: Setting • Workbook Lesson: Bonus Setting Exercises: Settings That Reinforce Characters • Students continue work on plot roller coasters and settings that reflect their characters and events.

Focus	Getting Ready for NaNo (One Week Prior to November)
Reading	Personal Free Reading
Literature Lessons	• Reading like a writer, noting characterization, conflict, plot, point of view, setting details, literary elements, and anything else that will serve as inspiration for the month of writing
Writing Lessons	• Narrative Leads
Application: NaNoWriMo Connections	• Workbook Lesson: Back to the Beginning • Set personal word-count goals, then sign the contract and complete the Personal Chart of Noveling Progress. • Break down goals into smaller, more manageable chunks by establishing a calendar. • Getting Ready for NaNo worksheet, and then set up My NaNoWriMo page in Virtual Classroom.

Figure 5.11 (continued) Sample NaNoWriMo Curriculum Integration for the Month of October

Possible Assignments and Grades During NaNoWriMo

- Complete the "Author Info" and "Novel Info" tabs on the My NaNoWriMo page.
- Post an excerpt and explain what *characterization techniques* were used.
- Post an excerpt showing use of_____ (imagery, irony, symbolism, or foreshadowing); explain what makes this excerpt a good example of that literary device.
- Post an excerpt that is a great example of an author's craft; explain which one it is and why you used it .
- Post your favorite excerpt on your "Novel Info" tab on the My NaNoWriMo page.
- Respond to various teacher posts throughout the month.
- If you are continuing to work on the grammar component of your curriculum while noveling, have kids post a short excerpt demonstrating application of the grammar skill being studied.

Possible Extra Credit Opportunities

- Create a blog post for classmates to respond to.
- Respond to a classmate's blog post.
- Post an inspirational message to keep your classmates going or to show some NaNo gratitude.
- Create a book cover and post it to your "Novel Info" tab.

Additional Lessons to Keep the Writing Flowing Throughout the Month of November

- WEEK 1: Review Dialogue—the rules and how to weave it into narrative text (because the juices are flowing and they may just need a reminder.)
- WEEK 2: Show, Don't Tell; Thoughtshots; Snapshots (because the details make the word count)
- WEEK 3: Exploding a Moment (because, in theory, by the end of the week, they should be getting close to the climax)
- Throughout the month: Writer's Craft (because it's fun, and this bring us back to our reading-writing roots)

(For more information on thoughtshots, snapshots, and exploded moments, see *Reviser's Toolbox* by Barry Lane [1999].)

Other Fun Activities to Think About for the Month:

- Host a write-in out in the community on a weekend or evening (we often do it at our local mall food court or bookstore).
- Host a T-shirt contest as a way to commemorate this special event.
- Online, find a partner classroom from another country, then participate in Word Wars and develop virtual pen pals and future writing partners.
- Contact the newspaper and local news organizations to get the word out about the amazing things you are doing for with students (and invite them to your I Survived NaNoWriMo celebration!).
- Get in touch with local businesses to let them know about NaNoWriMo and see if they would be willing to contribute any products or certificates for kids who meet their word count goals.
- Buy a roll of raffle tickets and give kids one each time they meet a word-count milestone. (Then, at the end of the month, pull the tickets to award prizes donated from the businesses in your area).
- If you attend a fall literacy conference (such as NCTE), pick up free books and have them signed by the authors with the greeting, "Congratulations, NaNo-Novelist!" (or some other personal message), and award the books to your top word-count writers or as raffle prizes.

Figure 5.11 (continued) Sample NaNoWriMo Curriculum Integration for the Month of October

> *Write a novel from beginning to end. I mean it. I don't care if it's the worst book in history, write a beginning, a middle, and an ending, and everything in between. You won't believe the magical power that will come over you once you've accomplished this task.*
>
> —James Dashner, author of the Maze Runner series, the Mortality Doctrine series, the 13th Reality series, and many other titles

goals, defeat blank-page fear, and craft and draft under pressure to build stamina and fluency. As an educator with more than twenty years of experience, I know of no other writing experience that provides as much bang for the buck as participating in NaNoWriMo.

After a month's distance from our novel-writing experience (typically, a snowy week in January for us), I have the kids read back through their novels to select a 500- to 1,800-word excerpt that they would like to continue to revise and develop for the remainder of the school year. This excerpt provides excellent practice for our future grammar lessons and the revision work that students will be expected to do on their own as they prepare their self-selections for publication later in the school year. See Appendix D to review the trajectory.

Chapter 6

Getting Back to ME (Writer's Notebook)

The seeds for all my stories come from my teen years. When I was a teen, I wrote in my journal almost every night. I often go back and reread those journals to remind myself what it feels like to be a teen. Some things, like technology, slang, and culture, change over the years, but the feeling of falling in love, of feeling betrayed or humiliated—those emotions are universal and time resistant. When I say that my characters' experiences mirror mine, I'm talking about emotional experience and resonance.

—Becca Fitzpatrick,

author of the Hush, Hush Saga, *Black Ice*, and *Dangerous Lies*

Whew! October was filled with anticipation, and November was such a rush. And, believe me, your students will be feeling it. Now that it's December, they legitimately need a break, not from writing, but from the intensity. And you may feel as if you have some unfinished curricular business that you would like to complete before the winter break. For that reason, I suggest that you look at the next three WWCs as strictly optional. With distractions from the upcoming holidays, breaks from school, and the likelihood of extended family encounters, Weekly Writing Challenges 9 through 11 give kids the chance to reconnect with their friends, their families, and themselves without completely losing their writing momentum. Although students referenced their writer's notebooks in November to trigger their memories of writing ideas developed in the month prior, they did very little writing in them. If you have time, ease students back into their

ME books (writer's notebooks).

Once the holidays are over, Weekly Writing Challenges 12, 13 and the bonus challenge of "What if . . .?" writing mark the final push for idea generation before students slow it down and reflect on their learning.

The WWCs in this chapter are inspired by middle grade and YA greats such as Cornelia Funke, Sue Monk Kidd, Cynthia Lord, Matt Christopher, Markus Zusak, Scott Westerfeld, Sarah Dessen, Margaret Peterson Haddix, and Becca Fitzpatrick, as well as Laurie Halse Anderson, Veronica Roth, J. K. Rowling, Rick Riordan, Kathryn Erskine, Suzanne Collins, Steve Sheinkin, Stephen King, Lois Lowry, and Gordon Korman. The lessons are somewhat personal, offering students a chance to reminisce about their past experiences, explore their present lives, and dream about the future. All of the strategies lead students to plumb their thoughts and memories for two purposes: First, they discover additional writing topics and territories to fuel their upcoming press toward publication. Second, they discover new lenses through which to view their experiences and new reasons for which to write about them. With the noveling experience under their belts, they begin to look at the world differently. It's not just about finding more topics and territories for writing; it's about helping students find out what is really important to them and teaching students ways to mine for these potential writing influences in their hearts, their minds, and out in the world.

Weekly Writing Challenge 9: Accumulating Artifacts

In WWC 9: Accumulating Artifacts (see Figure 6.1), I ask students to mine their physical memories for tiny keepsakes that hold meaning. The items that students tend to collect for this exercise include photos, movie or concert ticket stubs, pressed flowers, award ribbons, and tags from new bedroom furniture, favorite sneakers, and clothes. Students who don't feel comfortable taping the original item into their ME books can take a picture of it (or I will scan a copy of it) and print it out so they can take the original home.

Students have many choices for how to approach the related writing. I always make sure that I show a personal model as an example. Often I begin by creating a web of written ideas around my artifact as a way of recalling memories associated with it. There is no right or wrong way to brainstorm. Some kids like to enlist the strategy of free association and jot down anything and everything that pops into their heads with regard to their artifacts, whereas others prefer to home in on sensory details from that one moment from their lives. The beauty of this challenge is that it typically brings up happy memories that flow effortlessly onto the page.

For example, Jackie decided to tape into her notebook a wristband from a recent trip she had taken with her family to Atlantis on Paradise Island in the Bahamas. Around her

Weekly Writing Challenge 9

"I start collecting like a squirrel. I start filling my treasure chest . . . I research and read, read, read, having piles of books . . . I scribble down notes, start to think of my characters . . . My whole wall is covered with cards of the set chapters I'm going to do."

—Cornelia Funke, author of
The Thief Lord, the Inkheart trilogy, and many other titles

"I tear pictures out of magazines and collect postcards, choosing images that fascinate me, and then I paste them on a board, which becomes a loose story board for my novel."

—Sue Monk Kidd, author of *The Secret Life of Bees*

On my desk, I keep a dictionary, a grammar book, books of photographs, a field guide of animals and plants, and other reference books, as well as objects and pictures from my settings."

—Cynthia Lord, author of *Rules*, *Touch Blue*, *Half a Chance*, and other titles

Weekly Writing Challenge 9: Accumulating Artifacts

THE CHALLENGE

- This week, go through your photographs, old movie ticket stubs, and other relatively flat artifacts from your life.

- Select three or more to glue or tape into Chapter 2, "Memories," of your ME book. You can scan the artifact and glue that in instead of the original. Then do your twenty minutes of writing for each.

- You may want to brainstorm thoughts about it around each artifact, and then you could explain why you picked it or why it is important, describe the memories associated with it, re-create a narrative scene, or develop a poem about it. .

Figure 6.1 Using symbols from their lives, students can write from personal experience.

wristband she wrote down details about her first time down a huge water slide into the shark-infested lagoon below. Her writing that accompanied the brainstorm was a tiny memoir that captured the fun and excitement of one moment.

Portland, on the other hand, found a baby picture of herself sitting in an exersaucer. Around her picture she generated a list of questions and observations that a baby might have. She approached her writing from the point of view of a baby, trapped in her baby seat, surrounded by jabbering adults, noisy toys, and deliciously messy food!

Michael taped in a photo of a trophy that he won in a martial arts tournament, and around his photo listed all of the sensory details he could remember from being in the middle of the ring in that huge arena. His vignette turned into a powerful exploded moment that really drew the reader into the excitement of his competition.

Weekly Writing Challenge 10: Mapping Out Memories

Weekly Writing Challenge 10: Mapping Out Memories (see Figure 6.2) is similar to WWC 9, except that students will now be writing from memory, not from an artifact. According to Ralph Fletcher, "Memories may just be the most important possession a writer has. As much as anything else, our memories shape what we write. Memories are like a fountain no writer can live without" (2003, 86). As the students have discovered during their noveling adventure, when they get backed into a corner and don't know what to write about, they can always tap into that endless fountain of memories. These anecdotal connections and personal reflections can draw the reader in, *regardless of the mode of writing*. Whether students are writing to find a story or writing in response to a test question, we must teach them the value of tapping into their memory fountains.

> *There has to be something about [your writing] that connects with you and something that you know will connect it to readers.*
>
> —Neal Shusterman, author of the Skinjacker trilogy, the Unwind series, and many other titles

Instead of having students simply share their artifacts and memories with one another, which they enjoy, I encourage them also to start thinking about their writing with an eye toward publication. The details, topics, and stories could be spun into longer pieces that span genres and appeal to a wider audience.

Manda, for example, selected the memory of getting her first cat. In her first draft, she wrote a happy little tale of girl + kitten = love. It was *fine*. It had some good feelings and details, and plenty of crafty stuff, but we both agreed that something was missing.

"I don't know what it is exactly," Manda began our writing conference. "I just feel like

Weekly Writing Challenge 10

"What usually happens is that I start with something that did happen to me, or to someone I know, and then build on it from there. I find with my writing that the beginnings are usually from real life, but you have to veer off into fiction pretty quickly or the story doesn't work. I think also that part of being a writer is just being tuned in to the world."

—Sarah Dessen, author of *Lock and Key*, *Just Listen*, *The Truth About Forever*, and other titles

"Most of my ideas come from my own experience."

—Matt Christopher, author of the Matt Christopher Sports Classics series and many other titles

"I started writing when I was sixteen. I'm thirty now. I get my ideas from fourteen years of thinking about it."

—Markus Zusak, author of *The Book Thief*, *I Am the Messenger Under Dogs*, and other titles

"I didn't fully realize it at the time, but during those early years of my life I was also amassing things to write about."

—Margaret Peterson Haddix, author of the Missing series, the Shadow Children series, and many other titles

"My first YA was Midnighters, about a group of small-town kids for whom time freezes every Midnight. That was inspired by memories of sneaking out at night in Texas and walking around in the emptiness and stillness of the wee hours. As a teenage memory, the idea only made sense as YA."
—Scott Westerfeld, author of *Afterworlds*, the Leviathan series, the Uglies series, and many other titles

Weekly Writing Challenge 10: Mapping Out Memories

THE CHALLENGE

Memories remain in your mind because there is usually a strong emotion associated with them.

- Think about the happy, sad, scary, and humbling moments that you will never forget.

- Select at least three memories to flesh out and re-create for the reader. Write these in Ch. 2, "Memories," in your ME book.

- Begin brainstorming with a sensory web or map.

- Then, as you write, include details from your five senses and your feelings to help the reader experience the scene right there with you.

Figure 6.2 Anecdotes and reflections recalled from memory can become good writing territories.

it's babyish, and like no one would really care."

"So, I guess we need to figure out how we can make them care, right?" I said. "Let's think about what you could do differently. What would you say the *point* is of your current writing piece?"

Manda thought for a minute, "I don't know; I guess just sharing a time when I got my cat."

"Geez, Manda, that even sounded boring when you said it!" I joked. We both laughed. "Why did that memory matter to you?"

"Well, because it was my first pet and I was really excited to get her."

"Okay . . . I totally got that from your entry, but I don't feel like that purpose alone is working for you, so let's dig a little deeper. Why were you so excited to get her? Besides the fact that it was your first pet?"

"I think because my sister always got everything first, you know, because she is older. I just wanted something that was mine—that I didn't have to share with her."

"I think anyone who has older siblings can relate to that," I said. "Do you have any specific memories about getting your cat that can help you make that point clear? Maybe a little bit of sisterly competition?"

"What do you mean about competition?"

"I have no doubt that your cat was smaller and way cuter than your sister's, right??

"Oh, my gosh, yes! And it was so funny, not because it made my *sister* mad, but *her cat* didn't like all of the attention that my new, supercute kitty was getting! He was so jealous! It was hysterical the things he'd do, like knocking my kitten off the counter and sitting on top of her when my kitten, Cleo, would sit on my lap."

"Now, *that* doesn't sound boring at all!" I said. "Based on your energy and the look on your face, I think you may have found your missing piece. If you are that excited just talking about it, then I have no doubt that your readers will enjoy reading it."

When Manda returned to her seat, she wrote a snarky piece full of personality and "anyone who owns a cat knows," moments about how *unhappy* her older sister's cat was when the new little puff of fur stole the show. Manda's humorous observations and witty style crossed genres and opened up the possibility for a more sophisticated audience.

Weekly Writing Challenge 11: Writing Down Your Dreams

Weekly Writing Challenge 11 (see Figure 6.3) was my somewhat-desperate attempt to find one more WWC to fill in the week and a half of school before December break. I needed it to be fun and lighthearted because we all know how kids get right before the holidays. They all have dreams of sugarplums (and cell phones, and tablets, and new video games and Nike

Weekly Writing Challenge 11

"Daydream. When you write, do so without worrying what your mother will think, unless you plan on having her, and her alone, read your manuscript."

—Becca Fitzpatrick, author of the Hush, Hush Saga, *Black Ice*, and *Dangerous Lies*

"Dream. Because when you daydream that will show you what is important enough to write about."

—Cynthia Lord, author of *Rules*, *Touch Blue*, *Half a Chance*, and other titles

"Ideas seem to creep into my head while I'm sleeping. SPEAK started in a nightmare. I've dreamed several critical scenes for other books."

—Laurie Halse Anderson, author of *The Impossible Knife of Memory*, *Wintergirls*, *Twisted*, and many other titles

"I write down most of my dreams. Dreams can be confounding, yes, but occasionally they drop something priceless into my lap. I got the whole ending of *The Secret Life of Bees* from a dream."

—Sue Monk Kidd, author of *The Secret Life of Bees*

Weekly Writing Challenge 11: Writing Down Your Dreams

THE CHALLENGE

- Throughout the week, make a deliberate effort to remember and write down your dreams.
- Keep your ME book by your bed and record as many details as you can remember about each dream in Ch. 3, "Writing from Life."
- Details might include specifics from the *setting*, *characters*, and/or *action* in your dream. Also consider the *feelings* you had during and after the dream. Be sure to note any *words/dialogue*, *sounds*, *smells*, and *colors* as well.

Figure 6.3 Students can probe the dream world for writing themes.

For WWC 11, set up your ME book like this:

Dream Question

[Before you go to sleep, write down a question you'd like answered in your dream; repeat it in your head over and over again as you drift off.]

Dream Details

[This part can be a list. Record people, objects, colors, smells, places, actions, and feelings that you can remember as soon as you wake up; feel free to add on if you remember more throughout the day.]

Writing About My Dream

[On this page, write from your dream. You have two choices:

1. You could write a narrative scene (story) based on what happened in your dream

OR

2. You could analyze your dream, explaining why you had it and what it meant by going online to http://www.dreammoods.com/ dreamdictionary/ (This webpage is on my website as well.)]

Figure 6.3 (continued) Students can probe the dream world for writing themes.

basketball sneakers) dancing in their heads, so why not use that to our writing advantage? After all, many writers tap into their dreams for inspiration, right? Novels such as *Twilight* by Stephenie Meyer, *Misery* by Stephen King, and classics such as Mary Shelley's *Frankenstein* and Robert Louis Stevenson's *The Strange Case of Dr. Jekyll and Mr. Hyde* came to light entirely from authors' dreams. We will leave no pillow unturned to build better writing fluency. The lesson associated with this WWC does take a little longer than the typical WWC introduction, because we need to take the time to make sure that the kids understand dreams and dream rhythms and how to harvest potential writing territories from them.

> *Ideas come in so many different ways . . . from an experience, a memory, or a dream; from seeing something and having it click perfectly in some distant part of your brain; or even just from a funny word or phrase.*
>
> —Elise Broach, author of *Masterpiece, Desert Crossing,* and *Shakespeare's Secret*

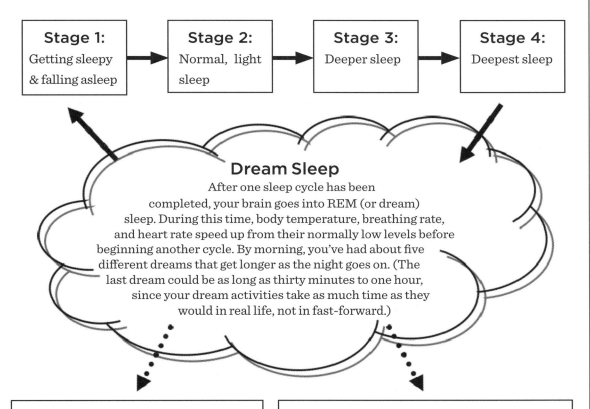

Writing Down Your Dreams:
Stuff to Know Before You Get Started

One Sleep Cycle takes eighty to ninety minutes to go through all four stages.

| **Stage 1:** Getting sleepy & falling asleep | → | **Stage 2:** Normal, light sleep | → | **Stage 3:** Deeper sleep | → | **Stage 4:** Deepest sleep |

Dream Sleep

After one sleep cycle has been completed, your brain goes into REM (or dream) sleep. During this time, body temperature, breathing rate, and heart rate speed up from their normally low levels before beginning another cycle. By morning, you've had about five different dreams that get longer as the night goes on. (The last dream could be as long as thirty minutes to one hour, since your dream activities take as much time as they would in real life, not in fast-forward.)

Does Everyone Dream?

Yes. Everyone has dreams, but not everyone remembers them. It depends in which part of the sleep cycle you awake. If you wake up during dream sleep, you will probably remember at least foggy details of your dream, but if you wake during any of the other stages, you are not actually dreaming, so there is nothing to remember. That's because your brain actually shuts off your memory controls while you are sleeping.

Why Do We Dream?

There are several different theories about why people have dreams. In ancient times, some people believed that this was their connection to the Gods. These dreams were to warn them of evil or temptation, or to serve as a guiding force in life. In some cultures, it is believed that we actually live within both worlds. In most cultures today, dreams seem to be regarded as the brain's way of processing or making sense of our daily experiences and feelings. For some, however, dreams can be truly inspirational! Many scientists, artists, and writers look to their dreams for creative ideas.

Figure 6.4 I want to make sure students understand how dreams occur before they start using dream memories for writing tasks.

Are You Ready to Be Inspired?

Obviously, we are going to be looking to our dreams for inspiration this week as we begin Weekly Writing Challenge 11: Writing Down Your Dreams. This one is definitely going to be a challenge, as this is not something that most of us are used to doing. You will want to keep your ME book (and maybe a flashlight!) by your bed, and you might want to plan on getting up just a few minutes earlier to have time to record all that you see in those midnight mind movies! Good luck and have fun with it!

Tips for Remembering Your Dreams:

1. *Get enough rest* (at least eight to ten hours every night). When you are overtired, you will sleep more deeply and have a more difficult time remembering your dreams.

2. *Before you go to sleep*:
   - *Review* what happened during the day; think about the things that are important to you.
   - *Write* down a dream question about one of those things in your ME book.
   - *Repeat* your dream question to yourself as you drift off to sleep, and tell yourself that you will remember your dreams when you wake up.

3. *When you wake up*:
   - *Lie completely still* (even stretching or turning can make dreams vanish).
   - *Keep your eyes closed and think* about the dream from beginning to end (visualize as much of it as you can).
   - *Ask yourself questions* about it: Where was I? Who was there? What did it look like? What happened? What did I do? Did anyone say anything? Was there a smell or odor I can recall? How did I feel? Did any part remind me of anything in my waking life?

Recording Your Dreams:

When you wake up in the morning (or in the middle of the night), once you have followed step 3 above, it is time to record everything that you can remember about your dream(s) in your ME book, Ch. 3: "Writing from Life."

1. Focus on jotting down your answers from the questions that you asked yourself before you got up. You could list or freewrite, but just try to recapture as many details as possible, including (but not limited to): the setting, characters, action . . . also names, people, numbers, or words said . . . as well as sounds, smells, colors, strong feelings, and any possible connections to your life. (five to ten minutes)

2. Throughout the day, you may recall more details . . . Be sure to add these to your notebook.

3. Later on, consider playing with your "dream notes" by doing one of the following: (1) Go to http://www.dreammoods.com/dreamdictionary/index.html to decode the possible meaning(s), then analyze your dream (what does it mean?) Or (2) go beyond freewriting to re-create part or all of your dream as a narrative passage or a poem. Who knows where it might lead?!

Figure 6.4 (continued) I want to make sure students understand how dreams occur before they start using dream memories for writing tasks.

To aid this process, I distribute a worksheet that helps students understand the dream cycle and use their "pillow talk" for writing themes (see Figure 6.4). I warn the kids that this particular writing challenge may require several attempts before one idea sticks around long enough to take hold. They can continue this over the holidays when they may have more time to sleep in and/or interrupt their sleep cycles without disrupting their entire schedule for the day.

This one writing exercise has inspired tales ranging from lost little sisters and aliens to basketball champions and armed robberies! At the end of the day, it's a fun writing territory that keeps kids talking about their experiences.

The Final Frontier

By this point in the year, January, the fun of the holidays has passed and it's time to buckle back down. The Weekly Writing Challenge entries now mark the final push for the development of ideas that were generated in the first semester. Afterward, students will be self-selecting their own writing pieces to take all the way through the process to publication, so we need to make sure that they have enough sustenance to fuel their journeys.

Because of the way I structure our workshop, based on the advice of our favorite authors, I keep open the possibility of adding to or changing our WWCs as new authors emerge with fabulous new insights worth trying. For now, however, the following three WWCs give students one final glimpse at the world as they know it. These lessons give students the chance to explore and research topics as possibilities for nonfiction or multigenre writing.

Weekly Writing Challenge 12: Lists: I Wonder . . . (and Others)

We start the last leg of the journey to publication with lists. Weekly Writing Challenge 12 (see Figure 6.5) massages the brain and coaxes all kinds of wonderful ideas to the surface. I begin this WWC's introductory lesson in the "Lists" section of students' ME books.

I select a few high-speed list topics from my List of Lists (see Figure 6.6), which I have collected over the years. I then give the kids timed jotting sessions (two to five minutes each, depending on their efforts and excitement) to create their own fast-paced, stream-of-consciousness, brainstormed lists from each topic. Once the students have several brainstormed lists completed, I let them share in small groups. During this time, they are all welcome to add to their own lists if they hear a good idea. Next, I introduce the author quotes and the Weekly Writing Challenge. I also make sure that I discuss my writing expectations for the week—the goal is to *write* about topics *from* their lists rather than just continue to generate new lists.

Weekly Writing Challenge 12

"Just start generating ideas and jotting them down like some kind of crazy idea-generating machine. Your brain will get used to spitting out five different plans at once, and you really won't get stuck."

—Veronica Roth, author of the Divergent series

"I just write what I want to write. I write what amuses me. It's totally for myself."

—J. K. Rowling, author of the Harry Potter series

Weekly Writing Challenge 12: Lists: I Wonder . . . (and Others)

THE CHALLENGE

Writing down lists is a strategy that all authors use to help keep track of possible writing ideas. In class, we are going to brainstorm a variety of lists in Ch. 7 of your ME book, "Lists."

- From these lists, you are to select at least three different items to write about throughout the week.

- You could freewrite, develop an opinion, tell a story, or write a poem.

- Be sure to really develop your details this week!

Figure 6.5 Making lists is a good way to develop writing ideas.

The lists serve multiple purposes for our young writers. At first, they are just lists of things to write about; this exercise also gets them back in the habit of brainstorming and writing on demand. The kids may not feel passionately about all the ideas, but this task ignites a spark.

Weekly Writing Challenge 13: Multigenre Writing

Once we have a spark, it's time to fan the flames. One of the ways I have learned to do this is by adding research. Professional authors often have to research to make certain that they get the details right, whether they are developing a setting, finding a telling incident for a historical or scientific novel, or writing an informational or argument piece for a literary journal, newspaper, magazine, or trade book. Including research in writing is an important skill that our students need to practice anyway, so why not make it matter to them by giving it an authentic purpose in our writerly work?

List of Lists

- Make a list of the things that you wonder about most with your family, relationships, society, the future.
- Make a list of the things that you wonder about most in the world in nature or history.
- Make a list of the big things that you see wrong in our world.
- Make a list of the things that you see that are right in our world.
- Make a list of the things that irritate you the most.
- Make a list of the things you hope to do or see in your lifetime.
- Make a list of things that make you sad.
- Make a list of hobbies and talents—these could be real or ones you wish you had. (If you wish you had them, tell why!)
- Make a list of the things that you hold most dear to your heart.
- Make a list of questions your parents would answer no to.
- Make a list of questions your parents would answer yes to.
- Make a list of compliments.
- Make a list of the things another person would say in response to the compliments.
- Make a list of insults.
- Make a list of the things another person would say in response to the insults.
- What makes a person ugly? Make a list of these qualities.
- What makes a person beautiful? Make a list of these qualities.
- Look closely at something. Compare it to other things. Make a list: "This thing is like . . ."
- Make a list of things to say to a person who is having an awful day.
- Make a list of the most interesting places you have been to.
- Make a list of extraordinary things you'd like to do someday.
- Make a list of the characters or story ideas you might consider writing about someday.
- Make lists of bests and worsts (fashions, hairstyles, school lunches, parent punishments, etc.).

Figure 6.6 Over the years I have compiled many ways to inspire list writing.

In Weekly Writing Challenge 13: Multigenre Writing (see Figure 6.7), we explore the role of research in writing for publication. As part of the lesson, we brainstorm authors and the research that they probably had to do in order to write with authority in their books. Obvious authors who come to mind are Rick Riordan, who the students suppose had to research ancient mythology; Gordon Korman, who must've had to research settings and various news articles to write any of the books in his Survival series; and Steve Sheinkin, who obviously researches, since his books are nonfiction thrillers. Kids are surprised to learn, however, that almost all authors have to do some research for every book they write in order to make sure that they get their facts straight for discerning readers.

The research was, and continues to be, the best part of the process! It's the perfect excuse to study the subjects I've always been interested in.

When I do find myself "stuck" I usually go back and do more research into my world, my characters, their motivation, etc., and it always spawns the next sentences. Always. Never fails!

—Alyson Noël, author of the Beautiful Idols series, the Immortals series, the Soul Seekers series, and many other titles

I share the research I did as I was writing my NaNo novel. For example, I needed to know if honeysuckles bloom in late June (they do!). I also needed to double-check that the part of the flower that you pull out to lick the "honey" off of is called a stamen, because it had been so long since I learned that back in science class. My character ends up in the hospital from a severe asthma attack, so I had to do the medical research to figure out what kinds of tests and procedures the doctors and nurses would follow and how they would converse with each other and my character's family. Through my research, I learned that an asthma attack is actually referred to as an asthma *exacerbation*, and that doctors use *spirometry* to test how well the lungs are functioning. I also added words like *pulse ox* (short for *pulse oximetry*, the procedure for gauging the amount of oxygen in the blood) and *pneumothorax* (the technical term for a collapsed lung) to my story to make the hospital scene more realistic. There are many instances when authors use research tools to improve their writing, regardless of the genre, and the biggest reason is that it makes the writing more authentic and believable to their readers.

Sometimes, through research, authors find information that can lead them in unplanned directions, and entirely new territories and genres for writing can emerge. This writing challenge can give students the opportunity to explore multigenre writing if that's where their research takes them.

From last week's WWC, Brittany had a lengthy list of "irks," as many of our seventh-grade girls do. In her list-writing exercise, she chose to rant about cell phones and driving—mostly about how annoying it is to be behind someone who is driving slowly, swerving, or continually braking all because they are talking or texting on the phone. She ended her writing piece with, "Put down your phone and drive!!" Obviously, this was a topic she felt very strongly about, so when WWC 13: Multigenre Writing came around, it was easy for her to pick a topic to research: distracted driving.

Once Brittany started sifting through the data, however, she was horrified by the statistics and was incited to act. In her entry, she wrote this:

Weekly Writing Challenge 13

"History, if you do it wrong, can be really boring, but if you look at the really fun stuff in history, it can be really be amazing and really exciting . . . A lot of the stuff I talk about is real and is from history."

"I always start with the research and look for interesting facts . . . I do a lot of reading. I read a lot; I go online. I find out all of these interesting things that I didn't know . . . And I decide which would be the most fun to put into the book. Then I outline it and I plot what I was going to say, and then I just start writing. And it was amazing—it just all came out!"

— Rick Riordan, author of the Percy Jackson and the Olympians series, the Kane Chronicles series, and many other titles

"As with any book, even fiction, it's important to do research so your story can be as authentic as possible."

—Kathryn Erskine, author of *Absolute Value of Mike*, *Mockingbird*, and other titles

"I tend, after I get the creative idea, to go into an almost nonfiction research period to fill in all of those huge blanks in what I am going to write about."

—Suzanne Collins, author of the Hunger Games trilogy, the Underland Chronicles, and many other titles

"I try to take historical facts and turn them it into books that read like thrillers, that are novels because people, especially young readers, when they hear history they might expect, 'Oh it's going to be boring. It's gonna be like my textbook.' But this is not. So I take true stories and turn them into sort of page-turners."

—Steve Sheinkin, author of the *The Notorious Benedict Arnold: A True Story of Adventure; Heroism & Treachery; Bomb: The Race to Build—and Steal—the World's Most Dangerous Weapon*; and many other nonfiction titles

Weekly Writing Challenge 13: Multigenre Writing

THE CHALLENGE

- This week, go through the lists that you made last week and select three different nonfiction topics to research. (Try to pick topics that you are genuinely interested in and/or topics that you could include in your stories in some way.)
- In the "Lists" chapter of your ME book, create three new focused lists of specific and interesting details about each topic.
- Below each list, include a brief statement on how you could incorporate these details into a piece of writing.

Figure 6.7 Authors often engage in research to ensure that their writing is factual.

For WWC 13, set up your ME book like this:

Topic

[Select one topic from your lists from last week that you find interesting and want to learn more about.]

Interesting facts I discovered from my research

[Google the topic; float around to reputable websites, searching for interesting information about your topic.]

[Note: Wikipedia is *not* a reputable site for research.]

[This part can be a bulleted list. Record as many different facts and details as you can.]

[Please Note Where Your Information Came From]

Writing about my topic

[On this page, write from your research.
You have two choices:

1. Explain how/where you would use this researched information in a specific piece of your writing. (Is there a scene you might add to an existing piece of writing that includes this information? Does the information you found ignite a strong opinion within you? Does this new information give you ideas for writing a brand-new informational piece? Explain them here.)

OR

2. If, after researching, you already know exactly how you want to incorporate this new information and you want to just write the scene, editorial, or article, go for it!

Whatever you decide, be sure to include the new information you discovered!]

Figure 6.7 (continued) Authors often engage in research to ensure that their writing is factual.

We've all seen them on the road . . . those cars that drive slowly or swerve suddenly, and at first you might wonder: 'Oh, are they ok?'—until you see that cell phone in the driver's hand. And then you know exactly why they can't drive: That driver is DISTRACTED. I used to think of using cell phones and driving as a personal pet peeve, mostly because when I am in the car with my mom, she always has something to say about stupid drivers. But I never realized that real, serious accidents are caused by texting (or talking) and driving. Literally thousands of people are killed each year—hundreds of them teenagers—and cell phones are to blame! I can definitely see me writing an editorial to the newspaper about this or maybe some other kind of persuasive writing to be published in a magazine. I think if a kid wrote about it, from our perspective, people might listen.

Josh is a history buff, and in his "fierce wonderings" list from the prior week he had several questions about the military and military life. In his research, he found a list of military commands and the basics of marching.

"I am so glad that I found this list of drill commands," he shared. "When I was writing my novel, my main character ended up enlisting in a militia against the rebel army. I didn't really know how to make his training seem real, but let's face it, I was just trying to get done all of my words for the day so I didn't have time to stop and research. I did bookmark a bunch of military sites so that I can go back and add in some details like the actual commands and maneuvers to my novel to make it seem more real."

> *It was in writing my adventure series that I discovered research. Before that, I'd relied heavily on experience, since I was so close in age to my characters at the beginning of my career. Research is awesome because it replaces the experiences you don't have.*
>
> —Gordon Korman, author of the Swindle series, *Schooled, Ungifted,* and many other titles

Although these list-writing and multigenre writing exercises may seem disconnected from the intensity of the writing we completed in previous WWCs, they encourage kids to reflect and think strategically about topics that will connect with readers.

Looking into the Reflection Pool

As we complete the first semester, we look over excerpts in our writer's notebooks. I like to move students through this process in two stages: The first stage identifies and teases out any additional writing ideas. The second stage helps the kids to identify their writing strengths and needs, as well as spy excerpts they would like to develop into publishable pieces.

The Extra Bonus Challenge: What If...?

"What if" writing is an amazingly freeing experience for adolescents. It's the do-over that they never get in real life. That's why we call the next writing assignment the Extra Bonus Challenge (see Figure 6.8). The "bonus" does not mean it's an optional writing exercise; the bonus stems from the fact that students get to read over all of their writing entries, and for each one, ask, "What if?" By asking that one question, they have the power to change history. The purpose of this final idea-generating strategy is to stretch writing territories one last time to squeeze out the last drop of possibility!

I ask students if they have ever had moments in their lives that they wish they could do over. My question is always answered with nods of acknowledgment and some not-so-subtle, "Oh, my God, YES!" responses. Then, I ask them to skim back through all of their WWC entries searching for memories, events, or character decisions that they'd like the chance to do over for a completely different outcome. After a few minutes of thinking, I ask them to turn to two clean pages in their writer's notebook that open to a spread. At the top of the left page, I instruct them to write the "what if" question and then generate a list of all of the things that would have been different, underneath the question. The students will use the right-side page to retell any part of their tale.

Jenna knew exactly which vignette she wanted to do over in life and on paper, and she dove right into this assignment. During writing time, I stopped by her desk.

"What are you working on?" I asked.

"Oh, it was a family trip to Costa Rica," she said.

"Costa Rica? Wow. Why would you want to do that over?"

"I feel like I wrecked a big part of that vacation," she said. "For me and my mom, anyway."

She flipped back a few pages in her writer's notebook. In one of her entries from WWC 10: Mapping Out Memories, Jenna had written about a vacation that her family took in Costa Rica. In her writing she describes being at the top of a platform in the middle of a rain forest, hooked up to ropes and pulleys for her zip-line canopy tour. Sounds amazing, right? It would have been, if only she had been brave enough to just step off the platform. Instead, Jenna freaked out, and she and her mom (and a less-than-pleased tour operator) had to walk back down the mountain and take a golf cart over to the site where her dad and brothers would be landing.

"That's like the one moment that I really regret in my life," Jenna sighed.

"Why, though? I mean, it must've been pretty scary, and you were pretty young."

"I was twelve, so I wasn't that young, and it shouldn't have mattered. My mom didn't get to do it either because of me. Now, I just feel dumb for not doing it. I mean, think about how cool that would've been. My brothers and my dad couldn't stop talking about it. We don't usually take those kinds of vacations, so who knows if I will ever have the chance to go back there."

"I have a feeling that you are going to remember that moment for a long time, and I hope that when you are facing a fear later on in life, you remember these feelings, and just go for it!"

Jenna smiled.

Weekly Writing Challenge

"I get my ideas from everywhere. But what all of my ideas boil down to is seeing maybe one thing, but in a lot of cases it's seeing two things and having them come together in some new and interesting way, and then adding the question 'What if?' 'What if' is always the key question."

—Stephen King, author of *The Stand*, the Dark Tower series, and many other titles

"Ideas come from your imagination. What triggers your imagination? Things that you read, see, overhear, dream, or wonder about. Anything that makes you think: 'What if . . . ?' is the start of a story."

—Lois Lowry, author of the Giver Quartet, *Number the Stars*, and many other titles

"How do I research and plan a story? It depends on the story and whether it's the kind of thing you can research . . . I am very much a 'what if' writer. All of my stories are 'what ifs.'"

—Gordon Korman, author of the Swindle series, *Schooled*, *Ungifted*, and many other titles

Extra Bonus Challenge: "*What If . . . ?*"

THE CHALLENGE

This week marks the final required creative notebook entries before you begin the process of selecting and writing pieces for publication, so dig deep and see where the power of "what if" takes you.

- Look back through all of the entries in your ME book that you have written so far. This includes your lists, your heart map, and anything else you may have written in there.

- Find three places where a "what if" question leads you in a new writing direction. (Ex: What if Grandpa hadn't died? What if I struck out instead of getting that homerun? What if I came home from my first day of school and my mom wasn't home waiting for me? What if I remembered to turn off the water?)

- Jot down your "what if" at the top of a new page in whatever section of your ME book makes sense to you. Then write by re-creating the setting in a narrative description. Write small . . . let the tiniest details develop the setting, allowing the reader to feel like he or she is there.

Figure 6.8 Students look back over their writing samples and ask "what if" to see if they can reimagine an experience.

"For now, though, go back to that moment—that moment of such intense fear that you couldn't let go—and write through it. Write right through the fear, and see what happens on the other side. You might surprise yourself."

Jenna quickly got to writing and produced a very strong piece for only twenty minutes of writing time:

I stood there on the wooden platform miles above the moist mossy jungle floor below trying to open my eyes and take in the view of the mountainside to the east and the volcano to the west. Don't look down! Don't look down, I thought to myself. Maybe it was easier to just keep my eyes closed all together. My dad was first to be hitched up to the cable. He would be pioneering our family down that thin, metallic path to our certain doom.

"Jenna, Daniel, Karl, be brave! Babe, make sure you get some good video!" Dad yelled over his shoulder as the tour guide checked his gear. "I'll see you at the next platform! Woo-hoo!" And he was off, yelling his way through the foliage.

My heart was beating so fast and hard that I could actually see it pulsing against my chest strap. I tucked my hair back under my helmet and tried to pull myself together. Deep breath in. Deep breath out. You can do this.

Karl was next. He's nineteen, so there was no way he's chickening out, especially since there were a few girls his age in our tour group. I swear I saw him wink at them as he took off down the zip line.

I realized that my turn was coming up quickly, and instantly, my knees turned to mush. I could feel my kneecaps sloshing around like the fruit in my grandmother's holiday Jello mold.

Deep breath in. Deep breath out. I can't do this.

Danny was up. He brushed past me on his way to the end of the platform and gave me the thumbs up and whispered, "You got this."

Before I had the chance to tell him that I definitely DID NOT have this, he was slipping his way down the line with a howl.

My turn.

When the tour guide called me over, I just stood there blankly, my feet glued to the platform. I wasn't going anywhere. I could feel the rest of the tour group watching me, waiting.

Deep breath in. Deep breath out.

I wiggled my toes inside of my sweaty, white Nikes, just to be sure that I still had the power of movement. I felt my mom's hands rest on my shoulders from behind. She spun me around and looked me right in the eye, breaking my fear-trance. "You are so brave. You can do this. I know it seems scary, but you will be so glad that you did it when you get to the other side. And . . . You don't want your brothers to show you up, do you?"

Without me even realizing it, while she was talking, my mom had shuffled me over to the edge of the platform.

"I'll be right behind you!" She kissed me on the top of my helmet, and handed me over to the tour guide.

Shallow breath in. Shallow breath out. Shallow breath in. Shallow breath out. I tried to say something, but my lips felt chapped and my throat was so dry. No, no, no, no, no! My mind screamed, but I didn't say a word.

Before I knew it, the tour guide placed my gloved hands above the pulley attached at my waist, and my hands instinctively clung onto it for dear life, and my heels dug into the wooden plank. No use. The tour guide gently slid me off the edge, and sent me on my way.

As the wind rushed past my face, I leaned my head back, peeled my eyes open and focused on one single white cloud above. My heart was still beating, but not out of fear. Out of adrenaline. What a rush! They were right!

I landed at the other end, right into my dad's arms. "That's my girl! Woo! Wasn't that awesome?!"

I smiled, still trying to catch my breath.

Mom skidded in behind me, "We did it, girl! I'm so proud of you!"

This was truly the best family vacation. Ever.

> *I've always thought up stories in my head, both to entertain myself and to keep myself from getting anxious. I was a very nervous child—always worried about something—and I discovered that inventing stories and creating new worlds and characters kept me from worrying so much. Worry is all about "What if?" But so is storytelling! Now I get to ask "What if?" as part of my job.*
>
> —Ingrid Law, author of the Savvy series

This "what if" exercise is one that can be done at any point in the writing process, from prewriting to drafting to revising. It's a way for young writers to get to the root and figure out what is most important for their characters or for themselves.

Weekly Writing Challenge 14: Reflecting on Writing

Although this is the shortest Weekly Writing Challenge, and it requires the least explanation, Reflecting on Writing (see Figure 6.9) is an extremely important personal exercise. As students read through their WWC entries, they are reading with an eye for potential, for both publication and improvement. Weekly Writing Challenge 14 gives students a chance to reflect on all that they have learned. It helps them to bring to the forefront the skills and strategies that they found helpful throughout the semester so that they can use those skills to develop upcoming manuscripts for publication.

Students also create a list of skills or concepts that they know they will need to work on throughout the second semester to add to the quality of their writing. In *Writing Workshop: The Essential Guide*, Ralph Fletcher and JoAnn Portalupi encourage this stage: "When they finish a piece of writing, ask them to reflect on the process that worked for them. Ask them to talk about problems they may have encountered and how they solved them. Encourage them to identify the strategies they used that worked" (2001, 111).

> *The talent for writing is a gift from God. The craft of writing is learned. The more you know, the better your chances to get published.*
>
> —Lurlene McDaniel, author of *Keep Me in Your Heart, True Love, Prey,* and many other titles

At the end of this WWC, we regroup as a class and create a chart of mini-lesson needs based on students' reflections from the week. Next to each mini-lesson, we also log the names of the in-class experts on that skill, so that students know which of their peers they can turn to for assistance or a peer conference session. This process helps me to plan for specific mini-lessons customized to the needs of my students. And, just as real authors look to their peers for support, it helps students recognize and use the writing talents of their classmates who have already mastered the skill.

This wraps up the first semester of writing workshop in our classroom and the third leg of our journey. The kids' tools have been sharpened, their lenses focused, and their bags have been packed with enough writing sustenance to get them started on the next phase of our expedition: destination publication.

Weekly Writing Challenge 14

> "Writing is all about mistakes. I mean, you can't write without making mistakes. And sometimes mistakes are things that you can really learn from. The biggest mistake is thinking that it has to be perfect. It doesn't have to be perfect. You can make it perfect later."
>
> — Rick Riordan, author of the Percy Jackson and the Olympians series, the Kane Chronicles series, and many other titles

> "The best writing requires some daring—a little literary skydiving. Look at your idea and ask yourself: how can I make this larger?"
>
> —Sue Monk Kidd, author of *The Secret Life of Bees*

Weekly Writing Challenge 14: Reflecting on Writing

THE CHALLENGE

This week you will be writing in Ch. 6 of your ME book: "Writing from Class." Each night for your twenty minutes of writing, you will write on one of the following. (They can be completed in any order).

- Reflect on your strengths and weaknesses as a writer. Be honest and specific. Be sure to offer examples.

- In what areas have you seen the greatest growth or improvements in your writing? Explain how and/or why the changes have occurred.

- Set goals and give yourself new challenges for continuing to develop your own writing. (This one can be a list.

Figure 6.9 This writing challenge encourages students to think about their writing strengths, weaknesses, and goals.

PART 4

Becoming Word Travelers: How Can I Become a Published Author Too?

Chapters 7, 8, and 9 in Part 4 share the technical tools that young writers need to cross the threshold into authentic publication. Students and teachers learn how to survey the young writer's market (via various media sources, including teacher-designed web searches) and prepare manuscripts that reflect thoughtful and deliberate revisions that mirror submission guidelines. Explicit instruction in goal setting and formatting is provided to keep students on track and to make sure their work looks professional. The possibility of publication has been the driving force behind all student writing this school year, and now it's time to see it through to the finish line and to give their voices wings out in the world.

Chapter 7

Publication Preparation

You have to be patient to be a published writer, and you have to practice humility, because the editor (or teacher) is nearly always right.

—Ridley Pearson,
author of the Kingdom Keepers series, the Starcatcher series,
the Neverland series, and many other titles

When I was a kid, I was an avid writer. Not in school—just for fun. My dad gave me a faux-leather portfolio, which I kept in my bedroom and filled with pages of poems and stories and ideas. Eventually, as my life became filled with the friends and activities that coincide with budding adolescence, my stuffed portfolio gathered dust.

That is, until the middle of my sixth-grade year. In language arts class, Mr. Martin required us to write an original story—at home, on our own time—with limited, if any, instruction on story arcs, characterization, or any of the lessons required for writing a story. Although we had several weeks to complete this assignment, I raced home and fished my beloved writing portfolio from my bottom desk drawer. Leafing through the pages, I found the idea that I wanted to use for my story. I got up extra early each morning, my thoughts already brimming with ideas. I wrote on the school bus, under the covers with a flashlight, and during every spare minute I could find.

When I was finished writing, I lugged my mother's old, manual typewriter out of the basement, heaved it upstairs and onto my desk, and filled my room with the tap, tap, tapping of progress. Finally, after about three days, yards of correction tape, and fifteen pages of work, I had completed my masterpiece, "Janet and the Wubble Bubbles." I remember being so proud to turn in my story to Mr. Martin five days early. I couldn't wait to have him read it and give me genuine feedback and validation for all my hard work. I marched up to the teacher's desk and handed it to him, with a gleaming smile.

"What is it?" he asked indifferently.

What is it?! It is my life's finest work, the masterpiece that I had been crafting day and night for the past two weeks!

I sheepishly admitted that it was my story, the one he had assigned. His response: "You didn't have to do *all that*."

Weeks later, he returned it to me with one red ink mark on the front. No comments. Not even the shadow of a crease where he would have turned the pages. Just a single letter: A.

I was crushed. I had gotten a "good grade," one that would surely make my parents proud, but it didn't *feel* good, and *I* didn't feel proud. I felt *insignificant*.

Flash forward eleven years . . . I was in my first year teaching seventh-grade language arts. Bogged down with basic classroom and paperwork management and daunted by the magnitude of covering the entire curriculum, I did the best I could. For each structured writing assignment in the curriculum, I taught the necessary form and conventions and modeled the writing process on the overhead projector. I gave the students at least three different topics to use for their drafts in each genre, and then I had each student select one draft to bring through the process of revising, editing, and publishing* (*translation: final graded copy). Then it was on to the next mandatory structured writing assignment. Pretty good for a first-year teacher, or so I thought.

There are two students from that first year whose memories still haunt me. The first was Charlie, an extremely bright and (dare I say it?) *annoying* student. Charlie was arrogantly achieving top-notch grades with virtually no effort and absolutely no heart. Grades were his only motivation. He could not have cared less about the learning. His writing was technically correct, but every piece lacked . . . *something*. Back then the domain scoring rubric was barely a glimmer in some academic's eye, so I couldn't pinpoint exactly what was wrong with his writing.

Even without what I know now as true *voice* in his writing, Charlie still got an A. In his mind, there was no need to learn or improve since he had already earned a top grade.

Adam, a student receiving special-education services, was in the same class period as Charlie. Adam was always tired and seemed disinterested in class. He rarely submitted work or participated. As a veteran teacher, it pains me to openly admit this. Because he was quiet and didn't cause any problems in this class of thirty-four students, he usually went unnoticed. After three and a half marking periods of Ds and Fs, Adam probably would be socially promoted to eighth grade anyway, so . . . I stopped worrying. I stopped pushing. I stopped bothering him at all.

One spring day, after dismissal, Adam stopped by my classroom and handed me a fifty-six-page manuscript entitled "The Shadow of the Sword."

Filling the silence that lingered in the air, Adam blurted out, "I've been working on this for a long time. I just finished it last night, and I thought you might want to read it."

Wow. There was nothing that I wanted to do more. I promised Adam that I would read it that evening, cover to cover. And I did. It was wonderful. Of course, there were age-appropriate mistakes with writing conventions, but I could see where he had added figurative language, varied his sentence structure, and used more active verbs, just as we had practiced in class. It was as if the entire year's lessons were reflected in this one final piece of writing.

There was no longer any doubt in my mind. I had let Adam down. I thought he was insignificant. This quiet, well-behaved kid had learned—almost in spite of me.

Here was the problem: My grade book did not have a place to reflect his learning. I could not let him make up three and a half marking periods of unsubmitted work with this final, unsolicited project. I sought the advice of my older, wiser department chair. She simply shrugged her shoulders and suggested I give him extra credit points. Adam ended the fourth marking period with a C.

In retrospect, I realize I didn't understand how to *teach* writing. I was taught how to assign it, but not how to teach students to craft it, revise it, and love it (or at least like it).

In *Write Like This*, Kelly Gallagher shares that "writing well does not begin with teaching students how to write; it begins with teaching students why they should write. Students who are taught how to write without being taught the real-world purposes behind authentic writing are much more likely to end up seeing writing as nothing more than a school activity—nothing more than a series of obstacles to overcome . . . When students see why writing is important in a post high school world, they are more likely to give writing the time and attention it deserves" (2011, 7–8).

That was the missing piece all along: purpose. In classrooms where publication *is* the inspiration, all students have the opportunity to learn from authors, teachers, and each other. They know what it feels like to be successful writers. Authentic publication gives students ownership of the process and the product of writing. It promotes self- and social awareness by offering students a stage for sharing their voices. Publication endures.

Looking back, with authentic publication as the inspiration for writer's workshop . . .

- I could have had a true audience for my childhood writing.
- Charlie could have found a reason to discover his voice.
- Adam could have been a part of a true writing community where he might have developed the confidence to share his writing and be recognized for his accomplishments.

Publication is the ultimate performance assessment—an insight I wish I had discovered before my first year of teaching.

A Place to Publish

Over the years, I've discovered that there is a place to publish nearly every kind of writing. Even when we are working on our "school writing," such as poems, book reviews, essays, and arguments, students have opportunities to share their work outside the classroom. Writing with the prospect of publication in mind naturally raises the bar on the quality of work for every assignment.

> *Read (bad stuff and good). Write (it's all bad stuff at first). Rewrite. And rewrite again. And all the while, be learning everything you can about the publishing industry in general and the genre you write in specifically. Start sending out short stories to magazines and keep all your rejection slips. Be proud to be involved in the process, and know that you're very brave.*
>
> —Shannon Hale, author of the Books of Bayern series, the Princess Academy series, *Book of a Thousand Days*, and many other titles

Figure 7.1 shows a list of publications and contests that accept student submissions. Teachers should also look for publications and contests supported by the local community, such as colleges, universities, libraries, and school parent-teacher organizations.

In Nancie Atwell's classroom, every young writer is expected to attempt professional publication. She believes that all students "need the experience of raising their voices in the big world at the same time that they try to understand and meet its standards" (1998, 100). My public school expectations are no different. My students are required to submit a minimum of three pieces of writing throughout the year for publication (one mandatory poem and two self-selected pieces from seeds in the writer's notebook).

I make time for a mini-unit on poetry, because it synthesizes much of what we have learned about reading and writing quality literature. Poems are short and manageable writing selections that reinforce word choice and punctuation to create meaning. Through poetry, kids learn to develop abstract ideas and figurative language and make them concrete through sensory details and imagery. Our poetry unit is the perfect place to introduce the publication process. They learn what it means to write for an audience beyond the classroom, as well as the importance of formatting work for publication.

Admittedly, poetry is scary for many kids. They think that it has to rhyme and have a strict meter or structure (like that of the diamante and haiku) or they believe that they're just not good at it. Most kids (boys, in particular) have never had a positive poetry experience. That's all about to change.

Publications for Young Writers: These are some of our favorite publications that accept student writing.			
Website	**Type of Publication**	**Title of Publication**	**Description**
www.poeticpower.com	Poetry Anthology	*A Celebration of Poets*	National poetry and essay judging (U.S. and Canada) with separate regional poetry and essay anthology publications • published as a hardback book • fall, spring, and summer deadlines • all grade levels
	Essay Anthology	*Celebrating What's Important to Me*	
www.anthologyofpoetry.com	Poetry Anthology	*Anthology of Poetry by Young Americans*	National poetry and short story anthologies • published as a bound book • one late fall deadline • also has "teacher's selection" • all grade levels
	Short Story Anthology	*Anthology of Short Stories by Young Americans*	
http://thisibelieve.org/guidelines	Essay Anthology/ Radio Broadcast	*NPR's This I Believe . . .*	NPR's famous radio broadcasts and anthologies • rolling deadlines • 350–500 words (three minutes when read aloud) • all grade levels
www.theclaremontreview.ca	International Literary Magazine	*The Claremont Review*	International print and online magazine • accepts poetry, short stories, plays interviews • two deadlines: spring/summer and fall/winter • ages 13–19
http://www.teenink.com/submit	Literary Magazine	*Teen Ink*	Monthly literary newspaper written entirely by teens • rolling deadlines • accepts various genres • ages 13+

Figure 7.1 Many publications and contests accept student submissions.

Contests and Competitions for Young Writers: These publications require students to compete against one another for publication and prizes. Many contests have entry forms and strict, specific deadlines. Theme, format, or genre may change from year to year, so check for the latest contests and competitions.			
Website	**Genre**	**Competition Sponsor**	**Description**
www.aadl.org/events/itsallwrite	Short Story	*Ann Arbor Book Festival and Ann Arbor District Library "It's All Write!" Contest*	Annual contest • story must be 1,300–3,000 words • submission form online • three winners in each age group receive generous awards • grades 6–12
http://thechallenge.dupont.com/essay	Essay	*DuPont Challenge Science Essay Competition*	Annual science essay contest • see website for themes, entry forms, and deadline • grades 7–12
www.vfw.org/index.cfm?fa=cmty.leveld&did=151&tok=1	Essay	*VFW's Patriot's Pen Youth Essay Contest*	Annual essay contest • see website for entry form, theme, guidelines, and deadline • monetary prizes awarded for top winners • grades 6–8
www.libraryofpoetry.com	Poetry	*The America Library of Poetry Contest*	Annual poetry contest; winners published in an anthology • entries accepted year-round (cut-off each year in spring) • one entry per student per issue • entry form needed with submission • grades 3–12
www.artandwriting.org/the-awards	Various	*Scholastic Art and Writing Awards*	Annual contest • teacher/students must register online • see website for various guidelines, registration, and awards • grades 7–12
www.writingconference.com/writer's.htm	Various	*Writers' Slate*	Annual contests • one spring and one fall deadline • winners published in online journal • all grade levels

Figure 7.1 (continued) Many publications and contests accept student submissions.

Poetry with Purpose

Because poetry topics and interests are so vast, and comfort levels of teaching poetry writing vary greatly, I hesitate to make specific recommendations and dole out poetry plans. I will say, however, that as with any type of writing, it is important to find mentor texts that complement your curricular goals.

- "Mimi's Fingers" by Mary O'Neal is an ideal choice for our poetry-writing unit. In the poem, Mimi is blind, so she "sees" not with her eyes but with her other senses. We begin our writing with a sensory web that requires us to describe a color using every sense other than sight. As we write, we are not only reinforcing imagery but also revisiting figures of speech such as similes, metaphors, alliteration, and personification. Figure 7.2 shows a model color poem we created as a class. Notice the vivid language and imagery.

Midnight Story

Cold, misty rain dampens the road
and smothers the embers
of the once-brilliant bonfire.
Smoke and clouds cloak the moon
as loneliness surrounds me.

Distant thunder rolls across
the midnight sky,
silencing the cricket's song,
leaving only the faded sound of ripples
drifting across the murky water.

The quiet murmer of the owl's wings
sweep the dim horizon
on a solo flight
to find the stars—
Deep midnight blue.

Figure 7.2 Students use "Mimi's Fingers" as the inspiration for poetry writing using sensory connections. Notice how the color, midnight blue, is experienced through the senses.

- A collection of sports poems will get like-minded students, including many boys, interested in poetry. I switch the mentor texts from time to time, but I keep these poems in my rotation: *Hoops* by Robert Burleigh (a picture book); "Fast Break" by Edward Hirsch; and "A Boy Juggling a Soccer Ball" by Christopher Merrill. Our prewriting for what I call "sound and action" poetry is a T-chart with *sounds* of the game on one side and *actions* on the other. This prewriting produces a more sophisticated use of onomatopoeia, as well as active verbs and hyperbole, to create a fast-paced poem that brings the reader right onto the court or field. Figure 7.3 shows model sports poems that we created as a class.

The Space Between

Bottom of the 9th: 2 outs
Batter steps into the chalked box
Taps dirt from his cleats—
Taps bat to the Plate, signaling the target.

Pitcher spits, gives catcher "the nod."
Eyes dart to 1st—checking the runner.
Batter digs in, lifts bat into position.
Pitcher winds up, releases—
Ball races to mitt, dodging bat . . .
A muffled thump releases a sigh:
      STRIKE ONE!
Man on first l-e-a-d-s, d
                       i
                         v
                           e
                              s, steals second.
Pitcher side-steps, pulls back the trigger,
Fires—fastball (clocked at 96).
Bat cracks—ball screams toward outfield.
Second to Third—
      Third to home (now 3–3).
Batter—now runner—rounds third, pounding home.
Crowd goes wild!
Dust fills the space
between player—and—plate.
  umpire lunges . . .
    leather on leather . . .
      "He's outta here!"

Figure 7.3 Our class sports poems emphasize sound and action through active word choices and creative punctuation and spacing techniques.

Sudden Death

The puck drops—
0–0 about to be shattered in O.T.
Sticks slash the face-off circle,
Struggling for possession.
Blades slice the frozen surface,
Leaving behind trails of scars.
Black circle g-l-i-d-e-s
—smooth—
Piercing

        The space between
                Players.

One stick strikes out: SLAPSHOT
Goalie: Blocks, clears,
Sending the bullet back into the battlefield,
Ricocheting off the Plexiglas.
Players scramble—CHECK—
Plowing into each other.
The puck emerges, racing toward the goal . . .
        The crowd is silenced . . .
          The buzzer sounds . . .
             "IT'S GOOD!"

Figure 7.3 (continued) Our class sports poems emphasize sound and action through active word choices and creative punctuation and spacing techniques.

- "I Was Sleeping While the Black Oaks Moved" by Louise Erdrich pairs well with Georgia Heard's Six-Room Image Poem writing lesson from *Awakening the Heart* (1999). The reading and writing here focus on the powerful connections between humans and their environment.
- "Tony Steinberg: Brave Seventh Grade Viking Warrior" by Taylor Mali is a powerful example of a contemporary elegy. (Search Vimeo for a short video interpretation of the poem with Taylor Mali reading the poem.)
- Nancie Atwell's *Naming the World: A Year of Poems and Lessons* (2006) contains poems from famous poets as well as students.

For each poetry lesson, we begin with a read-aloud and then close reading and analysis. I explain the poetry-writing task and then model the entire process of writing a poem. Students will refer to these model poems while writing poems on their own in the "Writing from Class" sections of their writer's notebooks. Because we aim to submit some of the poems for publication, I need to make sure that their work stands out. We start with free verse, and I set some ground rules:

1. Absolutely NO RHYMING. It limits the creativity, and often sounds too sing-songy and unsophisticated.
2. Play with white space to create a visual flow on the page.
3. Final drafts should:

    *   be 16–21 lines long (those are standard publication guidelines).
    *   include *imbedded* examples of imagery (but do *not* write *I feel, I see, I smell,* and so on).
    *   include a variety of figures of speech and parts of speech.
    *   include deliberately crafted word choices and active verbs.
    *   NOT contain *you* or *your* (this is a tough one, but it's not a choose-your-own-adventure book, so no second-person point of view).
    *   include complete thoughts and correct punctuation (yes, poetry does still need to be grammatically and mechanically correct).
    *   include deliberate and creative punctuation choices to help develop mood (e.g., ellipsis, commentary/em dash, colon).

I take the time to model the revision process so that students understand the work required in crafting fine poetry. To do so, I begin with a mini-lesson on punctuating poetry and playing with white space. Figure 7.4 lists the main points we discuss in the mini-lesson.

> *The first step in writing my book was a purely creative phase. After that, however, came the grind of editing the manuscript into readable material. It was there that I learned how to produce graceful and grammatical prose.*
>
> —Christopher Paolini, author of *Eragon* and the rest of the Inheritance Cycle series

I select either a poem sample that I wrote or a student's poem in progress to work with in the mini-lesson. I need a poem that requires a bit of work—one that visually doesn't resemble a poem yet and needs better or more concise word choices. I try to decide on the poem that I will use the day before this revision lesson so that I have time to type it up and double-space it. I can then distribute copies to the class for ease of reading and revising. Figure 7.5 shows the phases of our lesson for this day. This poem stemmed from Heard's Six-Room Image Poem lesson.

I read the poem aloud twice. The first time through I ask students to listen for places where my voice naturally pauses. I tell them to place a slash at the end of each word where

Punctuating Poetry & Playing with White Space

Poetry Punctuation Tips

- As a general rule, all poems should contain punctuation. Period.
- Punctuation is not based on line length, breaks in lines, or white space.
- Poem punctuation follows the same rules as paragraphs:
  - Use end punctuation at the end of a sentence (not the end of a line).
  - Use commas for introductory words, phrases, and clauses; in compound sentences; for items in a list; for out-of-place adjectives, verbs, and adverbs.
  - Consider adding interesting punctuation to add emphasis without adding extra words, including: — (em/commentary dash), . . . (ellipsis), and : (colon).

Tips for Playing with White Space and Creating Consistent Line Lengths

When you begin writing poetry, you may find that your poems look more like blobs of paragraphs than finished poems. Visually, poem lines should be shorter than paragraph lines, not stretching all the way across the page. You want to try to create a visual flow where lines are fairly short and tight; you also don't want one or two lines that jut out way beyond the others. Here are some tips to create a visual flow to your poem:

1. Read your poem aloud. As you read, listen for places where your voice naturally pauses, and put a slash (/) there. These will become your line breaks.
2. Now look for places to breathe life into your words. Play with the white space to make them d ^{a} n ^{c} e on the page. Have fun with it:

   - The word *alone* could be on a line by itself.
   - The word *drift,* could literally d
                                         r
                                           i
                                             f
                                               t down the page.

Figure 7.4 I encourage students to think of poems as art. They should be both aurally and visually stimulating, in addition to being grammatically correct.

Round 1

Prerevision, Step One: Examining the Original

Trees engulf us as the water trickles over the rocks. The light shines onto the water through gaps in the leaves. In those spots you can see the many fish swimming happily. When we enter the light our shadows stretch out shortly. As we walk through the water splashing gently we hear a variety of birds chirping and bugs making many different relaxing noises. The kids outside scream happily playing games. I stare in the water and wonder, "Where do all of the fish go in winter? Do they migrate, do they hibernate, or do they just die? What happens to the beautiful water after dark? I sit relaxed by the trickling water.

Prerevision, Step Two: Marking Up the Poem

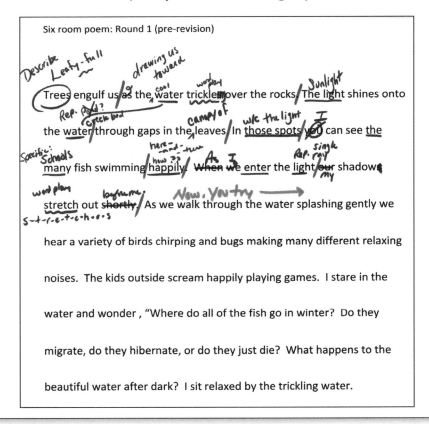

Figure 7.5 Through our poem revision process, students make poetry come to life on the page.

Round 2

Midrevision
Part One: My Partial Revision from Class Discussion

Leafy-green trees engulf us,

drawing us toward the cool water

t r i c k l i n g over the rocks.

Sunlight shines onto the creek bed

through gaps in the canopy of leaves.

In the light, I can see schools of fish darting—

here—

—and—

—there.

As I step into that single ray,

my shadow s-t-r-e-t-c-h-e-s out before me.

=== Revised to here; now you try!

Remember: Trade up for better word choices, remove unrelated or unnecessary details, check for complete thoughts (no fragments!), punctuate for power, and play with white space.

Figure 7.5 (continued) Through our poem revision process, students make poetry come to life on the page.

Final Revision: Student Sample

The World Before Me

Leafy-green trees engulf me,

drawing me toward the cool water

t r i c k l i n g over the rocks.

Orange evening sunlight shines onto the creek bed

through gaps in the canopy of leaves.

In the light, I can see schools of fish darting—

here—

—and—

—there.

As I step into that single ray,

my shadow s-t-r-e-t-c-h-e-s out before me.

I carefully *slosh* through the water,

ankle

deep

causing birds and bugs to lift off with excitement.

Far off in the d i s t a n c e,

kids GIGGLE and PLAY,

while I stare at my wrinkled reflection, now

s-p-e-c-k-l-e-d with minnows, **contemplating**...

Where do the fish go once the world turns cold?

Do other animals join them by the light of the moon?

Relaxed, I sigh and sit, perched, taking in this world.

By: Halle, Anna, Amin, and Connor

F Period

Figure 7.5 (continued) Through our poem revision process, students make poetry come to life on the page.

I pause. These slash marks will become our line breaks. For the second read-through, I ask the students to listen again for those pauses to make any changes or additions and also to keep their eyes and ears peeled for word choices and punctuation we will need to revise and places that naturally lend themselves to playing with white space.

After students have fully revised their own self-selected poem from our unit based on the criteria, I teach them how to prepare their poems for submission (see Appendix E). This is important, because some editors and publishers won't bother to read a submission if the writer hasn't followed the guidelines. For this lesson, I take the class to the computer lab so they can actually set up their margins and footers as I instruct them on the formatting. I also show them how to create visual interest in Microsoft Word by introducing them to the subscript and superscript keys, showing them how to expand and condense text, and helping them with other spacing issues that arise as they make words come to life on the page by playing with the white space.

I deliberately choose the organization Creative Communication (www.poeticpower. com) for this assignment because we have found that the odds of being accepted for publication here are greater than for many other opportunities available to kids. (Creative Communication accepts the top 45 percent of the entries for each contest based on overall quality and content.) After our intensive poetry instruction, the vast majority of my students make the cut. Many of my students even find that they enjoy writing poetry, which is great news because Creative Communication has several seasonal deadlines. The multiple submission deadlines enable me to time our initial poetry unit so that my students who have found a gift in poetry writing can write and submit another poem when they get to self-select writing genres. Students who prefer informational or persuasive writing will also be able to use this outlet later in the year to submit their work, because this organization sponsors both essay and poetry contests.

Savoring the Thrill

Publication matters to students far beyond any test score or marking-period grade. It is tangible evidence that they have accomplished something that few can claim: *I am a published author*. Publication builds confidence in all future academic endeavors. It is validation that what they have to say matters—beyond the classroom and out in the real world. I have found that this is particularly true for those students who rarely get recognized for their academic accomplishments.

I will never forget the letter that I received from Brian's mom. Brian was a struggling learner in my language arts class in both seventh and eighth grade. Overall, he was not a stellar student, but he had been published twice, so he was obviously willing to put in the work to get a job done. When he moved up to high school, no doubt there were some preconceived notions about Brian's abilities in English from his new teacher based on his Individualized Education Plan (IEP). According to Brian's mom, one day he was taking a little longer than the rest of the class to complete an assignment, and when he was asked if he needed help, he responded indignantly, "You know, I *am* a published author—*twice*! I think I can figure *this* out!" Brian's mom went on to write that although she did talk with him about speaking that way to an adult, she also expressed how proud she was of her son for his confidence in his abilities when others assumed he was capable of less, and for his willingness to soldier on to complete the task unassisted.

As any published author will tell you, the more submissions sent in, the greater the odds of acceptance. But what happens if a student doesn't get published? There is never a guarantee. The reality is that many of the world's finest authors have had to deal with repeated rejection before acceptance. Although I share this logical nature of the business with my students, it can be a challenge for them to accept rejection in this age of entitlement, where "everybody gets a trophy." Fortunately, because they are submitting to "kid-friendly" publications, the publishers are both kind and reassuring to the young writers who don't make the cut, encouraging them to keep writing and not to give up on their dream of becoming a published author (an extremely rare occurrence in the adult market today).

> *For two years I received nothing but rejections . . . I would go to sleep at night feeling that I'd never be published. But I'd wake up in the morning convinced I would be. Each time I sent a story or book off to a publisher, I would sit down and begin something new. I was learning more with each effort. I was determined. Determination and hard work are as important as talent.*
>
> —Judy Blume, author of *Deenie*; *Are You There, God? It's Me, Margaret*; *As Long as We're Together*; and many other novels

From the beginning, I try to keep my writers optimistic by letting them know that I will give them all the tools that they will need to be successful. I let them know that while we are in this phase of our writing workshop, I will take on the role of *editor* rather than teacher, and I will help them to develop their writing and make decisions that will increase their odds of acceptance.

The *real* question that kids want answered regarding publication rejection is this: *How will my grades will be affected if I don't get published by the end of the year?* Ugh. I know that most teachers would love to have classes full of students who want to learn for learning's sake, but because schools place such emphasis on grades and assessments it's no wonder students become preoccupied with these evaluations. I think it's important to keep in mind that grades do not reflect a student's *potential*, only their past. I want all of my students to write well, and I believe they all can with time and training.

In *Writing Essentials*, Regie Routman writes that "when expectations are high, the work is interesting, and sufficient demonstrations and support are provided by knowledgeable teachers, *all* students succeed—the second language learners, the students with learning disabilities, all writers who struggle" (2005, 57).

Too often, struggling students like Brian and like Adam, whom I described near the start of this chapter, are shortchanged when we require them to do less writing or to do so with lower expectations for the quality of the work. If we can affirm that "writing is *hard*—so hard that it has been called the most complex of all human activities," as Kelly Gallagher does, and "highlight the difficulty as an opportunity for them to create something truly rewarding," our students will learn that "writing is rewarding *because* it is hard" (2006, 16). It's time that all students have the opportunity to reap the real, intrinsic rewards of a job well done, instead of relying on teachers doling out false recognition in the form of grades alone.

> *I enjoy writing and it is hard. It's hard for everyone to write well. I have to rewrite over and over again, so that on average it takes me a year to write a book.*
>
> —Avi, author of *Catch You Later, Traitor; Nothing but the Truth; Sometimes I Think I Hear My Name*; and many other titles

Here are some key facts about publication that we should share with students:

In the real world, editors don't care about a student's grades. They don't care how "smart" students are or what modifications are dictated in an IEP. They don't care if a student comes from an affluent family and dresses well or if he or she is homeless, surviving off the generosity of others. The beautiful thing about authentic publication is that it levels the playing field for all students. What *The Voice* has done for singers, authentic publication does for writers, giving children the freedom to show off their talents by writing about whatever is most important at that moment, and to do it in their own style without being judged before they've even had a chance to succeed.

As the teacher, I may never know whether a student gets published. Because I choose to submit bulk PDF entries of my students' poems to Creative Communications during our poetry unit in mid-February, I *do* have the luxury of being notified which of my students have been accepted. This is precisely why I select this publication for our first attempt. This way, I have a record of submissions and I can stay on top of my students to return the appropriate permissions paperwork once they are accepted. However, many publishers, including some that the kids may choose select to submit their personal workshop writing to later in the year, only require home addresses, so I may not know about an acceptance unless the student chooses to tell me. Because of the timing, students typically find out about acceptance for their end-of-year personally selected workshop submissions during the summer months, when we are not in school.

Publication is not up to me, so acceptance can't be included as a grade. All I can do is try to set up my students for success by supporting them through the process with mini-lessons and conferences, and by helping them to select the most appropriate platform for submission.

A rejection may not reflect the editor's opinion of the writing. It may mean that the publisher is not looking for such material at this time, on this topic, or in this style. Students need to survey the reader's market to be sure their topic and genre are relevant before beginning this round of the writing and submission process. It is equally important to research potential publication opportunities in the writer's market as well as magazines, ezines, and blog sites to which students subscribe. (See Chapter 8 for more on surveying the reader's and writer's markets.) When researching the writer's market, kids need to *carefully read the submissions guidelines* to see what each editor is specifically looking to publish. In some cases, it may be necessary to query the editor prior to sending any manuscript. That's why teachers need to be involved in the process of identifying the most appropriate publishers based on the students' particular topics, genres, or styles. Over the years, I have gotten to know which publications are better suited for my "hard-core" writers—those who write with a style and passion that is well beyond their years (*Teen Ink* is a great publication for them)—and which publications are better for my novices (Creative Communications is the best for these).

> *Write what you love—don't feel pressure to write serious prose if what you like is to be funny. You are a reader as much as a writer, so write what you'd want to read.*
>
> —Cassandra Clare, author of the Shadowhunter Chronicles (the Mortal Instruments series) and other titles

Good writers get rejected all the time. Search online for a list of authors and books that were rejected before being accepted by another publisher (J. K. Rowling, Meg Cabot, and Judy Blume just to name a few!) and share it with your students. In our classroom, we learn from the authors who come before us. Most of them have a *lot* of experience with rejection, but they also have so much inspiration to offer to young writers, which can keep students motivated despite discouragements.

Teacher as Writer

I would be remiss if I didn't mention the significance of *teacher as writer* in this process. Just as we need to model writing side by side with our students, we also need to make a practice of submitting our own work. The adult market can be fierce, but be fearless. Show students that it is okay and even beneficial to learn to deal with rejection. I humbly share my own rejection pile with my students. Doing so respects the community of writers that we've developed from the beginning, and it builds trust that we are truly in this together. Teachers don't have any greater chance of being accepted for publication than their students do; they need to experience the joy of acceptance and the agony of rejection to fully understand what their students will experience in this process. Remember: If you never submit your work, you will never be published. That goes for students and teachers alike. I tell my students each year: "Write . . . as if each word could be the one that makes you famous."

That's our classroom motto. If the writing doesn't make them famous, it definitely makes them better writers. What really matters is that all students learn to express ideas that matter to them. Yes, we are seeking to create memorable literature every time we write. And, yes, we would all love to experience the glory and pride that comes with being accepted for publication. But our major goal is learning to write honestly, passionately, confidently, and fluently. At the end of the year, I want my students to look back over their words and think, "Wow, I actually wrote that?" And then I can nod and say, "Yeah, you did."

Chapter 8

Researching and Revising for Publication

Writing is hard work, work that relies on learning and applying a varied set of skills, and finding out what those skills are, learning and practicing them, is always better than waiting around for inspiration.

—Cassandra Clare, author of the
Shadowhunter Chronicles (the Mortal Instruments series) and other titles

During the second semester, the students are essentially on their own as they apply every lesson learned to their self-selected writing projects. The challenge is getting those notebook seeds to sprout, grow, and eventually blossom into publishable manuscripts. This semester is either the most exciting or most frightening part of the school year, depending on a student's interest in writing, self-confidence, and time-management skills. As teachers, we must do everything in our power to scaffold learning to set up every student for success.

By this point in the school year, it's early spring and we've already spent a great deal of energy developing poetry that sings. Now we need to help students who are interested in other genres find their rhythm.

Before surveying the writer's market and preparing manuscripts for submission, I slow things down for a week with an "audience lesson" that we use to survey the *reader's* market. All writers must develop an awareness of audience, and for publication it could be the difference between receiving an acceptance letter and a rejection letter. Nancie

Atwell shares that "a sense of audience—the knowledge that someone will read what they have written—is crucial to young writers. Kids write with purpose and passion when they know that people they care about reaching will read what they have to say. More importantly, through using writing to reach out to the world, students learn what writing is good for. Writing workshop isn't a method for filling up folders with 'pieces.' It is a daily occasion to discover why writing matters in their lives and in others' and what it can do for them and the world" (1998, 489).

Discovering the Importance of Audience

Prior to beginning the lesson on audience, we have a class discussion about the television sitcoms and podcasts the students watch, particularly those geared toward preteen and teen audiences. These days, their attention leans toward popular Disney Channel, Nickelodeon, and Cartoon Network shows as well as Netflix and many teenage podcast and Internet productions. (If your school district gives you permission to view an episode for educational purposes, plan a "discovery lesson," where students try to figure out the episode's plot elements based on what they already know about plot structure. Such a lesson is more engaging for them than the teacher telling them the plot structure.)

In our discussion, we talk about the basic formula writers and producers use to develop their plot-driven productions. Because the formula is so similar to the traditional short story arc we studied earlier in the year, this discussion serves as a refresher for students who are thinking about publishing short stories. It also helps us to bridge the gap between story idea and audience relevancy.

A typical sitcom is written for a thirty-minute time slot. Eight to ten minutes are used for advertising and credits, and the remaining twenty to twenty-two minutes are reserved for the story line (see Figure 8.1). Obviously, the plot needs to be tight and resolvable in that brief time frame, which is a good lesson for short story writers, who will have to abide by submissions guidelines that include a word-count cap.

I next assign the media challenge for the week:

- Watch three different TV sitcoms (or a combination of sitcoms and podcasts). Try to watch a variety of programs that target the same audience your writing targets.
- Maintain a log in the "Writing from Class" section of your ME book. (The worksheet shown in Figure 8.2 could also be used as a log.)

After the week of media research is completed, we come together as a group to compile the results. We create a class list of the lessons that the protagonists learned in the sitcoms and the issues/subjects/purposes of the podcasts. We also add any lessons or issues that the class believes kids in this age group would find beneficial or relevant in order to gain a better

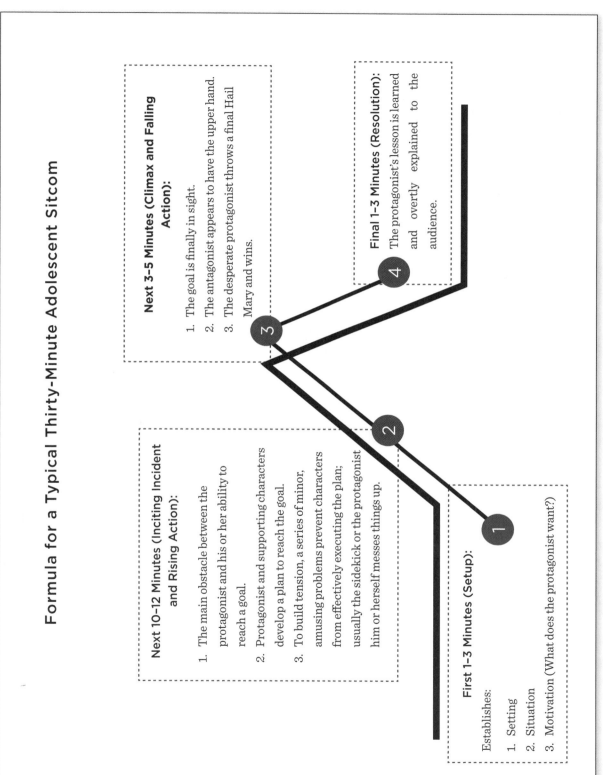

Formula for a Typical Thirty-Minute Adolescent Sitcom

First 1-3 Minutes (Setup):

Establishes:

1. Setting
2. Situation
3. Motivation (What does the protagonist want?)

Next 10-12 Minutes (Inciting Incident and Rising Action):

1. The main obstacle between the protagonist and his or her ability to reach a goal.
2. Protagonist and supporting characters develop a plan to reach the goal.
3. To build tension, a series of minor, amusing problems prevent characters from effectively executing the plan; usually the sidekick or the protagonist him or herself messes things up.

Next 3-5 Minutes (Climax and Falling Action):

1. The goal is finally in sight.
2. The antagonist appears to have the upper hand.
3. The desperate protagonist throws a final Hail Mary and wins.

Final 1-3 Minutes (Resolution):

The protagonist's lesson is learned and overtly explained to the audience.

Figure 8.1 The formula for a typical sitcom aimed at adolescents is similar to story arcs commonly featured in short stories.

Sitcom Analysis		Podcast Analysis	
What was the name, date, and time of the show?		What was the name and original release date of the podcast?	
What was the social issue addressed?		What was the social issue addressed or the purpose of the podcast?	
Who is the target audience (age, gender, social class, etc.)?		Who is the target audience (age, gender, social class, etc.)?	
Why is this issue important to this audience?		Why is this issue/ purpose important to this audience?	
What message should the audience get about the issue? Was it clear?		What message should the audience receive? Do you think it was clear? Was it appropriate for the audience?	
What do you think about how the writers/ producers handled the issue? What did they do well? What would you have done differently?		What do you think about how the writers/ producers handled the subject matter? What did they do well? What would you have done differently?	

Figure 8.2 Using this sheet, students can analyze the audience targeted in sitcoms and podcasts.

understanding of our target audience. Through our studies, we have found that bullying/ standing up to bullies, honesty (as an important aspect of a person's character), and peer pressure (and staying true to oneself) were all prevalent themes. The podcast subjects included a variety of how-to topics focusing on fashion/hair/makeup, sports, and comedy. This activity prepares students well for the final task, surveying the reader's market. Students work individually or in pairs to complete the chart shown in Figure 8.3.

Weekly Writing Challenge 15: Surveying the Writer's Market

Knowing their audience helps students focus when selecting possible publication targets. Weekly Writing Challenge 15 focuses on researching the writer's market (see Figure 8.4). Although we've been writing in our ME books for months, knowing that every word could potentially be published, our mission becomes more serious when we start selecting actual publications to target. The energy in the classroom when I introduce this Weekly Writing Challenge is an intoxicating cocktail of excitement, panic, joy, and fear. My introduction of WWC 15 is inevitably met with wide eyes, blanched faces, and subtle fist pumps accompanied by a barely audible, yet resounding *yes!* They realize that this is the real deal. Although it is only March, this is the final long-term project that they will have as seventh graders. During the next three months, they will plan, draft, revise, edit, and format two self-selected writing pieces for publication.

Referring to the lists shown in Figure 7.1 in the previous chapter, students use the Possible Publications template shown in Figure 8.5 to complete WWC 15 as they analyze the submissions guidelines for selected publications.

No matter how many publication possibilities I have compiled, I take time each year to update my lists. It's important to have the most current submission guidelines, weed out dead links, and find new opportunities that were previously unavailable. My own research helps me to guide my students to suitable matches. I post all opportunities as either "Student Publications" or "Contests & Competitions" on my classroom website.

Weekly Writing Challenge 16: Cultivating a Seed

Once students have decided on their best publication opportunities, they start setting goals. I expect them to work toward publication during our weekly workshop time in school *and* for twenty minutes three times per week at home. Weekly Writing Challenge 16: Cultivating a Seed makes that expectation clear (see Figure 8.6).

If your classroom budget permits, I highly recommend preparing a folder for each child that includes the following items in order to help keep your students organized throughout their publication process:

Understanding Audience: Surveying the Reader's Market

In order for authors to be truly successful, they not only need a great idea and the words to make it come to life on the page but also have to identify an audience who will *want* to read what they write. This week, your task is to explore the world of your intended audience.

Who is your intended audience?   Age/grade: _____ Gender: girl   boy   both

What matters most to kids in this age/gender group? Be specific.

Think about issues related to:

- family:

- friends:

- "stuff" (material goods/name brands):

- activities:

- school (social and academic):

- their future:

- their world (issues/concerns):

What's hot now for kids in this demographic?

1. What *TV shows* are most popular for this audience?

   Why? (Really. Why are these shows so popular with this group?)

2. What *products* are advertisers marketing to this audience?

3. What *books* are the current top sellers for this audience?

   Important themes, concepts, topics, genres, etc., in these books:

What's missing for kids in this demographic?

1. Are there any needs that this group has that are not being addressed? (In other words, is there a gap that you could fill with your writing?)

[On the back: *How will you use this information to guide your writing for publication?*]

Figure 8.3 Students deepen their understanding of audience by analyzing prospective readers of their own writing.

Weekly Writing Challenge 15

"The publishing industry is set up to weed out those who don't want it badly enough. Figure out how badly you want it."

"Follow agent and editor rules."

—Becca Fitzpatrick, author of the Hush, Hush Saga, *Black Ice*, and *Dangerous Lies*

"If you love to write, then write. Don't let your goal be to have your novel published, let your goal be enjoying your stories. However, if you finish your story and you want to share it, be brave about it. Don't doubt your story's appeal. If you are a good reader, and you know what is interesting, and your story is interesting to you, then trust in that."

— Stephenie Meyer, author of the Twilight series, *The Host*, *Life and Death*, and other titles

"Publishing is a tough business, one that is always changing, and the road is often long, and bumpy, and riddled with rejection. But if you really want it, you just have to keep going, reminding yourself that it only takes one 'Yes!' to get you where you want to be!"

—Alyson Noël, author of the Beautiful Idols series, the Immortals series, the Soul Seekers series, and many other titles

Weekly Writing Challenge 15: Surveying the Writer's Market

THE CHALLENGE

Now that you have a pretty good idea of which writing "seeds" from your ME book have publication potential, it is time to survey the writer's market to see where you could possibly send your writing to get published.

1. Log on to my eboard and click on "The Real Deal" Post-it in the "7th Grade English" tab.
2. Click on either "Student Publications" or "Contests & Competitions" to pull up a listing of all of the possible places that might accept your writing for publication. Read through each listing. If you find one that interests you, click on the web link for more info.
3. Throughout the week, you must record a list of three opportunities for publication on the Possible Publications worksheet from class. Be sure to include all necessary information (you can print extra sheets online).

Figure 8.4 To have a good chance of success in publishing, students study the writer's market for their work.

Possible Publications List: Surveying The Writer's Market

To make sure that you select the best possible sources with the greatest potential for getting your writing published, it is important that you familiarize yourself with the writer's market and the guidelines for each publisher. Peruse all of the publication opportunities that I have gathered for you. Then select three places that you feel are most likely to accept your work. Once you have narrowed down your choices, fill in the guidelines below (complete one for each of your top three choices).

Name: _____ Date: _____ Period: _____

Choice # _____ Publication Guidelines

Title of publication/contest:	
Name of editor (if given):	
Address:	

Target audience:	**Word count max/min:**
Target themes:	**Target genres:**

Additional information to include in cover letter or manuscript:
My ideas/plan for submitting to this publication or contest:

My ideas for developing and submitting my writing:

My Writing	Piece #1:	Piece #2:	Piece #3:
Genre			
Theme			
Audience			
Additional work I will do to get it ready for publication			

Figure 8.5 Students use the Possible Publications list to keep track of potential publication opportunities for their writing.

Weekly Writing Challenge 16

"Whether you intend to write a few paragraphs or a longer piece, think about the structure of your work before you begin. What do you want to say? What information do you need to convey? If it is a report, decide how to arrange the information. For short stories, have a clear idea of how you will start, what will happen, and how it will end. This will allow you to focus on the actual writing, so you are not trying to invent the story at the same time."

—Christopher Paolini, author of *Eragon* and the rest of the Inheritance Cycle series

" . . . you need to work your bootie off . . . Don't worry about how good it is yet. Just write. Then write some more. By doing this alone, you will improve drastically."

— James Dashner, author of the Maze Runner Series, the Mortality Doctrine series, the 13th Reality series, and other titles

"Most importantly, pick an amount of time each day, 30 mins, 1 hour, and sit down and DO IT."

—Ridley Pearson, author of the Kingdom Keepers series, the Starcatcher series, and many other titles

"I've learned that if I wait for the perfect moment to write, I won't write very often. So I just try to write through it and usually it gets better as I go along."

—Ally Condie, author of the Matched series, *Atlantia*, and *Summerlost*

"Read all the time and write every day. Don't get discouraged."

—Gary Paulsen, author of *Hatchet, Brian's Winter*, and many other titles

"Writing is as much about discipline as it is about creative inspiration."

—S. E. Hinton, author of *The Outsiders*; *Rumblefish; That Was Then, This Is Now*; & many other titles

Weekly Writing Challenge 16: Cultivating a Seed

THE CHALLENGE

The expectations have changed, and now it is up to you to apply all that you have learned to truly make your writing worthy of publication. The time has come for you to be in charge of your own writing destiny.

- In class, you have been given a workshop checklist that you must complete for every writing assignment prior to submitting your work to an editor for publication. You can print out extras online if needed.

- Each step along the way must be completed, then signed and dated by both you and the teacher.

- Pace yourself. I expect you to write in class during workshop time, and at home at least three times per week. To make your work worthy of publication, commit to plenty of revision.

Figure 8.6 This writing challenge sets the expectation of fierce revision with the aim of publication.

- one two-pocket folder with prongs
- one plastic sheet protector
- one pencil
- one small stack of sticky notes
- one calendar sheet (easily created on Microsoft Publisher or similar program) with dates of days off from school, field trips, field days, and any other school events that might preclude productivity; the students will use these calendars to break their publication projects into manageable chunks
- two Writer's Workshop Process Checklists (see Appendix B)
- two Writer's Workshop Project Planning Sheets (see Appendix F)
- one sheet of Teacher Conference Cards (see Appendix G)
- one laminated RADaR Revision Card, printed two per page (see Appendix H)
- two Peer Conference Forms on colored paper (see Appendix I)
- one laminated Color Editing Card; I print these out in full color, two per sheet to save ink and paper, and then I laminate them so that they can be reused each year and for other assignments (see Appendix J)

I can reuse the majority of the folders, sheet protectors, and laminated pages from year to year, so it is worth the initial time and expense. If budget constraints prevent this, consider asking for the items as part of the beginning-of-year student supply list for your class and simply hold on to these items until the second semester. To set up each folder, clip the plastic sheet protector into the prongs, and then slide in the calendar, conference cards, revision card, editing card, pencil, and sticky notes. Then place one checklist and one planning sheet in each of the two folder pockets.

First, we talk through the calendar, noting holidays and other occasions that will limit academic time. In addition, because each student has two Writer's Workshop Process Checklists (Appendix B) to complete (feel free to modify for individual students as needed), we walk our way through the fifteen steps of the checklist and note on the calendar days by which they should reach specific milestones in order to meet the class deadline. Students then take the time to break the workload into manageable chunks, jotting down goals for completion of tasks in school and at home.

Some students find it easier to keep track of their work by labeling the two folder pockets Work in Progress and Done, because they like the idea of moving items from one to another upon completion. Others prefer to keep each process checklist and all of the work associated with it in its dedicated pocket. Any way is fine by me as long as each student can keep his or her work organized.

We still have our regular curriculum to finish, but I keep Workshop Monday intact, and I add extra workshop time wherever I can make room. If I happen to be out for a day, the students don't give the substitute teachers any problems because they know that they will be getting time to work on their publication pieces. Working on the steps of their publication process checklists also becomes our new "sponge activity" for the semester, and the kids really take to the idea so that they can get ahead or get caught up if they finish regular classwork assignments early.

Choosing Genres

Each student can select from any of the following genres: short story, memoir, three poems, essay (compare/contrast, argument, or informational), editorial, book review, or any other writing genres that come to light through WWC 15. To begin, students choose the topic, the mode, and the audience for each piece of writing. They must carefully review the publication options that they've collected while surveying the young writer's market, decide how they can reach a specific audience, and define their own writing tasks by looking through the seed ideas already planted in their writer's notebooks. Students should review their prior entries, considering how they can build on and expand them into fully developed, publishable pieces, with explicit submissions guidelines and audiences in mind. It is essential that students develop their own plans so they have ownership of their projects. The Writer's Workshop Project Planning Sheet (Appendix F) assists them.

Connor, one of my stronger writers one year, was really into superheroes. So naturally, he decided to write an original story about two brothers who obtain shape-shifting powers. As traditional superhero lore would dictate, these brothers become enemies: one decides to use his newfound powers for evil and the other chooses to defeat his brother and save the earth. In many middle school English classrooms, this kind of writing would be considered nonsense unworthy of recognition. But Connor's passion and creativity elevated the mundane to magnificent. His planning sheet (see Figure 8.7) shows how seriously he thought about the lessons and mentor texts that would be most valuable. He also indicated additional research he would need to do to make his details realistic and specific writing skills he would need to improve.

After the students have completed the planning sheet, they are ready to begin tackling the fifteen "author-proven steps," which are designed to foster a natural transfer of the skills we have learned throughout the year into a publication-worthy submission. This process encourages the students to write with an awareness of craft, vocabulary, and audience. Keep in mind that students will have worked on most of these steps individually while revising their novel excerpts (see Appendix D).

The checklists will serve as guides through the process, but it is up to each student to establish the time line for completion. (In some cases, particularly for magazines that have rolling submissions for various themes and annual contests, a student's time line may also mean abiding by a deadline that supersedes any classroom-imposed deadline.)

The structure of our workshop time will now be changing. I release control over lessons and pacing to the students to make their own decisions about how to best utilize their time to

Writer's Workshop Project Planning Sheet

Name: Connor _____

Before beginning your personal workshop project, complete and submit this planning sheet in preparation of your writing conference. I can't wait to hear about all of your writing plans!

1. Prewriting Plan: I will write a short story about
   Brother shape shifters who learn that they have this
   power by accident after something bad happens. I decide
   to use this power for evil, the other uses it for good. In the end,
   they battle each other

2. How I plan to use my Writers' Notebook:
   entries from:
   —Writing from the heart p.15
   —artifact no.2 p.58
   —emulating text p.93

3. Lessons I plan to refer to from my Resource Guide:
   —whole craft section
   —Varying sentence structure notes

4. Additional instruction I may need:
   S-V agreement w/ prep phrases - 1st unk a that

5. Mentor texts &/or authors I can refer to as I write:
   Neal Shusterman - Everlost series

6. Additional things I may need to research for this writing:
   —what it would feel like as molecules change
   —which animals or object are the strongest
   —Best things for conducting electricity

7. Possible publication places include (and potential audiences):
   Anthology of short stories by young Americans
        Beyond Centauri

8. Peers I can go to for specific needs:
   ✶ Riley is awesome at that

Additional questions/comments/concerns:
   making time/finishing on time

Figure 8.7 Looking at Connor's planning sheet, I can see that he has thoughtfully considered the reader's and writer's markets for his work of fiction.

reach the goal of submitting two new writing pieces for publication by the end of the school year. On most workshop days, I will still start out with a mini-lesson on craft or process, and the conference time will be based primarily on their individual needs. I do a traditional "status of the class" check at the beginning of each workshop period so that I can compare what everyone will be working on for the period to my Class Checklist Progress Roster (see Figure 8.8).

Staying on Track

Students who can keep themselves on track can self-advocate for specific needs by filling out a Teacher Conference Card (see Appendix G) to meet with me directly. The Conference Cards help me and the students know who's up and who's on deck as I move around the room for my conferences. If I see from the cards that a few kids have the same issue or are ready for the same mini-lesson, I will pull them all together a small-group session instead of one-on-one. Conversely, if I notice that a student is not making much progress and he or she has not scheduled a conference, I intervene. During the first-round checklist writing, it is not uncommon for kids to get behind, but it's not difficult to get them back on track.

> *Set goals and work to achieve them . . . I also set daily writing goals (words per day) when I'm in first draft writing mode, and that really helps keep me on task. You don't have to get all Stephen Covey crazy about it, but goals do work.*
>
> —James Dashner, author of the Maze Runner series, the Mortality Doctrine series, the Thirteenth Reality series, and other titles

Shawn, for example, was really struggling writing a memoir about his uncle's funeral. He had selected to write this piece based on one of his "Writing from the Heart" entries in his writer's notebook. Two weeks (that's three workshop class periods) after the start of the project, Shawn *still* hadn't completed his prewriting, let alone his rough draft. I called him up to the conferring table to see what was up. Because he was writing about an event that was so important to him, he wanted to be "honest" about everything that happened. In short, he was overwhelmed by all the ideas that kept popping into his head. Many of them were *funny*—definitely *not* the tone he was going for. He kept rewriting openings and reorganizing his details to try to get back on track. I could see the frustration and panic in his eyes, so I picked up my pen and scratched out the word *memoir* that I had written next to his name. Above it I wrote: *short story*.

Shawn didn't know how to react to my actions. "But, I am writing a *memoir*. This is important."

"I don't know what to tell ya, Shawn," I said. "Your heart's not in it, and your brain clearly has another story that it *wants* to tell. So let it."

A Period Checklist #1	Prewriting	1st Draft	Crafts/Strategies	Vocabulary	RADaR Revisions	Revision #1	Read Aloud	Peer Conf.	Revision #2	Color Editing	Manuscript	Letter to Editor	SASE/outer E	MAILED	Reflection	DEADLINE MET
Garrett 3 poems	3/10	3/21	3/21	3/31	4/7	4/7	4/14	4/14	4/21	4/28						
Melissa memoir	3/3	3/17	3/24	3/24	3/31	4/7	4/7	4/7	4/14	4/21	4/28	4/28	4/28	4/28	4/28	☆
Caitlyn 3 poems	3/10	3/24	3/24	3/24	3/31	4/7	4/14	4/14	4/14	4/21	4/28					☆
Casey short story	3/3	3/17	3/24	3/24	3/31	4/7	4/7	4/7	4/14	4/14	4/21	4/21	4/21	4/21	4/21	★
Justin essay	3/3	3/17	3/17	3/17	3/31	4/7	4/7	4/14	4/21	4/21	4/28					
Emily short story	3/3	3/24	3/31	3/31	4/7	4/7	4/14	4/14	4/21	4/21	4/28					
Farryl short story	3/10	3/24	3/31	3/31	4/7	4/7	4/14	4/14	4/21	4/28	4/28	4/28	◯			
Sona 3 poems	3/3	3/10	3/17	3/17	4/7	4/7	4/14	4/7	4/14	4/14	4/21	4/28				☆
Brett ① Novel	3/24	4/14	4/21	4/21	4/28											
Alex short story	3/10	3/24	3/24	3/31	4/7	4/7	4/14	4/14	4/21	4/28						
Julia essay	3/3	3/10	3/17	3/17	4/7	4/7	4/7	4/7	4/21	4/21	4/28		N/A			
Jennifer short story	3/10	3/24	3/31	3/31	4/7				4/21	4/28						
Brooke 3 poems	3/3	3/10	3/10	3/10	4/7	4/14	4/14	4/14	4/21	4/28						☆
Shawn short story	3/17	4/7	4/7	4/7	4/14	4/21	4/21	4/21	4/28							
Stephen short story	3/3	3/24	3/31	3/31	4/7	4/14	4/14	4/14	4/21	4/21	4/28		N/A			
Joy memoir	3/3	3/17	3/24	3/24	4/7	4/7	4/14	4/14	4/14	4/21	4/21	4/21	4/21	4/21	4/21	★
Daemon 3 poems	3/10	3/24	3/31	3/31	4/7	4/14	4/14	4/14	4/21	4/28						
Ahmed essay	3/3	3/10	3/17	3/17	3/24	4/7	4/14	4/14	4/14	4/18	4/28					☆
Bertram short story	3/17	3/31	4/7	4/7	4/14	4/21	4/21	4/21	4/28							
Stephanie 3 poems	3/10	3/24	3/24	3/24	3/31	4/7	4/7	4/7	4/14	4/14	4/21	4/28				☆
Shannon 3 poems	3/10	3/24	3/31	3/31	4/7	4/7	4/14	4/14	4/21	4/21	4/61	4/28				☆
Greg short story	3/17	3/31	4/7	4/7	4/14	4/21	4/21	4/21	4/28							
Kenny 3 poems short story	3/17	4/7	4/14	4/14	4/21	4/28	4/28	4/18								
Marissa memoir	3/10	3/24	3/31	4/7	4/7	4/14	4/14	4/21	4/21	4/28						☆
Kelly short story	3/3	3/10	3/17	3/17	4/7	4/7	4/7	4/7	4/14	4/21	4/28	4/28	◯			
David short story	3/3	3/17	3/24	3/24	3/31	4/7	4/7	4/14	4/14							
Michael short story	3/10	3/24	3/31	3/31	4/7	4/7	4/7	4/14	4/21	4/21	4/28	N/A	4/8			☆
Vashina short story	3/3	3/17	3/24	3/24	3/31	4/7	4/7	4/7	4/14	4/21	4/21	4/21	4/21	4/21	★	
Sarah 3 poems	3/3	3/17	3/17	3/17	3/31	4/7	4/7	4/14	4/21	4/21	4/18	N/A				☆
Cassidy 3 poems	3/3	3/17	3/24	3/24	3/31	4/7	4/7	4/7	4/14	4/21	4/28	4/28				☆

Figure 8.8 Using the Class Checklist Progress Roster to record completion dates, I can track the progress of all students.

"But..."

"Give it a try. Let's see where your story goes. Sometimes writing about your life can be stifling because you are limited by what really happened. When you *tell a story*, the sky's the limit. It can turn out however you want. You could even make a funeral...well...funny."

Shawn took off. He still wrote about *a* funeral; just not *the* funeral. And by allowing himself to write freely without being tied to the facts of reality, he was able to make up for the time lost and get himself back on track with very little additional redirection.

As you can see from Figure 8.8, Brett was also behind. It took him six weeks just to finish his first draft. I wasn't concerned. Brett is an avid reader and writer. He had really enjoyed the novel-writing experience and he had a great sci-fi idea he wanted to explore, based on one of his entries from his "Lists" and "Multigenre" writing. Because novels are so labor- (and paper-) intensive, we agreed that he would complete this *one* writing project for publication instead of two. We adjusted the checklist by adding additional craft strategies and vocabulary. Brett and I also agreed that it would be unfair to ask his classmates to read his entire novel, especially when they would likely still have their own work to complete. We decided that a good solution would be to select two to three excerpts or sections that were particularly important (definitely the exposition and the climax—the two most important scenes to editors), and have a peer or sibling read and conference with him on those. On his calendar, Brett mapped out his time line for completion.

Kenny, on the other hand, had fallen down the rabbit hole with a short story that he was writing from scratch. He had actually started with one of his seed ideas, but his imagination had gotten the best of him. So far it had taken him two weeks to complete his story arc and character chart and by week five he was still working on the exposition. Kenny probably could've used his time more wisely, but the story had just gotten way bigger than he could handle. He had a decision to make: continue his story at an accelerated pace or switch gears completely and try something new. He had done very well in the poetry unit, and he had enjoyed writing poems, so Kenny opted to abandon his story and give the three poems a shot. He did end up finishing and submitting his poems, but unfortunately for his second manuscript, he decided to return to the story to try to finish it. He never did.

In his reflection, Kenny noted that he learned two important lessons:

1. I should have never picked up this story for my second checklist. I was being lazy, and figured that I could just finish it because I already started it. I was wrong.

2. Procrastination is NOT my friend.

In the real world of writing, these things happen. Plans change, deadlines pass, new opportunities develop; it is not the end of the world. Publication is a messy process.

Our goal is to instill positive writerly habits, but we must remember that at the end of the day we are teaching *kids*. As teachers, we should be consistent with the expectation of a quality product, and we need to be flexible with the kids and their process if they are to succeed. Workshop time in my classroom can look different for each student.

Colin was a student in my last ninety-minute block of the day. (I am fairly certain that the timing of his arrival to my classroom coincided with his morning meds wearing off.) Once our second semester workshop time hit, there was no way that he (or I) was going to be able to tolerate ninety minutes of independent work. Together with his parents, Colin and I came up with a proactive plan to help him independently succeed. He spent every workshop Monday of the second semester seated at a desk at the far end of my conferencing table. It wasn't a punishment, and I wasn't micromanaging his time. Colin simply could not focus on his work if I wasn't physically right there. I also allowed him to politely interrupt me—even midconference with another student—any time he had a serious question. I know that may sound rude, but we found that if he couldn't ask the question as it popped into his head, he'd become stifled at the prospect of moving on and shut down completely for the rest of the period. The consequences of that were far worse for Colin and for the rest of the class than the momentary interruption.

> *Let people read your work. Not just ANY people, mind you, but people you trust to give you honest and constructive feedback. And when you get that feedback, don't be so stubborn that you can't listen to it. You're young and you don't know everything; I know that because I'm young too. But that's okay, because you have time to learn.*
>
> —Veronica Roth, author of the Divergent series

Jennifer and Kennedy were extremely productive when they had the freedom to work together and spread out in the hallway. This does not work for many kids, but these two girls needed to talk through and seek validation from one another. They were a true writing team. As they wrote just outside the classroom door, I could hear them reciting lines to each other, asking, *Does this dialogue sound realistic? Can you picture this in your head as I read this? Do you think I should separate this into two sentences?* They helped each other come up with the best possible wording. They used their time wisely every week during workshop time, and they pushed each other to keep going outside of class to create writing worthy of publication.

As you can imagine, during our second-semester workshops, my students spend a lot of time working autonomously (alone or with their peers), without teacher direction. This 20 percent of independent work feeds and nourishes the 80 percent of classroom and curriculum work that they continue to accomplish all year, reinforcing the true concepts of *autonomy, mastery,* and *purpose.* Students must define a task, outline the pace of the process, and monitor and adjust in order to accomplish a goal: publication. The purpose, this prospect of sharing a piece of themselves with the world through publication (and, of course, the prospect of fame and infamy!), motivates them to complete the task. Figure 8.9 shows the Workshop Wall, where I include the steps leading to the destination.

> *One thing I have used with every manuscript I've revised is checklists.*
> —Veronica Roth, author of the Divergent series

Let's take a look at each of the steps in the process.

Step 1: Prewriting/Organizing

Prewriting is the natural first stage in any writing process. Throughout the year, all students have some exposure to freewriting and brainstorming as well as practice using more structured organizers. For example, students could revisit writer's notebook entries and brainstorm ways to expand them into fully developed pieces, or they could freewrite to figure out exactly what they want to say about a particular topic of interest or event from an earlier writing challenge. When students require a bit more structure, I refer them to their resource guides or to the Workshop Wall, where they will find a variety of organizer templates that we've used in class for previous writing assignments. These include plot structure and character charts unveiled originally during our NaNoWriMo writing escapade; poem organizers, such as sensory webs, sound-and-action T-charts, and Georgia Heard's Six Room Poem organizers from our poetry unit; and various informational and persuasive organizers from our essay-writing exercises. Feel free to add your own prewriting organizers and strategies to your own classroom Workshop Wall.

Step 2: Write First Draft

In writing their first drafts, students have to pay close attention to submissions guidelines and classroom-established expectations as they write. They must take notice of editors' word-count ranges for prose and line counts for poetry. I also advise students to review the front page of the peer conference form for a rundown of all of the required elements for each genre. Beyond that, the primary task is to get the butt in the chair and write. Period. There's no way around it. This is by far the longest, most time-consuming step, but it is also the most rewarding. Tell your students not to rush. If a first draft is well crafted from the beginning, completing the remaining steps will be far more satisfying. During this stage, I encourage my students to begin in old school pencil-and-paper fashion. I have found that jumping too soon into word processing actually limits the amount of revision magic that takes place later. As they take the time to transfer their work from paper to computer, their writerly brains will find it difficult to simply transfer their work word for word onto the screen. Naturally, their inner editor wants to revise, fill in gaps, and switch word choices as they type. I have found that kids who go straight from prewriting to word processing rarely go back through what they've typed with the attention to detail shown by those who draft on paper.

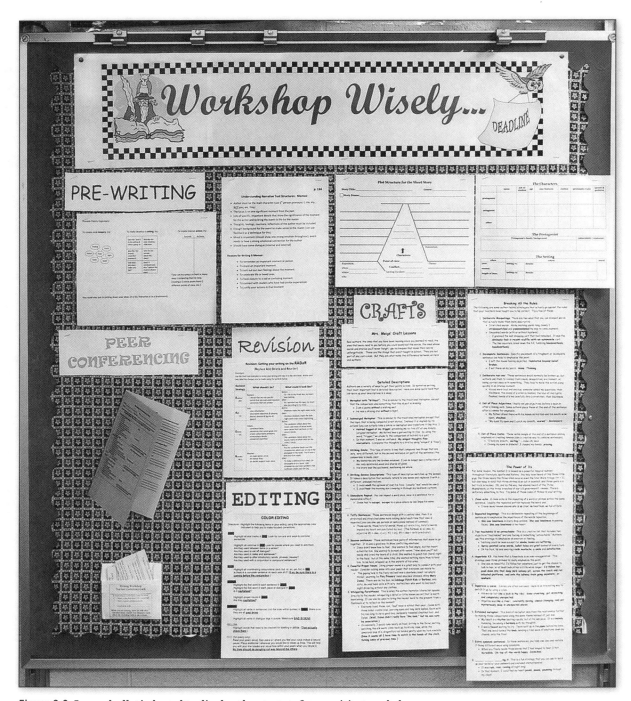

Figure 8.9 I use a bulletin board to display the stages of our writing workshop.

Troubleshooting: What if I get writer's block?

First, remind them that they wrote novels, so this isn't the first time they've been to this rodeo. Show them that you have the utmost confidence in their abilities, and you know they've got this. Or you could just make a big poster with author Philip Pullman's famous words about writer's block, put it on your wall, and refer students to it as needed:

> The most valuable thing I've learned about writing is to keep going, even when it's not coming easily. You sometimes hear people talk about something called "writer's block." Did you ever hear a plumber talk about plumber's block? Do doctors get doctor's block? Of course they don't. They work even when they don't want to. There are times when writing is very hard, too, when you can't think what to put next, and when staring at the empty page is miserable toil. Tough. Your job is to sit there and make things up, so do it. (https://www.randomhouse.com/kids/catalog/author.pperl?authorid=24658&view=sml_sptlght)

Step 3: Incorporate Writer's Crafts and Strategies

According to the National Council of Teachers of English's updated "Beliefs About the Teaching of Writing," entitled "Professional Knowledge for the Teaching of Writing," students "need to be aware of stylistic options and larger language choices that will best articulate their ideas and produce the most desirable impression on their readers" (NCTE 2016). Throughout the year, we collect some examples of amazing writer's craft to give students choices for bringing their work to life for their readers. During our NaNoWriMo and workshop mini-lessons, I share these techniques, along with others that I have collected or created, and place the craft examples into three categories: Breaking All the Rules, Detailed Descriptions, and The Power of Three. Here are a few samples for each:

Breaking All the Rules. Although these examples seem to flout the writing rules we stress in school, I try to show how authors can thoughtfully break the rules for effect:

- *Incomplete sentences:* "Something about him makes me feel like I am about to fall. Or turn to liquid. Or burst into flames." Veronica Roth, *Divergent*
- *Out-of-place adjective*: "Out of the corner of my eye, I see Peeta extend his hand. I look at him, unsure." Suzanne Collins, *The Hunger Games*

Detailed Descriptions. Authors use a variety of methods to get their points across. One of the most important methods is crafting detailed descriptions that make the reader sit up and take notice. Examples include these:

- *Striking senses descriptions:* "The moon drips through my window." Laurie Halse Anderson, *Winter Girls*

- *Powerful proper nouns:* "Jerry introduces us to his assistant—a perky graduate student named Debbie, who is wearing rainbow-striped overalls the likes of which I haven't seen since old *Brady Bunch* reruns." —Wendy Mass, *A Mango-Shaped Space*

The Power of Three. The number three resonates in literature, sports, and history. Consider the three little pigs, three blind mice, or the three musketeers. Examples include these:

- *Sequential simile:* "*That's great, just great* Max mutters <u>interrupting</u> me <u>chopping</u> off my words <u>letting</u> them fall onto the path like dead leaves." —Sharon Creech, *Heartbeat*
- *Close-echo:* "I wait for the lie detector <u>to</u> flare red, <u>to</u> beep, <u>to</u> reveal that I'm lying." —Marie Lu, *Prodigy*

Other authors' strategies that are fair game include literary elements such as flashback, foreshadowing, symbolism, and imagery. Students are expected to incorporate a minimum of six different craft techniques or literary elements for each of the two checklists (two in each of the three poems, and more for a single novel). Through our NaNo novel excerpt revisions, they have learned how to seamlessly weave craft into their writing to authentically reflect the literature that they read. And now they get to show off their knowledge by doing it on their own.

Step 4: Add Vocabulary Words

By this point in the school year, nearing the fourth and final marking period, we are no longer collecting vocabulary words from our nightly reading. Instead, we are looking for natural ways to integrate these words into our writing. Assuming that students have submitted their five vocabulary words for each of the due dates assigned, they should have eighty-five to one hundred personal vocabulary words to choose from. Now they must include a minimum of nine new words in each of the two checklist projects (three in each, if they select three poems). To integrate their vocabulary words, students can either substitute simple words for more sophisticated vocabulary words, or they can take the time to develop new sentences or paragraphs using vocabulary words. Each of the words selected should be just a notch above the student's average written or reading vocabulary.

Step 5: Make RADaR Revisions

RADaR is an acronym describing the four steps that real authors use when they revise their own writing, and it is a revision strategy that my students learn to use from their very first writing assessment of the school year. RADaR stands for *Replace, Add, Delete,* and *Reorder.* It was originally developed by Kelly Gallagher and Jeff Anderson in Pearson's

Writing Coach, but I came across this innovative strategy in Gallagher's *Write Like This* (2011). I love using this technique, because it is so simple for me to teach and for my students to grasp and use time and time again. See Appendix H for the chart my students use as a reminder of the task at hand. Using the RADaR process, students don't just pretend to revise for the sake of checking off a step; they actually make revisions that improve the original version of the writing in the same way that real authors do.

Step 6: Type Revision 1

Students' handwritten pages undoubtedly are full of cross-outs and carets and sticky notes, so it's time to clean up the copy on the computer.

Troubleshooting: What if I'm already done? Or What if it's already good?

Optional Next Step: Revision Precision (see Appendix K). After the students have typed their work, it becomes much easier to read, but because it looks so fresh, the clean copy may actually make it *less* clear where additional revisions may be necessary. If students feel they're finished at this point, you can share this idea to help them become more aware of sentence flow and word choices. This strategy is especially effective for *already-pretty-darn-good* writers who need to move to the next level. I encourage them to revisit the sentence analyzer and equalizer lessons (recall Appendix D) from our novel excerpt revisions. When they have completed their three-column organizer and graph, students work in pairs to look for ways to revise their sentence structures and lengths. Without fail, students who

> *I always read it aloud to myself because I very much believe that you hear whether a sentence is wrong.*
>
> —Cornelia Funke, author of *The Thief Lord*, the Inkheart trilogy, and many other titles

complete this optional next step of "revision precision" find numerous places where they can step up their writing game.

Step 7: Read Aloud (to Yourself and to a Peer)

As a teacher of writing, I can't even tell you how many times I was grading a paper and wanted to scream, "Did you even read this?!" Now I don't have to, because I've made it a part of our process. Reading aloud exposes the gaps in writing that the "silent reading brain" naturally fills in. It gives kids the opportunity to catch their mistakes and omitted words and ideas before a peer or teacher (or editor!) can.

Troubleshooting: What if I feel weird reading my work aloud in class?

I have several sets of whisper readers, also known as phonics phones, which are available for about ten dollars online or can be made from PVC tubing and curved connectors. I love these devices, because they enable students to tune out distractions as they read their

> *As a beginning writer, I had to learn to trust my own creative instincts, but at the same time, gather a handful of trusted readers who would tell me the unmitigated truth. I had to learn how to detach enough from my work to listen genuinely to their advice and criticism, to see my work through their eyes. It is a difficult thing to sort out, but with practice I figured out how to stand by my best, most authentic impulses and words, while letting go of or revising the parts of my work that really were wrong, extraneous, unaffecting and plain mediocre.*
> —Sue Monk Kidd, author of *The Secret Life of Bees*

work aloud quietly, catching interruptions in flow or meaning.

Step 8: Peer Conference for Ideas and Flow

As students read aloud their writing (step 7), they should check off the boxes that pertain to the mode of writing on the front cover of the Peer Conference Form (see Appendix I). Then, as they read aloud a second time to a peer, their partners can complete the inside of the form, offering suggestions for improvements. The writers must make improvements based on peer feedback, log the revisions on the back of the form, and then share the revisions with the original peer reviewer. Both the peer and writer must sign off on the back of the form.

Troubleshooting: What if I get to the peer conferencing step when I am at home with no peers around?

Inevitably, some of my students find themselves at this stage while they are at home after school hours or over a weekend or longer break, so what do they do then? Although parents *can* serve as peer conferring partners, it is not ideal. They haven't been in class with us, and they have their own ideas about "what's best" that don't often complement their child's plan. In addition, parents typically want to focus on conventions rather than idea development and flow. To prevent that battle, students can e-mail their work or upload their work into Google Docs or Dropbox and invite a friend to complete the peer review digitally.

Step 9: Complete Revision 2

Once students have made the necessary revisions after peer conferencing, I encourage them to save this copy with "—revision 2" added to the end of the file name. I also remind students to click Save As instead of simply Save, so that they can keep track of their progress. If, for example, a student ended up cutting a scene because, according to a peer, it didn't fit the rest of the story, that student could always pluck that chunk of extraordinary-but-not-quite-fitting text from a prior revision and use it elsewhere. As a writer myself, I can't tell you how many times I have gone back to early drafts looking for a certain scene that I had previously cut in order to give it new life in another text. This step may seem redundant, but it helps to have a clean copy with all of the revisions included as we move on to the next phase: editing.

Step 10: Color Edit

This step takes place late in the process so that students can feel the freedom to write with abandon in order to get all of their ideas, craft, and creativity on the page. Now is the time to take it from just being *creative* to also being *correct*. According to NCTE, "Conventions of finished and edited texts are an important dimension of the relationship between writers and readers" (2016). That is precisely why our young authors need to learn to edit their own work. "Readers expect writing to conform to their expectations. In public texts written for a general audience, contemporary readers expect words to be spelled in a standardized way, for punctuation to be used in predictable ways, for usage and syntax to match that used in texts they already acknowledge as successful. They expect the style in a piece of writing to be appropriate to its genre and social situation. " NCTE warns, "Too much emphasis on correctness can actually inhibit a writer's development.

> *You have to be willing to rewrite. I didn't become a good writer until I learned how to rewrite. And I don't just mean fixing spelling and adding a comma. I rewrite each of my books five or six times and each time I change huge portions of my story.*
>
> —Louis Sachar, author of *Holes, Fuzzy Mud, Small Steps, Card Turner*, and many other titles

By the same token, without mastering conventions for written discourse, writers may find their efforts regarded less highly by readers they wanted to influence"(2016).

Here is where we achieve that balance. Up to this point, students have been allowed to write freely and creatively, and now they must strive to make sure that the text is correct— or at least developmentally correct enough for an adolescent to submit to a real editor beyond our school's walls. Color editing is the best self-editing tool that I have ever used (see Appendix J). It completely changed the way that both my students and I feel about the editing stage, because it works. Students are always amazed by the number of errors they can find—and fix—on their own. It is empowering for them to know that they have the capability to skillfully produce writing that meets the expectations of the real world. Throughout the course of the year, students prepare for this completely independent step by performing each of the editing tasks in isolation in various school writing assignments as they master the specific grammar, sentence structure, and punctuation skills along the way. We also practice using color editing in its entirety on our NaNo novel excerpts just weeks before we begin our checklist endeavor, so that students can feel prepared to go it alone. Once they reach this step in their checklists, students gather colored pencils, a red pen, and color-marking sheets from their folders. Then they read through their own work several times, focusing on one color-editing task for each read-through. By the time they are finished focusing, finding, and fixing, the work will be more polished.

Troubleshooting: I am color blind

This is a legitimate concern, and it's one to which teachers need to be sensitive. Some kids can't see any color while others experience loss of certain colors on the spectrum and/or have difficulty distinguishing colors. I have had some students who actually can't see pink at all, and those who have a tough time discerning differences in the hues of blues, greens, reds, and purples. Please note that the colors that I have chosen for the color-editing sheet are arbitrary, having no actual meaning. They were only selected because the first year that I used this method, I had packs of highlighters with these colors. (I have since found that colored pencils work better, because they don't smudge or bleed and some can be erased.) It's not important to use certain colors. The point is to *correct mistakes*. The colors serve as a visual tracking device for both students and teachers to see what has already been checked and corrected. Feel free to switch the colors as you see fit. As long as the students are going through the process one color at a time, color blindness should not be an issue with this task.

> *Maybe you found the "actual writing" part easy, and revisions difficult. The problem there is that editing and revisions are also writing. They are just as necessary a part of the process as banging out a first draft.*
>
> — Cassandra Clare, author of the Shadowhunter Chronicles (the Mortal Instruments series) and other titles

Troubleshooting: I hate editing

No writer loves this stage of the process, but that doesn't make it any less necessary. Even students who think about "just pretending" to color edit realize very quickly that it's just not worth it. After all, if they have to put in that much effort to display that many colors on a page, they might as well just do it right. Best of all, teachers can see at a glance whether a student has effectively completed the task by both coloring and correcting.

Step 11: Format Manuscript

For our purposes, the term *manuscript* refers to our submission-ready writing. Appendixes E and L show our manuscript formatting guidelines for poetry and prose, respectively. Because we have already modeled poem formatting, most kids will pick up on this process fairly quickly. I typically provide small-group instruction, as needed, with kids who are ready for this step. Because prose formatting has so many nuances, it is much easier to gather four to six kids around my computer with their school laptops in hand so that I can explain step by step exactly where to go on the toolbar to follow line spacing guidelines and to create headers and footers. This time, when students click Save As, the file name should include "—final draft" after the title.

Troubleshooting: What if I don't format properly?

Following directions and procedures is an important skill to learn in any industry. We must reinforce quality control in the classroom. If we want publishing professionals to take students seriously, their work must meet the standards. All students are capable of completing this step properly.

Step 12: Write Letter to Editor

Letters that accompany submissions show that students have taken the time to carefully consider audience. Appendix M shows a generic letter to the editor that can be used as a template or customized to better reflect your classroom or an individual student. The notes on how to write the letter will go in students' notebooks for reference, but typically I also post a downloadable Word document version on my web page. Students can then simply pull up the letter template, fill in the blanks, and print it out to save time and to keep the formatting intact.

Troubleshooting: What if the publisher only accepts e-mail submissions?

If the publisher only accepts e-mail submissions, students should do the following:

- Take note of what must be entered in the subject line in order to get the correct editor's attention.
- Plan on using the body of the letter to the editor template as the body of the e-mail, making sure to keep the greeting addressed to the editor.
- Send the manuscript as an attachment to the e-mail. Before attaching and sending, do one last Save As with a file name giving the student's last name and title of writing piece (*"last name—title"*).
- Skip step 13 on the workshop checklist. Check with the teacher before hitting Send so he or she can mark the submission on your checklist and will know not to expect a snail mail version. Send, and then print a copy of your e-mail as evidence of completing steps 12–14.

Step 13: Prepare for Mailing

Students must print *two copies* of both the manuscript and the letter to the editor. My advice here is to have the student print one copy of both the letter and manuscript at first so that you can skim through quickly to look for any glaring errors in formatting that will need to be fixed *prior* to sending out. After those errors have been corrected, the student has the go-ahead to print out the second copy of the letter and manuscript. One of the copies will be kept in the student's folder for his or her own records and/or for teacher assessment, and the other copy will be put on hold for a moment as we prepare the envelopes for mailing. Students will need two envelopes and two stamps for this step. If

> *Publishing is a tough business, one that is always changing, and the road is often long, and bumpy, and riddled with rejection. But if you really want it, you just have to keep going, reminding yourself that it only takes one "Yes!" to get you where you want to be!*
>
> —Alyson Noël, author of the Beautiful Idols series, the Immortals series, the Soul Seekers series, and many other titles

your school is willing to pay the postage for the outside envelope, then only one stamp will be necessary for the self-addressed stamped envelope (SASE) (see Appendix N). I encourage students to bring in stamps from home, and I also buy a book or two and allow students to purchase them at face value. I introduce my early finishers to the Mailings tab in Word, and I show them how to professionally print a self-addressed envelope, which will be used as the SASE, and an outside envelope that will be used for mailing. I have an older, stand-alone printer that is not connected to the network that I reserve exclusively for this task so that none of the other print jobs will be interrupted as we format envelopes. The students to whom I have taught this process will now become my "envelope experts," which frees me to continue working with other students.

Step 14: Send

Because the work will look more professional with fewer folding attempts, *I* take the student's manuscript and letter and fold them into thirds. I also fold the SASE into thirds. I *do* let the student stuff the SASE inside of the folded manuscript/letter and place all that inside the outer mailing envelope, and I definitely let them do the licking and sticking to seal the envelope! Then it is time for the ceremonial walk of pride. I ring a bell and announce the student who is sending his or her work off for publication. The student then walks his or her letter down to the office to the sounds of envious, cheering peers to place that envelope filled with possibilities in the outgoing mail. Ahhh. The sweet sounds of accomplishment! For students completing e-mail submissions, I ring the bell after they have shown me the printed confirmation of the e-mail they've sent.

Step 15: Complete Self-Reflection and Exit Conference

Self-reflection is the final stage in the process, but it is one that should not be forgotten. Reflection gives students the chance to think about their personal writing processes (metacognition). The hope is that each student will carry new understanding into future writing assignments. Completing a second checklist right on the heels of a self-reflection on the first, students can immediately turn around and apply all that they learned (and avoid what they discovered did not work for them). They feel like professionals who know the ropes. They are much more focused and willingly seek assistance from peers rather than running to me with every struggle or concern.

Chapter 9

Assessing the Journey

My husband and I are very proud to report to you that our daughter Sarah's poem, written as one of your assignments last year, was accepted for publication by Creative Communications for their Poet's Contest Anthology. She has also been entered into a drawing for a prize of $3000!!!

Sarah is a quiet unassuming kid who is not well endowed with self-confidence. After she read her letter, she was humming with glee as she tried to get to sleep! This recognition will give her a needed boost! Thank you so much for the support, encouragement and excellent instruction you provided to our daughter last year.

—Proud parents of an author published in the seventh grade

To my mind, the greatest reward for completing the journey to publication should be finishing a long-term, self-directed task and meeting professional standards—truly embracing the notion of autonomy, mastery, and purpose. But, this is school. And in this setting, anything that requires as much effort and time as we have invested in the pursuit of publication demands a grade. Ultimately, you must decide whether to evaluate the writing process, evaluate the writing product, celebrate a job well done, or combine the three. Let's consider some options.

Evaluating Process

At the beginning of the second semester, I printed two blank Class Checklist Progress Rosters (see Figure 8.8) for each class participating in the publication process, to help me keep track of student progress for both of the required publication pieces. Each roster includes a column for each of the fifteen steps in the publication process. Throughout the semester, I can use these as comparison points for my status of the class, as mentioned in Chapter 8. I also use them to note the dates of completion for each step of the Writer's Workshop Process Checklists (Appendix B).

Once we get to the end of the semester, and ultimately the end of this publication process, I will have accurate records that reflect student process and completion. Using this information, I can either calculate a separate grade for each of the two student Process Checklists based on the number of steps completed (twelve out of fifteen, for example), or I can weigh each of those checklists based on the school district's requirements for writing during the marking period.

Note: If you decide to assign different point values for each of the steps on the students' Writer's Workshop Process Checklists, be aware that some students may aim for the minimal amount needed to earn an average grade rather than strive to meet the more demanding goal of publication. In addition to whatever calculation method you choose, you could also add points based on whether students complete all the items on their checklists by the deadlines you've established.

Evaluating Product

I recommend using a rubric (one that you've already used in your classroom or have found online) for evaluating each genre of writing. Obviously, you would need to give this out to students at the beginning of this project rather than at the end, so that they can use it to further guide their writing. If choosing to evaluate product, I recommend giving the students the appropriate rubrics at your first writing conferences of the second semester to put directly into the workshop folders mentioned in Chapter 8, to avoid any confusion. Additionally, you will need to have students print out two copies of each of their final manuscripts—one for submission and the other to be graded. Don't worry too much about making corrections or offering constructive criticism on the writing at this point. Your students will already have submitted their final manuscripts for publication, so they won't be using your feedback to improve their work, which is the point of feedback. Keep the comments positive and commend them for their hard work and growth. As for the final grade on each writing piece, consider aligning the points or the weight of the assignment according to your district's required writing percentages for the marking period.

Celebrating a Job Well Done

Here are some options for celebrating the year of writing:

1. Students can place their final writing in a folder and take the portfolio home to share.
2. Students can include all drafts from their Process Checklists and their final manuscripts in an all-inclusive, end-of-year writing portfolio and take it home to share.
3. You can host a portfolio party at school. Parents can attend and enjoy light refreshments while their children share their writing and reflect on their growth. Figure 9.1 shows a Parent Response Form that I have used to encourage more give-and-take between parents and their children after this sharing.
4. You can host a portfolio party for just your class. Instead of individual sharing, students can display their portfolios on tables and desks. Using packs of sticky notes, students can leave positive remarks on peers' work as they move around the room like a carousel. Of course, you should also invite administrators and even other teachers or classes to make this a true celebration.

I like to combine the three evaluation practices I've just described. Each year, I give my students a *process grade* for the steps they complete and add weight to the overall score, because it involves more time and commitment than anything else we will have completed in the final marking period. However, depending on the magnitude of the latest and greatest end-of-course assessments that I am required to administer by my district and depending on the amount of time that we have left at the end of the year (this fluctuates due to the number of snow days we accumulate during the winter), I may or may not evaluate the final *products*. Honestly, I may not have time to do it,

> *The process of publishing well was not exactly a breeze, but to see my poem in that year's edition of* Celebrate *made me quite proud of myself. This course helped me enhance my voice not only as a writer, but as an author.*
>
> —Kelly, published author in both seventh and eighth grade

and I also believe that the editors who receive my students' submissions will provide an evaluation more exacting than any grade I provide. In any case, I always *celebrate* their accomplishments in some way. They have earned it. My students have spread their wings, and their words have taken flight!

Parent Response Form

Date: _____   Student Name: _____

As you know, your child has worked very hard on developing this End-of-Year Writing Portfolio. From the beginning of the year, we have talked about writing for authentic audiences. Now you are the audience. Take some time to sit down with your child to review his or her portfolio. Feel free to talk to your child about the specific pieces and why they were included. You can even have him or her read a favorite piece to you. When you are finished, please take a few moments to respond to the questions below. Thank you!

1. Which writing piece was your favorite? Why?

2. In what area did you see the largest growth in your child's writing?

3. In your opinion, what are your child's greatest writing strengths?

4. In what writing skill areas do you think your child still needs work?

5. In the space below, please jot down overall comments about your child's work:

Parent Signature:_____

*PLEASE NOTE: This form is a required piece that **must** be submitted with the final portfolio.

Figure 9.1 To guide parents in reviewing their children's work, I provide some helpful tips.

Our Trip Ends

The end of this journey is really just the beginning. As the year closes, my students leave our classroom knowing that they can tackle any task ahead. My hope is that throughout the course of the school year, all of my students will have developed some important and enduring skills:

- The ability to notice the details, the craft, and the word choices that authors use to bring words to life, and a desire to make their own writing sing in the same way.
- The resourcefulness to seek mentors and models as inspiration for improving their writing.
- A personal writing process that works for them.
- The ability to accept challenging tasks and the determination to accomplish goals.
- Strong planning, organization, and time-management skills.
- An awareness of the need for cultivating a writing community that includes both peers and authors as mentors and guides.
- An understanding of what it takes to write well and the impetus to make this a goal for their own writing.
- The desire to analyze and understand the audience for their writing.
- The confidence to submit their work for publication.

Publication helps young writers understand that words have power. After launching hundreds of kids into authorship during two decades in the classroom, I continue to be inspired by their desire to share their work with a world beyond school. Together we learn as we write, side by side, discovering new crafts and techniques and new outlets for our expressions.

I have a plaque in my office that contains these words: "It is good to have an end to journey toward; but it is the journey that matters, in the end." I am not sure about the source of the quote, but I believe it aptly describes the publication process. It *is* the journey, and not the destination, that really matters when we are guiding adolescents. In education there will always be road blocks and speed bumps (and testing requirements and political agendas) that distract us from our goals, but as educators we can't allow these diversions to move

> *What makes a writer different from an author? Anyone can write and everyone should have the opportunity to become an author. An author is a writer who takes that extra step and transforms their writing into something more. Being a published author, even though it was a lot of work, has had a huge impact on me. I now feel more confident about my writing and know that writing requires hard work but in the end, I also know I can produce work I can be proud of.*
>
> —Melissa, who became a published author in seventh grade

> *I always give one word [of advice], and the word is: finish. The word is finish because I think the difference between being a person of talent and being a writer is the ability to apply the seat of your pants to the seat of your chair and finish. It means you'll sit there and work out the details, and work out the next transition, and that you'll have the discipline to transform talent into a written story, book, whatever.*
>
> —E. L. Konigsburg, author of *The View from Saturday* and many other titles

us so far off course that we forget why we were drawn to the profession: to make a difference in every child's life.

Now is the time to plan your expedition. Pack your bags, because we are off on the journey of a lifetime. This time, we'll make it matter.

Appendixes

✎ WWC 1: Notable Quotables and Wonderful Words

1. What book were you reading when you found this amazing quote?
2. What made you stop and write this quote down? What did you like or find interesting about it?
3. Which word choices caught your eye? Why?
4. From what you have read, would you say that this book is "good"? What is it about this author's style that makes it "good" reading?

✎ WWC 2: Emulating Text (A Springboard into Writing)

1. What was special about the original piece of writing that you jotted down in your writer's notebook?
2. How did you decide to emulate it? (Did you write from a line? Imitate the author's vivid word choices or style? Take the idea and make it your own?)
3. Where did your ideas come from for your writing?
4. Do you think this snippet of text has the potential to be further developed into a full-length piece?

✎ WWC 3: Writing from the Heart

1. What item from your heart map did you choose to write about?
2. Why is this topic important to you?
3. How did it feel to write about it? Did you put those feelings into your writing?
4. Was the topic easy for you to write about? Why/why not?
5. What examples of luscious language did you include from WWCs 1 and 2?

✎ WWC 4: Writing from Life I: Current Events

1. What did you select to write from? (The headline, article, ad, or other?)
2. How did it make you feel when you first read your selection? What affected you most strongly about it?
3. How did you choose to write off of this selection (express an opinion? make a connection? create your own narrative scene or poem based on the text in the article or headline?)?
4. Was it easier or more difficult to write from the newspaper than it was to write from literature as you did in WWC 2? Why?
5. Can you see taking this writing any further?

✎ WWC 5: Creating Characters

1. Why did you choose these people to write about?
2. Do you think that any of the attributes that you homed in on will make for good/interesting character traits for characters in your upcoming novel?
3. How did you try to develop tone through your word choices? Was word choice effective in letting the reader know whether he or she should like or dislike this character?

✍ WWC 6: Eavesdropping: Recording Life as It Happens

1. Where were you when you overheard this conversation?
2. Was there anything interesting that you noticed about the relationship between the people involved?
3. As you re-create the scene into a true narrative piece of dialogue, what other "showing details" did you/ could you include to help the reader "see" what's really going on between the people? (Think about gestures, posture, eye contact, setting, and so on.)
4. Do you see any potential writing seeds from these dialogue exchanges?
5. Did this WWC give you a better feel for how real people actually speak to one another?
6. What can you take from this experience that you will remember when you write character dialogue in your novel next month?

✍ WWC 7: Writing from Life II: A Tour of My World

1. What were your initial questions about your location? What did you notice about the setting that made you wonder about that?
2. Did any of your writings surprise you with the direction they headed?
3. Do you feel that as you wrote this time, the setting ended up revealing something about a character or situation?
4. What will you take away from this conflict and setting lesson that you will remember to apply in writing your novel next month?

✍ WWC 8: Stop (and Listen): Tools for Developing Setting

1. Why did you select the settings that you chose to write about?
2. Which senses were easiest to include in your writing? Which were the most difficult?
3. How did using sensory details (imagery) help you to re-create the scene?
4. What luscious language, craft, or figures of speech did you find creeping into your writing? Did it seem easier to include these things in this WWC than in others? Explain.

✍ WWC 9: Accumulating Artifacts

1. Tell me about this artifact. What compelled you to include it in your writer's notebook?
2. What feelings or memories did it stir up in you?
3. Do you think that other kids have similar experiences while growing up? Could that idea encourage you to write about this for a larger audience?

✎ WWC 10: Mapping Out Memories

1. Why was this memory important enough for you to write about?
2. Was it difficult or easy for you to get all of the sensory details and feelings down on paper for this memory? Explain.
3. Tell me about the memory, with as much detail as you can without reading from your notebook. I notice that you seem to feel _____ as you speak about it. Were you able to convey that emotion and all those details in your writing?
4. What else could you add to make the memory feel more real for the reader?

✎ WWC 11: Writing Down Your Dreams

1. How closely did you follow the before, during, and after sleep instructions? Do you think it made a difference?
2. Were you surprised by any of your dreams? Was anything going on in your life that might explain them?
3. Did you notice any patterns to anything that you saw, smelled, felt, or did?
4. What did you choose to do with your dream information? Why?
5. Do you see any potential for writing beyond this WWC?

✎ WWC 12: Lists: I Wonder . . . (and Others)

1. Which items did you select to write about from your lists? Why?
2. What did you choose to write? (Freewrite? Opinion? Narrative scene? Poem?) Why?
3. Because you had to focus on details for this WWC, talk about your process in doing that. What strategies did you use? What luscious language did you incorporate?

✎ WWC 13: Multigenre Writing

1. Why did you select this topic to research?
2. Is there a scene you might add to your novel or another existing piece of writing that includes this information?
3. Does the information you found ignite a strong opinion or the urge to write more?
4. Does this new information give you ideas for writing a brand-new informational or narrative piece?
5. As an author, how do you see yourself using research within your possible publication pieces?

✎ Extra Bonus Challenge: *What If . . . ?*

1. Did you discover anything about yourself (personally or as a writer) as you completed your "what if" writing?
2. What was your original entry? How did you change it? Why?
3. Did this WWC open any doors for your writing that you might have otherwise just passed by?
4. Do you see any potential for writing beyond this WWC?

WWC 14: Reflecting on Writing

1. When you look back on what you have written in your writer's notebook, does anything surprise you?
2. So far this year, how do you think you have grown or changed as a writer?
3. Do you notice any areas where you feel you could improve, add, or change something?
4. What were the fun parts, hard parts, rewarding parts, and frustrating parts of keeping up your writer's notebook?
5. Which genre do you feel most comfortable writing? Why? Would you rather stretch yourself in a less comfortable genre or just write in one that feels more natural?

WWC 15: Surveying the Writer's Market

1. Which contests or publications do you think are most appropriate for your style of writing and the topics you choose? Why?
2. Which contests or publications really seemed interesting to you? Why?
3. What are the specific submissions guidelines for the publications you have selected?
4. What writerly things do you know you will need to focus on in order to have your work accepted for publication? Which mentor text(s)/ author(s) will help to keep you grounded in your work? Which peers will be most valuable for you to turn to as you prepare your work for publication? Why?

WWC 16: Cultivating a Seed

1. You have so many entries in your writer's notebook. Why did you select this one as a possible springboard into publication?
2. What are some of your ideas for developing this piece even further?
3. Which other strategies that we have focused on in the Weekly Writing Challenges could you infuse into this piece as you work toward completion?
4. Which writer's crafts are you thinking about incorporating to bring your writing to life?
5. What do you think you will need from me (teacher) to help the publication of this piece become a reality?

Appendix B: Writer's Workshop Process Checklist (Page 1)

Name: _____

Teacher Initials   Date

[ ]   1. Prewriting/Organization: [ ]   journal brainstorm   [ ]   organizer   [ ]

[ ]   2. Write 1st draft: (working title_____)   [ ]

[ ]   3. Incorporate specific writer's strategies and craft: [ ]

Strategies used: [ ]   _____

[ ]   _____

[ ]   _____

[ ]   _____

[ ]   _____

[ ]   _____

[ ]   4. Add vocabulary words: [ ]

[ ] _____   [ ] _____   [ ] _____

[ ] _____   [ ] _____   [ ] _____

[ ] _____   [ ] _____   [ ] _____

[ ]   5. RADaR revisions completed   [ ]

Appendix B: Writer's Workshop Process Checklist (page 2)

Teacher Initials

Date

| | 6. Revision 1 complete | |

7. Read aloud: ☐ self ☐ peer _____

8. Peer conference for ideas and flow

☐ peer (s): _____

9. Revision 2 complete

10. Color editing

11. Manuscript formatting

Specifics to include for publication:

_____

_____

12. Letter to editor

Specifics to include for editor:

_____

_____

13. Prepare for mailing ☐ SASE ☐ outside envelope

14. Sent out in mail

Appendix B: Writer's Workshop Process Checklist (Page 3)

Teacher Initials   Date

| | 15. Self-reflection (below): |

(a) I chose to write this piece because . . .

(b) Writing this piece was challenging/moderate/easy for me because . . .

(c) The problems that I encountered along the way were . . .

(d) Strategies that worked for me included . . .

(e) Things I want to remember for future writing assignments . . .

(f) Compared to my other writing assignments, I would rate this a ____

because . . .

Appendix C: Getting Ready for NaNoWriMo! (Page 1)

Your journey to noveling fame begins in just a few short days. Your homework tonight is to prepare for your book jacket by answering the following questions:

1. Write down the e-mail address that you will be using to create your NaNoWriMo YWP account:

   _____

2. What will your username be (be creative!)?

   _____

3. Write down a password that will be easy for you to remember:

   _____

4. What is your word-count goal (must be between 7,000 and 15,000 or more)?   _____

5. Briefly describe what your novel will be about:

6. Describe yourself in an interesting and writerly way:

7. What are your hobbies (besides noveling, of course)?

Appendix C: Getting Ready for NaNoWriMo! (Page 2)

8. What authors inspire your writing? Why?

9. What is your favorite music to listen to while you are writing?

10. What survival methods are you planning to use to get through the month and meet your goals?

11. What do you do when you are not noveling?

1. Go to www.ywp.nanowrimo.org

2. Click on **Sign Up**. In the **Create New Account** tab, fill in:

    ✓ Username

    ✓ E-mail address

    ✓ Select the appropriate grade level (**Middle School**) from drop-down menu

    ✓ Choose **Young Writer**

    ✓ Read, then **Accept**, Terms & Conditions

    ✓ Answer the math question

    ✓ Click **Create New Account**

3. **Open a new tab** in your web browser

    ✓ Sign in to your personal e-mail account

    ✓ Open the mail from NaNoWriMo

    ✓ Click on the link to establish your password

    ✓ When the dialogue box opens, type in your *new password* (*make it your student ID*)

4. On the left-hand tab bar, click on **Join a Classroom**

    ✓ Find our classroom by entering the virtual classroom name your teacher has chosen into the Search box

    ✓ Select your teacher's virtual classroom name from the drop-down menu

    ✓ Click **Join**

5. On the top tab bar, click on **My NaNoWriMo**

6. On the left-hand tab bar, click on **Edit User Settings**.

    ✓ Scroll down to **Time Zone** and select the closest current time (if it's morning, it will be easy to figure out; if it's afternoon, add 12 to the current hour)

    ✓ Scroll down to **Private Message Settings** and select **Allow Private Messages** (this will allow you to participate in NaNo Mail and our classroom blog posts)

    ✓ Click **Submit**

    ✓ Later (on your own, with parent permission), you can upload a photo, add a signature line for your e-mails, or change your e-mail account

7. On the left-hand tab bar, click on **Edit Novel Info**
   - ✓ In Word-Count:
     - ➢ Skip **Current Word-Count** (This will be automatically calculated later when uploaded into the **word-count validator**)
     - ➢ Fill in your **word-count goal**
     - ➢ Skip the **word-count validator** for now
   - ✓ Skip **Novel Excerpt** for now (you can update this later once you've written some of your novel)
   - ✓ Fill in:
     - ➢ **Novel Title**
     - ➢ **Novel Genre**
     - ➢ **Novel Summary**
     - ➢ Later (on your own, with parent permission), you can upload cover art
   - ✓ Click **Submit**

8. On the left-hand tab bar, click on **Edit Author Info**
   - ✓ Check that grade level is correct
   - ✓ In the **BIO** box, type in that writerly info about you from the "Getting Ready for NaNoWriMo!" questionnaire
   - ✓ If you have done NaNo before, check the appropriate dates; if not, skip this step
   - ✓ Everyone must fill in:
     - ➢ **Author/book inspiration**
     - ➢ **Favorite music to novel by**
     - ➢ **Hobbies**
   - ✓ Click **Submit**

Appendix D: Post-NaNoWriMo Novel Excerpt Revision (Page 1)

The Sentence Analyzer and the Equalizer are really the only two tools that our young novelists will need to make their novel excerpts exemplary pieces of literature. The lessons here provide a natural means to teach all of the grammar and revision lessons that you likely would be incorporating into your classroom for the second half of the year anyway, and students' excerpts provide the perfect setting for practicing and refining skills in a context that matters to them. Below is a chart explaining how I use these strategies for the curricular and academic needs specifically of my students. Feel free to customize based on your own classroom experiences.

Lesson	Procedure	Additional Instruction/Materials
	Selecting a Novel Excerpt	

Selecting and Printing the Novel Excerpt	Have students follow these steps:
	
	1. Skim through your entire novel, searching for a 500- to 1,800-word excerpt meets these standards:
	
	  • Stands on its own with a natural beginning and end and makes sense in isolation (may need to add in or take out details in step 2)
	
	  • Is engaging; as the writer *and* a reader, you should feel excited about it
	
	  • Introduces at least one well-developed character that the reader can identify with (positively or negatively)
	
	  • Has some important action; something has to *happen* that your readers will care about
	
	2. Revise any obvious errors, eliminate what is not needed, and add in any additional details that will make it work to fit the requirements as a stand-alone piece. Then save this excerpt both on a flash drive and on the school network as "Novel Excerpt."
	
	3. Print it out double-spaced (or, if possible, triple-spaced so that you have the room to revise).
	
	4. Number the beginning of every sentence (not the lines—the *sentences*) within the excerpt in pencil (easy to fix mistakes if they occur); Note: if a sentence is accidentally skipped, say, between sentences 13 and 14, just add an *a* to the missed sentence (13a) to avoid renumbering completely.
		• **See NaNoWriMo workbook** page "Choosing an Exceptional Excerpt"

	The Three-Column Sentence Analyzer: The Root of Revision	
Setting up the Columns	Have students begin a Three-Column Sentence Analysis Organizer for the excerpt by following these directions: 1. Fold 1–2 pieces of loose-leaf paper in thirds lengthwise, creating three columns. (Tip: roll the paper lengthwise until you can see a lowercase *e* at the end, then squish it flat.) 2. At the very top right corner of the page, write your name (and number the pages if you need multiple) 3. To the left of the vertical pink margin, number the lines according to how many sentences are in the excerpt (i.e., if you have fifty-three sentences in the excerpt, then number lines 1 to 53, using the front and back of the loose-leaf paper). [Note: Please feel free to introduce the columns in *any* order that makes instructional sense for your classroom. I typically have students complete all three columns before I do any additional instruction.]	

Appendix D: Post-NaNoWriMo Novel Excerpt Revision (Page 2)

Lesson	Procedure	Additional Instruction/ Materials
Sentence Analysis Column 1: Graphing the Rhythm of Writing: *The Equalizer*	1. At the top of column 1 (to the right of the vertical pink margin), have students record the number of words in each sentence. 2. Ask students if they have ever seen a digital equalizer while listening to music. Explain how the equalizer basically shows the ups and down—the rhythm—of the music. (You can find dozens of videos of equalizers on YouTube as examples.) Be sure to discuss how, if all of the bars were short or if they all were long, the music would be boring. Our ear craves variety. And it is the same with language, both spoken and written. 3. Distribute graph paper. Have students hold the page vertically (portrait) and then draw an x and y axis about three blocks in and up, running the length and width of the page. The axes make the framework for a line graph. 4. Have students label the x axis (horizontal) with "Sentences" and the y axis (vertical) with "# of Words per Sentence." 5. Have students number the *boxes* (not the lines!) along the **x axis** to correspond with the number of sentences in the excerpt (be sure to add in any line mistakes as well (i. e., 13a). Note: Students may need to add more pages. Have them skip the first few blocks on the additional page and tape it on from the back so that writing is not impeded; continue numbering along the **x axis**. 6. Along the **y axis**, number the *lines* (not the boxes!) according to the longest sentence length. (Again, add paper if necessary.) 7. Have students use a highlighter to create a bar graph showing the number of words in each sentence. 8. Once the bar graph is complete, have students draw two horizontal lines across the bars, one at the 5 on the y axis and one at the 15 on the y axis. The students will pay special attention to the bars that fall below the "5-word" mark and above the "15-word" mark in the next few steps. (These numbers are arbitrary, but they seem to work pretty well for my students; you can feel free to change the numbers according to your classroom needs.) This becomes their Writing Equalizer, a powerful visual tool demonstrating the rhythm of their writing. From this, students can clearly see where they need to add more variety to their text. To encourage productive, lesson-based revision, you could work with the equalizers in these ways: • Create an interdisciplinary lesson where students figure out what percentage of their sentences have more than 15 words (look for bars above the 15-word line), which have between 6 and 15 words (look for bars that end between the 15- and 5-word lines), and which have five or fewer words (look for bars that end below the 5-word line). The goal is to identify sentences that they could lengthen and shorten, and places where they could add new sentences in order to shoot for roughly 25 percent on the upper and lower ends and 50 percent in the middle (obviously mixing up the lengths throughout the piece). • Review sentence **fragments** and **run-ons** and have students double-check for fragments below the 5-word line and run-ons above the 15-word line. • Review descriptive **parts of speech** (adjectives, adverbs, prepositions/phrases) to add length and detail where needed based on line lengths. • Review **sentence structures** (simple, compound, complex, compound-complex) and use this as a springboard to introduce the Revision Precision lesson (Appendix K). This will help students figure out how to switch up their sentence structures to add length and/or variety. • Introduce and practice more complex grammar, such as **verbals** (gerunds, participles, and infinitives) as a way to modify sentence structure.	• YouTube music equalizer videos • Graph paper (may need to review math graphing terms) • Your grammar lessons on parts of speech, sentence structures, run-ons and fragments, and verbals, etc. • Revision Precision (Appendix K)

Appendix D: Post-NaNoWriMo Novel Excerpt Revision (Page 3)

Lesson	Procedure	Additional Instruction/ Materials
Sentence Analysis Column 2: The First Three Words	In column 2, students will write down the first three words in every sentence. Here's why: • Once students have completed this column, they can highlight repeated words to help students visually see the repetition that otherwise would have gone unnoticed, and that provides motivation to change them. • They can also note the subject and verb (if they are present) in the first three words to bring awareness to the lack of sentence structure variety, especially if each sentence begins with the same pattern: s-v, s-v, s-v (in addition to teaching the **sentence structure/sentence variety** lessons mentioned above, it is also a great time to review **subject-verb agreement** rules).	• Your grammar lessons on sentence structures, sentence variety, and subject-verb agreement
Sentence Analysis Column 3: Verbs	In column 3, students will write down the verbs in each sentence [action, helping, and linking (not verbals)]. Here's why: • Once students have completed this column, they can highlight boring and repeated verbs to help students visually see the lack of creativity that otherwise would have gone unnoticed, and that provides motivation to switch out those verbs and add variety. • Looking at the verbs in isolation helps students to make sure they have used **consistent verb tense,** and it is a great time to work on **eliminating passive voice.**	• Your grammar lessons on consistent verb tense and eliminating passive voice

Appendix E: Poem Formatting for Publication

1. Remove class heading w/name, date, period if previously submitted for a grade.

2. Be sure margins are set to 1 inch.

3. Type your name either under title or after poem.

4. Poems should be *single spaced*. (**Be sure to *remove space after paragraph!***)

5. The entire page can be 12 or 14 point Arial or Times New Roman font.

6. *You* (*not your computer*) must decide if you want the beginning of each line capitalized or not.

7. *Center* or *left align* all of your text.

8. Create a *footer* with your complete address, school, grade, and teacher.

   (Be sure to check submissions guidelines to see if you need to add additional information.)

Example:

> # Poem Title
> ### by My Name
>
> Poem poem poem poem
> poem poem poem poem poem,
> poem poem poem poem
> poem poem poem poem poem.
>
> Poem poem poem poem
> poem poem poem poem poem,
> poem poem poem poem
> poem poem poem poem poem.
>
> Poem poem poem poem
> poem poem poem poem poem,
> poem poem poem poem
> poem poem poem poem poem.
>
> 123 My Street, City, State Zip, My School, Grade, Teacher

Appendix F: Writer's Workshop Project Planning Sheet (Page 1)

Name: _____ Period: _____ Project #: _____

Before beginning your personal workshop project, complete and submit this planning sheet in preparation for your writing conference. I can't wait to hear about all of your writing plans!

1. Prewriting Plan: I will write a _____ about

2. How I plan to use my writers' notebook:

3. Lessons I plan to refer to from my notes on craft, grammar, writing, or reading:

4. Additional instruction I may need:

5. Mentor texts and/or authors I can refer to as I write:

6. Additional things I may need to research for this writing:

7. Possible publication places (and potential audiences):

8. Peers I can go to for specific needs:

Additional questions/comments/concerns:

Writing Workshop
Teacher Conference Card

_____

is requesting a conference today because:

❑ I have a checklist item I've completed

❑ I have a quick question about: _____

❑ I need help with: _____

*While you are waiting, move on with other checklist items, consult your notes, check the workshop wall, or ask a friend.

Appendix H: RADaR Revision: Getting your writing on the RADaR
(Replace Add Delete and Reorder)

Directions: Use this chart and examples to revise your writing and take it to the next level. Within your text, label the changes you've made using the symbols noted in parentheses.

Revision Strategy	What should I do?	What could it look like?
Replace (RP)	Replace . . . -words that are not specific -words that are overused/repeated -sentences that are unclear	*Before*: As I ran to the finish line, my heart was beating. *After:* As I sprinted to the tape, my heart was pounding in my chest.
Add (A)	Add . . . -new information -descriptive adjectives and adverbs -literary devices and figures of Speech	*Before:* Shadows made the night seem scary. *After:* Ominous shadows made the dark night seem even more frightening.
Delete (D)	Delete . . . -unrelated ideas -sentences that sound good, but create unity/clarity problems -unnecessary details -unwanted repetition	*Before:* The candidate talked about the issues, and many of those issues were issues that had been on the voters' minds. *After:* The candidate talked about the issues, many of which were on the voters' minds.
Reorder (RO)	Reorder . . . -to make better sense -for better flow -so details support main ideas	*Before*: Put the sunflower seeds over the strawberries, which are on top of the pineapple in the bowl. You'll have a delicious fruit salad! *After:* To make a delicious fruit salad, cut pineapples into a bowl. Add strawberries and then sprinkle a few sunflower seeds over the top.

Helpful Symbols for Making Changes	ﻭ = delete	⋀ = insert or add
≡ = capitalize	/ = make lowercase	¶ = indent paragraph

The Author's Apprentice: Developing Writing Fluency, Stamina, and Motivation Through Authentic Publication
by Vicki Meigs-Kahlenberg. Copyright © 2016. Stenhouse Publishers.

Workshop Preconference Form

Author: _____ Title: _____

Genre: _____ Publication: _____

Author: Before you request a peer conference, reread your text to be sure you have included all required elements. *Make necessary changes prior to your conference*

Informational/Persuasive Writing:

- ❑ Lead/hook
- ❑ Introduction
- ❑ Thesis/claim
- ❑ Clear organizational structure
- ❑ Evidence to support thesis/claim
- ❑ Development and explanation of evidence
- ❑ One controlling point
- ❑ Use of transitions
- ❑ Strong, deliberate word choices
- ❑ Citations/works cited (if necessary)
- ❑ Conclusion
- ❑ Thoughtful closing

Topic:

Thesis/claim:

- ❑ **I have double-checked submission guidelines to be certain that my piece is suitable.**

Narrative Writing:

- ❑ Strong lead
- ❑ Clear, organized plot elements
- ❑ Obvious conflict
- ❑ Use of dialogue (internal & external)
- ❑ Character development
- ❑ Plot development (3+ complications in RA)
- ❑ Setting development (as a reflection of character)
- ❑ Use of literary devices (symbolism, irony, flashback)
- ❑ Consistent point of view
- ❑ Satisfying resolution

Main Conflict (problem/desire):

Theme (life lesson):

Memoir:

- ❑ Author reflections
- ❑ Clear purpose

Poetry:

- ❑ Clear point grounded in reality
- ❑ Imagery
- ❑ 3+ different figures of speech
- ❑ 16–21 lines
- ❑ Luscious language
- ❑ Effective use of line breaks
- ❑ Deliberate use of capitalization and lower case
- ❑ Playing with white space
- ❑ Complete sentences have punctuation (, . ?)
- ❑ Creative use of punctuation (— : . . .)

Topic:

Purpose:

- ❑ **I have double-checked submission guidelines to be certain that my piece is suitable.**

Peer's Name: _____ Intended Audience (age/grade): _____

Title: _____ Genre: _____

Please listen for the following while reading, and then provide feedback on each.

✑ A Great Lead/Hook/Opening Line

❑ The author really captures your attention and made you want to read on.

Suggestions for revisions: _____

_____

✑ Descriptive Language

❑ The author uses imagery (sight/sound/touch/smell/taste) to help you to visualize.
❑ The author uses deliberate word choices and strong verbs to make the meaning mostly clear.
❑ The author makes good craft choices.
❑ The author's vocabulary choices are fitting to the text.

Suggestions for revisions: _____

_____

_____

✑ Idea Development

❑ The author uses a balance of showing and telling.
❑ The author has left no holes or lingering questions about the story.
❑ The author has included enough details that you can relate to the text in some way.

Suggestions for revisions: _____

_____

_____

✑ Organization

❑ The author has developed the order of the events or ideas in a way that makes sense.
❑ The author has included no events or ideas that seem out of place for this text.

Suggestions for revisions:_____

_____

_____

After reading, please answer the following questions:

1. What is the *point/main idea* of this text? Did the author stick to it from beginning to end?

_____

_____

_____

_____

2. Were there any areas that simply *didn't make sense*? How could the author fix this issue?

_____

_____

_____

_____

3. What image, idea, phrase, or sentence sticks out in your mind the *strongest*? Why?

_____

_____

_____

_____

4. Do you feel the text is appropriate for the intended audience? Why?

_____

_____

_____

_____

5. Do you feel the title is fitting for the piece? Why?

_____

_____

_____

_____

6. Other comments or suggestions:

_____

_____

_____

_____

Post-Conference Form

I revised my writing by:

1._____

2._____

3._____

4._____

5._____

6._____

7._____

8._____

9._____

10._____

- -

Peer responder: After the author has made revisions, reread the writing piece and comment on revisions.

Praise:

Push:

Signatures

Author:_____Peer:_____ Date:_____

The Author's Apprentice: Developing Writing Fluency, Stamina, and Motivation Through Authentic Publication
by Vicki Meigs-Kahlenberg. Copyright © 2016. Stenhouse Publishers.

Appendix J: Color Editing Card

Directions: Highlight the following items in your writing using the color indicated to help you to make focused corrections. Focus on **one color at a time** from beginning to end. As you go along, be sure to correct any errors.

PINK:
- Highlight all end marks in pink. Look for run-ons and ways to combine sentences.
- Highlight all commas in pink. Look for places where you need to add them.

    - Are they used between items in a series?
    - Are they used to set off dialogue?
    - Are they used in dates and addresses?
    - Are they used after introductory words, phrases, and clauses?
    - Are they used with a conjunction in compound sentences?

BLUE:
- Highlight all coordinating conjunctions (and, but, or, so, yet, for) in blue.
- Is there is a complete sentence on each side of it? (**If so, be sure there is a comma before the conjunction.**)

GREEN:
- Highlight the first word in each sentence in green.
- Highlight the first word in each piece of dialogue in green.
- Highlight proper nouns in green.
- Are they **capitalized**?

PURPLE:
- Highlight all verbs in sentences and dialogue tags (not the ones within quotes/dialogue) in purple. Make sure they all have **consistent tense**.
- Eliminate **passive verb choices** where possible.
- **Eliminate repetition** where possible.

YELLOW:
- Highlight words and homophones that need to be checked for spelling in yellow. **Then actually check them for spelling.**

RED (for poetry only):
- Read your poem aloud, then place a slash (/) where you feel your voice makes a natural pause. Place additional **slashes** wherever you would like to break up lines. This will help you with your line breaks and visual flow within your poem when you retype it. **No lines should be dangling out way beyond the others.**
- Circle your use of "playing with white space." **Is word/letter placement clear? Does it add to the meaning?**

Gary Provost on the rhythms of sentence length:

This sentence has five words. Here are five more words. Five word sentences are fine. But several together become monotonous. Listen to what is happening. The writing is getting boring. The sound of it drones. It's like a stuck record. The ear demands some variety. Now listen. I vary the sentence length, and I create music. Music. The writing sings. It has a pleasant rhythm, a lilt, a harmony. I use short sentences. And I use sentences of medium length. And sometimes when I am certain the reader is rested, I will engage him with a sentence of considerable length, a sentence that burns with energy and builds with all the impetus of a crescendo, the roll of the drums, the crash of the cymbals—the sounds that say listen to this, it is important. (1985, 60–61)

<u>**Ways to Revise Sentence Length:**</u>

1. Combine two or more existing sentences.
2. Add more details—words, phrases, clauses—to an existing sentence (see notes on switching up sentence structures and verbals).
3. Break existing long sentences into several shorter ones.
4. Add brand-new sentences of varying lengths between chunks of sentences of similar length.

Appendix L: Prose Formatting for Publication (Page 1)

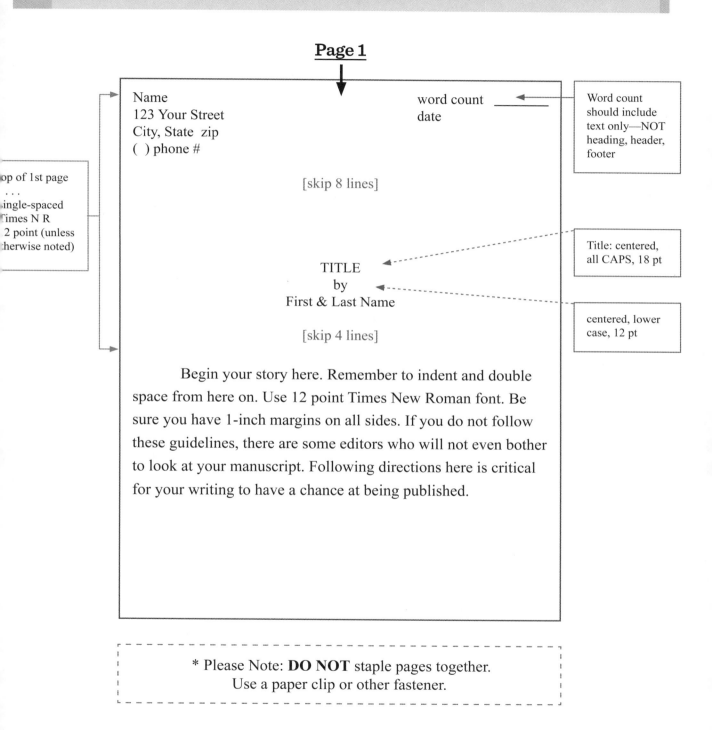

Page 1

Name
123 Your Street
City, State zip
( ) phone #

word count _____
date

Word count should include text only—NOT heading, header, footer

[skip 8 lines]

op of 1st page
. . .
ingle-spaced
Times N R
2 point (unless
therwise noted)

TITLE
by
First & Last Name

Title: centered, all CAPS, 18 pt

centered, lower case, 12 pt

[skip 4 lines]

Begin your story here. Remember to indent and double space from here on. Use 12 point Times New Roman font. Be sure you have 1-inch margins on all sides. If you do not follow these guidelines, there are some editors who will not even bother to look at your manuscript. Following directions here is critical for your writing to have a chance at being published.

* Please Note: **DO NOT** staple pages together.
Use a paper clip or other fastener.

Every Page After Page 1

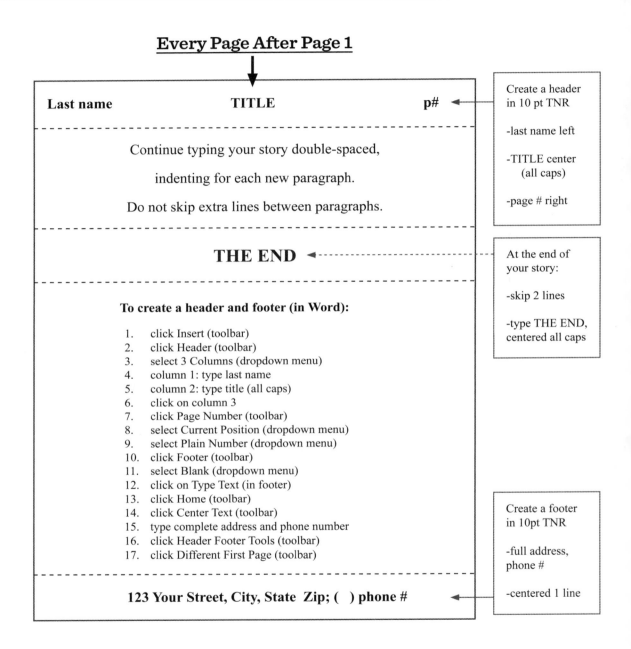

Last name	TITLE	p#

Continue typing your story double-spaced,

indenting for each new paragraph.

Do not skip extra lines between paragraphs.

THE END

To create a header and footer (in Word):

1. click Insert (toolbar)
2. click Header (toolbar)
3. select 3 Columns (dropdown menu)
4. column 1: type last name
5. column 2: type title (all caps)
6. click on column 3
7. click Page Number (toolbar)
8. select Current Position (dropdown menu)
9. select Plain Number (dropdown menu)
10. click Footer (toolbar)
11. select Blank (dropdown menu)
12. click on Type Text (in footer)
13. click Home (toolbar)
14. click Center Text (toolbar)
15. type complete address and phone number
16. click Header Footer Tools (toolbar)
17. click Different First Page (toolbar)

123 Your Street, City, State Zip; (   ) phone #

Create a header in 10 pt TNR

-last name left

-TITLE center (all caps)

-page # right

At the end of your story:

-skip 2 lines

-type THE END, centered all caps

Create a footer in 10pt TNR

-full address, phone #

-centered 1 line

Appendix M: Sample Letter to the Editor

[Entire letter is single-spaced; be sure to remove space after paragraph if typing it yourself.]

Please Note:
If you are submitting to an editor in the adult market, DO NOT INCLUDE YOUR GRADE, SCHOOL OR TEACHER. Instead, simply say that you are a student who is attempting professional publication.

Tab over
8–10 times

123 Your Street
Your City,   State   Zip
Date to be sent

skip 4 lines

Editor (if you know editor's name, use first and last w/ Mr., Ms., etc., comma, Editor)
c/o Publication Company
123 Their Street
City, State Zip

skip 2 lines

Dear Editor: (if you know editor's name, use last name w/ Mr., Ms., etc. in place of Editor)

skip 2 lines

I am a (*spell out the grade*) grade student at (*type in full name of school*) School in (*city*), (*state*). In my English class with my teacher, (*teacher's name*), we are attempting professional publication of a piece that we have written this year. I have selected a (*genre*) entitled ___(*put title in italics here*)___. I think that it would be perfect for ___(*put publication in italics here*)___ because ___(*give a specific, convincing reason here*)___ . ___(*add in any additional information that is required based on submission guidelines here*)___. Thank you for your time and consideration. I hope to hear from you soon.

skip 2 lines

Tab over same amount as heading

Sincerely,

skip 4 lines

Your Name

enclosures: (*title of piece*), SASE

Appendix N: SASE
(Self-Addressed Stamped Envelope)

1. **Fold** envelope into thirds.

2. Halfway down center column, **print** name and complete address in blue or black ink or send it through the printer.

3. Place **stamp** in upper right corner.

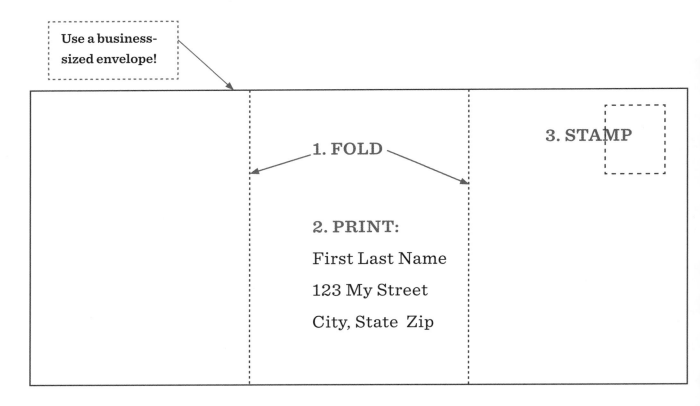

Bibliography

Anderson, Jeff. 2011. *10 Things Every Writer Needs to Know*. Portland, ME: Stenhouse.

Atwell, Nancie. 1998. *In the Middle: New Understandings About Writing, Reading, and Learning*. 2nd ed. Portsmouth, NH: Boynton/Cook.

_____. 2002. *Lessons That Change Writers*. Portsmouth, NH: Firsthand/Heinemann.

_____. 2006. *Naming the World: A Year of Poems and Lessons*. Portsmouth, NH: Firsthand/Heinemann.

Beers, Kylene. 1998. "Choosing Not to Read: Understanding Why Some Middle Schoolers Just Say No." In *Into Focus: Understanding and Creating Middle School Readers,* ed. K. Beers and B. G. Daniels. Norwood, MA: Christopher-Gordon.

Burleigh, Robert, and Stephen Johnson. 1997. *Hoops*. San Diego, CA: Silver Whistle.

Cowan, Catherine, and Octavio Paz. 1997. *My Life with the Wave*. New York: Lothrop, Lee & Shepard.

Dorfman, Lynne R., and Rose Cappelli. 2007. *Mentor Texts: Teaching Writing Through Children's Literature, K–6*. Portland, ME: Stenhouse.

Duncan, Lois. 1984. *Ransom*. New York: Dell.

Ellis, Linda, and Jamie Marsh. 2007. *Getting Started: The Reading-Writing Workshop, Grades 4–8*. Portsmouth, NH: Heinemann.

English Language Arts Standards. (n.d.). Retrieved March 01, 2016, from http://www. corestandards.org/ELA-Literacy.

Faulkner, Grant. 2012. E-mail interview, August 27.

Fletcher, Ralph. 1993. *What a Writer Needs*. Portsmouth, N.H.: Heinemann.

———. 2003. *A Writer's Notebook: Unlocking the Writer Within You*. New York: HarperTrophy.

Fletcher, Ralph, and JoAnn Portalupi. 1998. *Craft Lessons: Teaching Writing K–8*. York, ME: Stenhouse.

———. 2001. *Writing Workshop: The Essential Guide*. Portsmouth, NH: Heinemann.

"Framework for 21st Century Learning - P21." 2015. Framework for 21st Century Learning - P21. http://www.p21.org/about-us/p21-framework.

Gallagher, Kelly. 2003. *Reading Reasons: Motivational Mini-Lessons for Middle and High School*. Portland, ME: Stenhouse.

———. 2006. *Teaching Adolescent Writers*. Portland, ME: Stenhouse.

———. 2011. *Write Like This: Teaching Real-World Writing Through Modeling and Mentor Texts*. Portland, ME: Stenhouse.

Heard, Georgia. 1999. *Awakening the Heart: Exploring Poetry in Elementary and Middle School*. Portsmouth, NH: Heinemann.

Heath, Chip, and Dan Heath. 2008. *Made to Stick: Why Some Ideas Survive and Others Die*. New York: Random House.

Henderson, Kathy. 2001. *The Young Writer's Guide to Getting Published*. Cincinnati, OH: Writer's Digest.

Lane, Barry. 1999. *Reviser's Toolbox*. Shoreham, VT: Discover Writing Press.

———. 2006. *Hooked on Meaning: Writing Craft Video Lessons That Improve Achievement on Writing Tests Through Authentic Instruction for Students Grades 3–8*. Shoreham, VT: Discover Writing Press.

———. 2008. *The Healing Pen: Writing Your Way to Inner Peace and Outer Transformation*. Shoreham, VT: Discover Writing Press.

Langer, Judith. A. 2002. *Effective Literacy Instruction: Building Successful Reading and Writing Programs*. Urbana, IL: National Council of Teachers of English.

Lehman, Christopher, and Kate Roberts. 2014. *Falling in Love with Close Reading: Lessons for Analyzing Texts—and Life*. Portsmouth, NH: Heinemann.

Lupica, Mike. 2014. *Fantasy League*. New York: Philomel Books.

Mali, Taylor. 2009. "Tony Steinberg: Brave Seventh Grade Viking Warrior." *The Last Time as We Are*. Nashville, TN: Write Bloody.

Miller, Donalyn. 2011. "Gearing Up for NaNoWriMo." *Education Week,* October 18. http://blogs.edweek.org/teachers/book_whisperer/2011/10/gearing_up_for_nanowrimo.html?qs=NaNoWriMo.

NCTE. 2016. "Professional Knowledge for the Teaching of Writing." *NCTE Comprehensive News*. http://www.ncte.org/positions/statements/teaching-writing.

Overturf, Brenda J., Leslie H. Montgomery, and Margot Holmes Smith. 2015. *Vocabularians: Integrated Word Study in the Middle Grades*. Portland, ME: Stenhouse.

Pink, Daniel H. 2006. *A Whole New Mind: Why Right-Brainers Will Rule the Future*. New York: Riverhead Books.

————. 2009. *Drive: The Surprising Truth About What Motivates Us*. New York: Riverhead Books.

Provost, Gary. 1985. *100 Ways to Improve Your Writing*. New York: New American Library.

Ray, Katie Wood. 1999. *Wondrous Words: Writers and Writing in the Elementary Classroom*. Urbana, IL: National Council of Teachers of English.

————. 2006. *Study Driven: A Framework for Planning Units of Study in the Writing Workshop*. Portsmouth, NH: Heinemann.

Rief, Linda. 2007. *Inside the Writer's-Reader's Notebook: A Workshop Essential*. Portsmouth, NH: Heinemann.

Routman, Regie. 2005. *Writing Essentials: Raising Expectations and Results While Simplifying Teaching*. Portsmouth, NH: Heinemann.

Sepetys, Ruta. 2011. *Between Shades of Gray*. New York: Philomel Books.

Sonnenblick, Jordan. 2005. "Now *That's* a Sandwich! How to Make Your Characters into *Characters*." *Drums, Girls, & Dangerous Pie*. New York: Scholastic.

Spinelli, Jerry. 1990. *Maniac Magee*. New York: Little, Brown.

Taylor, William. 2011. *Practically Radical: Not-So-Crazy Ways to Transform Your Company, Shake Up Your Industry, and Challenge Yourself*. New York: William Morrow.

Tovani, Cris. 2000. *I Read It, but I Don't Get It: Comprehension Strategies for Adolescent Readers*. Portland, ME: Stenhouse.

Yancey, Rick. 2013. *The 5th Wave*. New York: G. P. Putnam's Son's.

Index

Page numbers followed by *f* indicate figures.